AF757578

Synaesthesia and Individual Differences

Synaesthesia is a fascinating cognitive phenomenon where one type of stimulation evokes the sensation of another. For example, synaesthetes might perceive colours when listening to music, or tastes in the mouth when reading words. This book provides an insight into the idiosyncratic nature of synaesthesia by exploring its relationships with other dimensions of individual differences. Many characteristics of linguistic-colour synaesthetes are covered including personality, temperament, intelligence, creativity, emotionality, attention, memory, imagination, colour perception, body lateralization, and gender. Aleksandra Rogowska proposes that linguistic-colour synaesthesia can be considered as an abstract form of a continuous variable in the broader context of cross- and intramodal associations. There has been a resurgence of interest in synaesthesia and this book will appeal to students and scientists of psychology, cognitive science, and social science, and to those who are fascinated by unusual states of mind.

Aleksandra Maria Rogowska is an Assistant Professor in the Faculty of Physical Education and Physiotherapy at the Opole University of Technology, Poland. Her research centres on synaesthesia but also includes the psychology of sport, art and addiction. Her work focuses on developmental paths for young adults, in particular undergraduate students.

Synaesthesia and Individual Differences

Aleksandra Maria Rogowska
Opole University of Technology, Poland

CAMBRIDGE
UNIVERSITY PRESS

CAMBRIDGE
UNIVERSITY PRESS

University Printing House, Cambridge CB2 8BS, United Kingdom

Cambridge University Press is part of the University of Cambridge.

It furthers the University's mission by disseminating knowledge in the pursuit of education, learning and research at the highest international levels of excellence.

www.cambridge.org
Information on this title: www.cambridge.org/9781107096189

© Aleksandra Maria Rogowska 2015

This publication is in copyright. Subject to statutory exception and to the provisions of relevant collective licensing agreements, no reproduction of any part may take place without the written permission of Cambridge University Press.

First published 2015

Printed in the United Kingdom by Clays, St Ives plc

A catalogue record for this publication is available from the British Library

Library of Congress Cataloguing in Publication data
Rogowska, Aleksandra Maria, 1970–
Synaesthesia and individual differences / Aleksandra Maria Rogowska, Opole University of Technology, Poland.
pages cm
ISBN 978-1-107-09618-9 (hardback)
1. Synesthesia. 2. Individual differences. I. Title.
BF495.R64 2015
152.1'89–dc23

2014042931

ISBN 978-1-107-09618-9 Hardback

Cambridge University Press has no responsibility for the persistence or accuracy of URLs for external or third-party internet websites referred to in this publication, and does not guarantee that any content on such websites is, or will remain, accurate or appropriate.

Contents

Plates

Figures

Tables

Introduction: is synaesthesia normal?

If a child says that the letter *G* on a toy brick has the wrong colour, it is most likely that this child is a synaesthete. In synaesthesia, which seems to be one of the most interesting and intriguing perceptual phenomena, sensory stimulation (or even imagining an inducer) can elicit an additional concurrent experience (or its mental representation). As such, synaesthetes may see sounds, smell words, taste colours, or feel tactile shapes when tasting food. These unusual experiences are involuntary, automatic, idiosyncratic, and relatively consistent over time. Some synaesthetes are surprised and disappointed when they recognize that others do not share their synaesthetic experiences.

Although it is very difficult to find two synaesthetes with identical combinations of synaesthetic associations, some general tendencies are common to all synaesthetes within a particular type of synaesthesia (e.g., linguistic-colour, music-colour, number-colour, time-space). Current research indicates remarkable similarities between synaesthesia and common cross-modal associations (e.g., Elias, Saucier, Hardie, and Sarty, 2003; Mulvenna and Walsh, 2006; Cohen Kadosh, Henik, Catena, Walsh, and Fuentes, 2009). Moreover, studies conducted among a random sample of participants revealed that synaesthetes are not easy to distinguish from non-synaesthetes (Simner, Mulvenna, *et al.*, 2006; Rogowska, 2007; Brang, Teuscher, Ramachandran, and Coulson, 2010). Synaesthesia seems to lie at the high end of a spectrum of cross-modal connections (Martino and Marks, 2001; Cohen Kadosh and Henik, 2007; Spence, 2011; Bien, ten Oever, Goebel, and Sack, 2012).

For over twenty years, scientific interest in synaesthesia has been constantly increasing. Although much research examining synaesthesia has been in the fields of neuroscience, medicine, cognitive science, linguistics, and art (Rogowska, 2011), research with reference to individual differences has been very scarce. However, this kind of research seems necessary in order to explain the nature of synaesthesia in its evolutionary context, research that may shed some light on the human development of perception, thought, and language (Ramachandran and Hubbard, 2001b).

Research on relationships between synaesthesia and various dimensions of personality could help to resolve problems with redefining synaesthesia (Simner, 2012a, 2012b) and appointing its boundaries, as well as with examining assignation mechanisms of synaesthesia in the fields of cognitive neuroscience (e.g., Hubbard and Ramachandran, 2005; Cohen Kadosh and Walsh, 2008; Rouw, Scholte, and Colizoli, 2011) and genetics (e.g., Barnett, Finucane, *et al.*, 2008; Asher *et al.*, 2009; Tomson *et al.*, 2011). Further explanation of how synaesthesia is mediated in the brain may aid understanding of the normal processes of perceptual awareness and multisensory integration (van Leeuwen, Petersson, and Hagoort, 2010). Recent findings suggest that theories of the brain mechanisms of grapheme-colour synaesthesia need to incorporate a broader neural network underpinning multiple visual features, perceptual knowledge, and feature integration, rather than focusing solely on colour-sensitive areas (Chiou, Stelter, and Rich, 2013).

Current neuroimaging research has demonstrated that some forms of synaesthesia are caused by enhanced cross-activation between brain areas specialized for the processing of different sensory attributes. There is some evidence of increased white-matter connections among regions known to be involved in typical cross-modal processes. For example, Rouw and Scholte (2007) revealed hyperconnectivity in brain areas that mediate the type of neurological 'cross-talk' inherent in synaesthesia. Synaesthetes may display enhanced modality-specific perceptual processing, in which hyperexcitability acts as a source of noise in the visual cortex that influences the availability of the neuronal signals underlying conscious awareness of synaesthetic photisms (Terhune, Tai, Cowey, Popescu, and Cohen Kadosh, 2011).

Furthermore, Rouw and Scholte (2010) showed that distinct neural mechanisms depend on the type of synaesthesia. Projector synaesthetes' experience is related to brain areas involved in perceiving and acting in the outside world (the visual cortex, auditory cortex, motor cortex) as well as frontal brain areas, whereas associator synaesthetes' experience is related to the hippocampus and parahippocampal gyrus, known for their role in memory. Therefore, the properties of subjective experiences are in accordance with the functional properties of the mediating brain mechanisms.

The investigations of Brang and Ramachandran (2010) on the eidetic imagery of the grapheme-colour projector synaesthete seem to support the enhanced cross-activation model. Using two classic cross-modal integration tasks, Brang, Williams, and Ramachandran (2012) revealed that grapheme-colour synaesthetes exhibit enhanced cross-modal interactions between the auditory and visual modalities, suggesting that the experience of synaesthesia in one modality generalizes to enhanced cross-modal processes in other modalities. Moreover, Hänggi, Wotruba, and Jäncke's (2011) study provided evidence for global hyperconnectivity within the synaesthete's brain. These researchers suggested that synaesthetic experience might be only one phenotypic manifestation of the globally altered network architecture in grapheme-colour synaesthesia.

The similarities in the personality attributes of synaesthetes and non-synaesthetes support the theory that synaesthesia may rely on mechanisms that are common to all people (Simner, Gärtner, and Taylor, 2011). Indeed, the results of a combined psychophysics transcranial magnetic stimulation and event-related potential (ERP) study (Bien *et al.*, 2012) provided evidence that synaesthesia represents the extremity of a spectrum of normal, adaptive perceptual processes that entail close interplay between the different sensory systems. Since neurological mechanisms such as hyperconnectivity are spectral, both synaesthetes and non-synaesthetes make similar systematic cross-modal pairings in behaviour tasks (Eagleman, 2012).

On the other hand, synaesthesia may be seen as a type of neural plasticity linked to more specific cognitive processes (Ramachandran and Hubbard, 2001a). Jawer (2005) proposed the application of the term 'sensitivity' to individuals who exhibit a greater susceptibility to a range of environmental factors including allergies, migraine headache, chronic pain, and chronic fatigue, as well as a high degree of anomalous perception, such as absorption, magical thinking, transliminality, or synaesthesia. A sensitive person may be characterized as creative, sensual, imaginational, intellectual, and emotional. Moreover, ambidexterity (the ability to use either hand) was found to occur more often among persons who consider themselves sensitive.

The main aim of the present preliminary study was not to find strong evidence for some current conception of synaesthesia, but rather to explore any new directions for further research. Here, synaesthesia was investigated in a wide context of individual differences in such dimensions as personality, temperament, intelligence, emotionality, gender, body lateralization, and cognitive capacities (e.g., attention, memory, imagery, colour perception). The other aspect of individual differences refers to the synaesthesia phenomenon. Synaesthetes may differ from each other in various features, including the following:

(1) The quantitative indices of synaesthesia:
- range of associations within particular categories of synaesthetic inducers (e.g., complete range of letters within the alphabet vs. selected letters)
- range of synaesthetic categories (e.g., grapheme-colour, music-colour, time-space)

- number of modalities involved within synaesthetic experiences (e.g., one modality in grapheme-colour synaesthesia vs. four modalities when music induces smell, taste, and touch sensations).

(2) The qualitative indices of synaesthesia:
- level of cognitive processes: sensory in lower synaesthetes (e.g., pain-colour) vs. semantic in higher synaesthetes (e.g., time-space)
- place of both inducer and concurrent experience occurrence (i.e., internal – as a mental representation – vs. external – as a sensory experience)
- feedback experiences (i.e., unidirectional inducer-concurrent experiences vs. bidirectional experiences).

Thus, the description of a subjective synaesthetic experience (Rogowska, 2011) may comprise various categories and types of a particular form of synaesthesia, such as intramodal, intermodal, bimodal, multimodal, analytic, synthetic, partial, comprehensive, sensory, semantic, perceptual, conceptual, internal (associators), external (projectors), unidirectional, and bidirectional. Idiosyncratic configuration of these types within one synaesthete might decide the place of an individual case on the weak–strong dimension of a synaesthesia trait.

Synaesthesia has usually been examined as a dichotomous variable, and in numerous studies, the strongest cases are compared with samples of 'non-synaesthetes'. Although this procedure is standard and 'safe', it does not seem to reflect the phenomenology of synaesthetic experiences and the existence of a wide set of individual differences between synaesthetes. Therefore, Chapter 1 of the present study examines whether linguistic-colour synaesthesia is a continuous and normal trait. A sample of 161 Polish undergraduates (including 82 women – 51%) between 20 and 44 years of age (22.67 ± 2.40) completed the Linguistic-Colour Association Test (L-CAT) – for full details on the participants, see Appendix A. The test consisted of 135 items in 10 categories: Colours, Fruits, Verbs, Adjectives, Months and Seasons, Days, Forenames, Pseudowords, Numbers, and Alphabet. The values of colours used in the test were transformed from the RGB (red, green, blue) model into the CIELab colour space before calculating the test–retest Euclidean distance. In this study, synaesthesia was regarded as a continuous variable according to two indices: consistency over time (*C*) and range of linguistic-colour association (*R*). The L-CAT scales revealed a normal distribution in *C* and a mixture of normal distributions in *R*. Exploratory factor analysis (EFA) extracted one factor for consistency of linguistic-colour associations, a finding that may point to a common basis for synaesthetic-abstract and common-concrete associations. The expectation-maximization (EM) clustering algorithm revealed two clusters of complete and selective associators.

The results of this investigation suggest that linguistic-colour synaesthesia is a strong abstract form of association on the concrete–abstract and weak–strong dimensions.

The range of linguistic-colour associations, as objective and quantitative indices of the strength of synaesthesia, was reconciled with subjective self-report qualitative methods, as described in Chapter 2. These studies also explored the relationships between linguistic-colour synaesthesia and self-related sensing, body lateralization, and gender. An objective method of examining the consistency of the linguistic-colour associations of the L-CAT was combined with participants' self-reports in the Synaesthetic Association Questionnaire (SAQ). Among 141 participants, 19 (13%) were arbitrarily recognized as linguistic-colour synaesthetes on the basis of both self-report and test–retest consistency methods. However, weaker types of synaesthesia may occur much more frequently, following a normal distribution. Although linguistic-colour synaesthesia was found to be associated neither with gender nor with body-sidedness, an interaction effect was revealed between gender and sidedness. Linguistic-colour synaesthesia seems to occur more frequently in one-sided women and lateralized men. Moreover, linguistic-colour synaesthetes reported poorer touch perception and more frequent migraine experience than non-synaesthetes. The results of these studies were explained in light of the compensatory hypothesis, with a possible contribution of the somatosensory cortex to the development of language skills.

Chapter 3 of the present study concerns the investigation of the relationship between linguistic-colour synaesthesia and cognitive capacities such as visual colour discrimination, visual and verbal memory, general selective attention (the d2 Test of Attention), and self-reported imagination. Sample A of the university student participants, including 11 linguistic-colour synaesthetes and 63 non-synaesthetes, completed a battery of tests and questionnaires assessing the strength of linguistic-colour synaesthesia (L-CAT), colour discrimination (the Visual Colour Discrimination Test), visual memory (the Benton Visual Retention Test), verbal memory (the Word List Recall Test), general selective attention (the d2 Test of Attention), and self-reported imagination (the Imagination Inventory).

Linguistic-colour synaesthetes outperformed non-synaesthetes in colour perception, verbal memory, general selective attention, and self-reported imagination. Moreover, synaesthetes demonstrated heightened engagement in experiences, which was significantly correlated to the strength of linguistic-colour associations. The pattern of these correlations was similar to the connection between absorption and linguistic-colour synaesthesia discussed in Chapter 4. These findings seem to suggest that synaesthetic mental representation requires increased cognitive resources of attention, imagination, and memory. However, the results of a cluster analysis indicated that individual differences in these cognitive abilities also exist among synaesthetes. The fundamental question regarding the explanation of synaesthetic mechanisms remains: are enhanced cognitive abilities the basis of the emergence of synaesthesia, or, alternatively, is synaesthesia an opportunity that facilitates the development of cognitive skills?

The relationships involved in linguistic-colour synaesthesia and individual differences in absorption, creative thinking, types of mind, and emotional and fluid intelligence were the main subject of the study described in Chapter 4. Sample A of 79 undergraduate participants, including 57 women (72%), completed the L-CAT to assess the consistency of synaesthetic associations over time, the Test for Creative Thinking-Drawing Production (TCT-DP), the Tellegen Absorption Scale (TAS), the Types of Mind Scale (TMS), Raven's Standard Progressive Matrices (SPM) as an assessment of fluid intelligence, and the Popular Emotional Intelligence Questionnaire (PEIQ). Linguistic-colour synaesthesia was found to be associated with both absorption and scale acceptation of emotion in the PEIQ. A second-order relation was also found by EFA. In the hierarchical model of *thinking*, the linguistic-colour associations were related to *openness to unusual experiences*, together with absorption and creativity, whereas in the hierarchical model of *association*, linguistic-colour associations were related to *internal associations*, together with absorption, fluid intelligence, and global types of mind. However, the study constitutes a preliminary analysis that needs to be supported by studies on much larger and more random samples of participants.

Chapter 5 covers a study examining whether synaesthesia is related to traits of temperament and personality. A total of 79 participants of Sample B, including eight linguistic-colour synaesthetes, completed the L-CAT, Big Five personality inventory (the Neuroticism Extraversion Openness Five-Factor Inventory (NEO-FFI)), and three temperament questionnaires: the Emotionality-Activity-Sociability Temperament Survey (EAS-TS), the Formal Characteristics of Behaviour – Temperament Inventory (FCB-TI), and the Pavlovian Temperament Survey (PTS). Participants of Sample A, including 11 linguistic-colour synaesthetes and 68 non-synaesthetes, completed the L-CAT and three-dimensional personality assessment, using the Eysenck Personality Questionnaire – Revised (EPQ-R). Synaesthetes differed from non-synaesthetes in higher conscientiousness and extraversion, and also in the balance of their nervous system processes. Synaesthetes showed a higher tendency to a predominance of strength of inhibition over excitation. Conversely, in non-synaesthetes, excitation dominated over inhibition. The L-CAT was correlated with extraversion and agreeableness in the NEO-FFI, with the Lie Scale of the EPQ-R, with anger from the EAS-TS in synaesthetes, and with sensory sensitivity in non-synaesthetes. Partial least-squares (PLS) regression was performed on the Sample B synaesthetes' results. This analysis showed that four higher-order latent variables (emotionality, arousability, sociability, and disinhibition) in the model accounted for 87% of the variance of the L-CAT and explained 99% of the variance of individual differences in personality and temperament.

It is important to note that there are some limitationss to the present set of studies. The main limitation is small sample size, so conclusions from the present study are not very strong. Among 141 students participating in the synaesthesia assessment, only 19 were considered to be linguistic-colour synaesthetes. Nevertheless, only half of the total sample (approximately 70 participants, including either 8 or 11 synaesthetes) were involved in studies described in Chapters 3, 4, and 5, which concerned relationships between linguistic-colour synaesthesia and individual differences in cognitive and personality dimensions. Although standard statistical methods were used, with an adequate level of significance for the small sample size, we should regard the results with caution. Thus, replication of the present research with a more random and much larger sample size seems necessary for further examination of the tendencies found in the present investigations. However, the results of the present study seem to be strongly related to one specific assessment, and this is a second limitation of the study. Thus, it is most likely that other research using alternative synaesthesia tests, as well as other methods of assessing personality, intelligence, and cognitive dimensions, may give different outcomes from the results found here. The third limitation of the study is that all of the participants were White and Polish (see Appendix A for more details). If linguistic-colour synaesthesia depends strongly on language, race, culture, and social context, the present results cannot be generalized for people from other countries and cultures. Future comparative studies conducted across several countries and cultural groups may resolve these issues. Finally, the present study relates to linguistic types of synaesthesia. The other types and kinds of synaesthesia (e.g., music-colour, touch-smell, ordinal-linguistic personification, mirror-touch, number-form) may involve distinct relationships with either personality or other dimensions of individual differences.

When we consider the limitations described above together, it seems appropriate to regard the present study as a preliminary case study, in which the same participants were involved in multiple psychological measures. This deep view of linguistic-colour synaesthesia in a wide context of other human traits seems be a unique opportunity to formulate general rules for the origination of both cross-modal and intramodal associations. Because association seems to be the most basic element of the thinking process, this kind of knowledge may shed light on the development of human intelligence and creativity. On the other hand, studying synaesthesia may help to explain cognitive disorders such as schizophrenia, unusual states of consciousness (e.g., aura vision, out-of-body experiences, mystical states), savant skills, and autism. Therefore, cross-sectional research seems necessary in the future.

I would like to thank Sean Day for his review of the first draft of the present book, and also the reviewers and the associate editor of *Behavior Research Methods* for their helpful comments and suggestions regarding the synaesthesia assessment. I would like to express my gratitude to Bożena Wojciechowska-Maszkowska for her assistance and to Oskar Rewucki for his technical aid with the L-CAT software preparation. I extend my sincere appreciation to Rebecca Taylor and Carrie Parkinson, editors at Cambridge University Press. Finally, I am grateful to Roman Kaźmierski for his sacrificial assistance during my work on this book, and my family, especially Alicja Pasierbska, for their support.

1 Exploring the structure and distribution of linguistic-colour associations in the concrete–abstract and strong–weak dimensions

1.1 Relationship between synaesthesia and common association

Synaesthesia is described in the scientific literature as an unusual, bizarre, and rare phenomenon (Hochel and Milán, 2008). Some researchers, however, express doubts about the mysterious nature of synaesthesia, observing a number of similarities between synaesthesia and common cross-modal associations (e.g., Elias *et al.*, 2003; Mulvenna and Walsh, 2006; Cohen Kadosh, Henik, Catena *et al.*, 2009). Indeed, several studies indicate that both synaesthetes and non-synaesthetes can associate high-pitched sounds with bright colours, and low tones with dark colours (Marks, 1989; Ward, Huckstep, and Tsakanikos, 2006; Spence, 2011). In addition, many non-synaesthetes can link spatial forms with days of the week or months in a similar manner to time-space synaesthetes (Makioka, 2009; Brang *et al.*, 2010).

The tendency of synaesthetes to connect colours with language (i.e., letters of the alphabet, numbers, words) is similar to that of non-synaesthetes (Hubbard, 1996; Simner *et al.*, 2005; Cohen Kadosh, Henik, and Walsh, 2007). A recent study (Brang, Rouw, Ramachandran, and Coulson, 2011) revealed that more similarly shaped graphemes correspond with more similar synaesthetic colours, stronger effects observed in individuals and more intense synaesthetic experiences (projector synaesthetes). These results support the cascaded cross-tuning (CCT) model of synaesthesia, implicate early perceptual mechanisms as driving factors in the elicitation of synaesthetic hues, and further highlight the relationship between the conceptual and perceptual factors of synaesthesia.

Furthermore, a recent study by Watson, Akins, and Enns (2012) revealed that the shape, frequency, and ordinality of individual letters have a secondary influence on synaesthetic colour assignments. This suggests that synaesthetic associations are acquired alongside learning the alphabet, with associations involving letter shapes, ordinality, and frequency made independently and idiosyncratically. Because these mappings of the structure of similarities between letters and colours are similar to those in numerous other cognitive and perceptual domains, the implication is that synaesthetic associations operate on principles common to many areas of human cognition.

Perhaps there is a common mechanism that accounts for cross-modal associations in both synaesthetes and non-synaesthetes. Some researchers propose that synaesthesia lies at the high end of a spectrum of cross-modal connections (Martino and Marks, 2001; Cohen Kadosh and Henik, 2007; Spence, 2011; Bien *et al.*, 2012). According to Martino and Marks (2001), weak synaesthesia represents common cross-modal associations that are dependent on individual experience and implicit knowledge about interactions between concrete objects (Marks, Hammeal, and Bornstein, 1987). Perceptual knowledge about objects and events is represented in terms of locations in a multidimensional and multimodal space. For example, large musical instruments (e.g., bassoon, cello, double bass) produce lower and milder sounds than smaller instruments (e.g., flute, clarinet, violin). Verbal processes thus access this graded perceptual knowledge, permitting an interpretation of synaesthetic metaphors according to the rules of cross-modal perception. Strong synaesthesia (Martino and Marks, 2001), also known as idiopathic, constitutional (Grossenbacher, 1997), or developmental synaesthesia (Harrison and Baron-Cohen, 1997), refers to idiosyncratically more abstract associations such as musical notation-colour (Ward, Tsakanikos, and Bray, 2006), time-space (Brang *et al.*, 2010), and ordinal-linguistic personification (Amin *et al.*, 2011; Simner *et al.*, 2011).

In this context, the problem of the distinction between synaesthesia and other forms of associations arises. What are the borders and the nature of the relationship between synaesthesia and common associations? Apart from being an inducer in the abstract–concrete dimension, a genetic basis seems to be another origin of synaesthesia and the acquisition of common and cross-modal associations. The rationale behind the genetic origin theory originates from some evidence that synaesthesia may run in families (Bailey and Johnson, 1997; Barnett, Finucane, *et al.*, 2008; Tomson *et al.*, 2011), and that the proportion of female to male synaesthetes reveals that more females than males report synaesthetic experiences (Baron-Cohen, Burt, Smith-Laittan, Harrison, and Bolton, 1996; Rich, Bradshaw, and Mattingley, 2005).

Although, at present, progress in the exploration of the genetic basis of synaesthesia can be noted (Bargary and Mitchell, 2008; Brang and Ramachandran, 2011), some reports appear to be inconsistent in their support for a strong genetic basis of synaesthesia. For example, Smilek and colleagues (Smilek, Moffatt, *et al.*, 2002; Smilek, Dixon, and Merikle, 2005), in two distinct case studies, revealed that in both male and female monozygotic twins, only one sibling was a synaesthete. Moreover, other studies (Simner, Mulvenna, *et al.*, 2006; Rogowska, 2007) on more random samples have failed to confirm the existence of gender differences in synaesthesia, and a more recent study on the genetic sources of synaesthesia did not provide any support for the X-linkage hypothesis (Asher *et al.*, 2009). Instead, current findings on synaesthesia indicate its genetic heterogeneity (Brang and Ramachandran, 2011; Tomson *et al.*, 2011).

Many synaesthetes claim that for as far back as they can remember they have always experienced synaesthesia in their daily perceptions. Although congenital synaesthesia seems to be present from earliest childhood and consistent over time, there is also evidence that synaesthesia may change over life (Spalding and Zangwill, 1950; Sacks, Waserman, Zeki, and Siegel, 1988; Simner, Mayo, and Spiller, 2009). Some types of synaesthesia could be evoked or obstructed by psychoactive substances (Ahmadi, Keshtkar, and Pridmore, 2011), post-hypnotic suggestion (Cohen Kadosh, Henik, Catena, *et al.*, 2009; Terhune, Cardeña, and Lindgren, 2010), or suggestive sensations (Biocca, Kim, and Choi, 2001; Schaefer, Noennig, Heinze, and Rotte, 2006). There are also well-known cases of acquired and post-accidental synaesthesia that occurs independently and unwittingly during adulthood because of biochemical brain changes, neurological dysfunctions, or permanent nerve damage, or as the result of an accident or disease, such as cancer, multiple sclerosis, or migraine (see Rogowska, 2011).

The explanations for different kinds and types of synaesthesia could depend on distinct neurocognitive and psychological mechanisms (Afra, Funke, and Matsuo, 2009; Novich, Cheng, and Eagleman, 2011; Sinke *et al.*, 2012). In accordance with the idea of the integrative or compensatory function, different kinds of synaesthesia could appear during various periods of human life that are critical for the development of perception (Rogowska, 2011). Because grapheme-colour synaesthesia is connected to knowledge of culturally acquired symbols and concepts (Nikolić, 2009), it cannot emerge at birth. Indeed, a study of a large, randomized population of children aged 6–8 years revealed that grapheme-colour synaesthesia emerged along a developmental path and evolved over time following environmental exposure to learned linguistic units (Simner, Harrold, Creed, Monro, and Foulkes, 2009). From comparison of its prevalence in children (Simner, Harrold, *et al.*, 2009) and adults (Simner, Mulvenna, *et al.* 2006), it can be concluded that grapheme-colour synaesthesia expands from childhood (1.3% of synaesthetes) and achieves more consistent inducer-concurrent mappings in adulthood (2.2% of synaesthetes), through stages of incremental acquisition.

Moreover, research has shown that grapheme-colour synaesthetic associations can be transferred and generalized into newly learned graphemes (Mroczko, Metzinger, Singer, and Nikolić, 2009; Asano and Yokosawa, 2012; Jürgens and Nikolić, 2012). Furthermore, Witthoft and Winawer (2006) showed that the particular synaesthetic associations between the English letters and colours, which were learned in childhood from a set of refrigerator magnets, were later transferred into the Cyrillic script in a systematic way. The colours induced by the Cyrillic letters were determined by their visual or phonetic similarity to English letters. In light of these findings, it seems appropriate to assume that synaesthesia arises as an effect of the interplay between genotype and phenotype.

The idiosyncratic character of synaesthetic experiences and the wide range of types of synaesthesia (Day, 2005; Novich *et al.*, 2011) seem to confirm this assumption. Synaesthesia could be an effect of an implicit learning process in those individuals who possess inborn susceptibility to it. There is some evidence that, at least in some synaesthetes, cross-activation occurs relatively early in perceptual mechanisms of visual processing (e.g., Barnett, Foxe, *et al.*, 2008; Brang and Ramachandran, 2010; Brang, Rouw, *et al.*, 2011). This may explain the involuntary character of synaesthetic associations in the majority of synaesthetes. Some people claim that they have synaesthetic experiences but have not had it confirmed experimentally, whereas others are convinced that they are not synaesthetes despite experiencing synaesthetic associations (Simner, 2012a).

1.2 Linguistic-colour synaesthesia as a form of linguistic-colour association

This study focuses on the linguistic form of synaesthesia in the context of common linguistic-colour associations. Research on a random sample showed that synaesthetes are not easy to distinguish from non-synaesthetes on the basis of measurement of test–retest consistency (Simner, Mulvenna, *et al.*, 2006; Brang *et al.*, 2010). Although examination of the consistency of synaesthetic experiences has been considered to be the behavioural 'gold standard' for determining the genuineness of the condition (Rich *et al.*, 2005; Asher, Aitken, Farooqi, Kurmani, and Baron-Cohen, 2006; Simner, 2007), it is now questionable whether consistency may be a good assessment of synaesthesia (Simner, 2012a, 2012b).

With the use of test–retest research procedures, synaesthesia is only arbitrarily confirmed in those individuals whose synaesthetic associations are around 80–100% consistent over time. However, studies on large groups of participants (Simner, Mulvenna, *et al.*, 2006) indicate that there exist individuals who appear to understand the nature of the condition, and who feel strongly that they experience it, but who fail to pass the consistency test because the vast majority of them are *in fact not synaesthetic at all by their own admission* (Simner, 2012a).

The present study uses another indicator of synaesthesia (beside the test–retest consistency of associations) – namely, the range of associations. This concerns the range of semantic categories involved in synaesthesia (e.g., some synaesthetes associate only forenames with colours, whereas others see all words in colours regardless of their category), as well as the range of word-colour associations within a category (e.g., number of coloured letters among all letters of the alphabet). It seems reasonable to expect that stronger synaesthetes would experience a more constant and greater range of word-colour associations than weaker synaesthetes.

The question of how to define synaesthesia (Simner, 2012a) and how to classify individuals as synaesthetes is related to the prevalence of synaesthesia in the general population (e.g., Rich *et al.*, 2005; Simner, Mulvenna, *et al.*, 2006; Banissy, Cohen Kadosh, Maus, Walsh, and Ward, 2009). There is great divergence in the estimation of synaesthesia, ranging in various studies from 0.05% of the population for linguistic synaesthesia (Baron-Cohen *et al.*, 1996) to 26% for time-space synaesthesia (Mann, Korzenko, Carriere, and Dixon, 2009). However, all of these studies examined synaesthesia as a dichotomous categorical phenomenon.

The present study, in contrast, considers synaesthesia as a continuous variable that is measurable on a quantitative scale that represents monotonically increasing values, depending on the number and strength of synaesthetic associations (Rogowska, 2011). It is assumed here that stronger associations are characterized by many elements of the category (e.g., all letters of the alphabet) and are relatively more consistent over time (e.g., letter *A* is always carmine). Weaker associations consist of a small number of elements and are relatively more unstable, depending on situation, mood, etc. According to the bell curve, if synaesthesia represents a normal distribution, the strongest cases of synaesthesia (scoring higher than 2 *SD* above *M*) are very rare (about 2% of the population), whereas the prevalence of the weaker form of synaesthesia may range from 34% (scores of 0–1 *SD* above *M*) to 14% of the population (scores of 1–2 *SD* above *M*), depending on the intensity of a synaesthetic trait.

If linguistic synaesthesia demonstrates a continuous normal distribution, this may have practical and theoretical consequences. Theoretically, synaesthesia could be viewed as a trait, and as such may be correlated and compared with any other continuous human trait. Synaesthesia might then depend on a specific configuration of an unknown number of traits

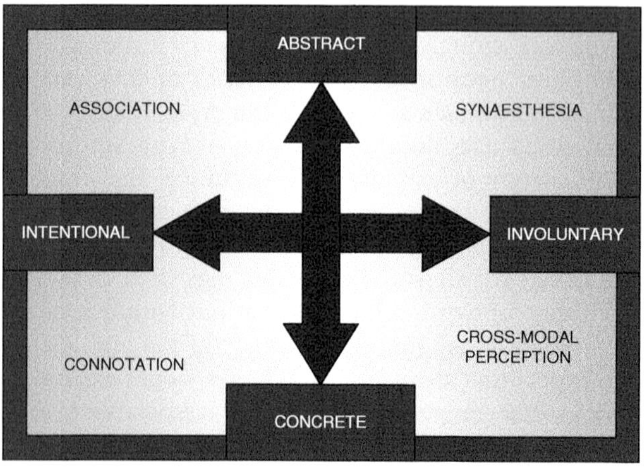

Figure 1.1 Hypothetical model of linguistic-colour associations.

and dimensions of individual differences. Research using parametric statistics can examine these presumptions. The main aim of the present study is to explore the structure of linguistic-colour associations on the concrete–abstract, involuntary–intentional, and strong–weak dimensions (Figure 1.1).

The concrete–abstract dimension refers to the linguistic type of inducer, whereas the involuntary–intentional dimension pertains to the emergence of colour concurrence. The weak–strong dimension may involve three features of concurrence: vividness (internal–external), consistency of associations over time, and range (selective–complete). Stronger associations could be characterized by more vivid external projections of concurrence, more stable associations over time, and a large number of associations within a linguistic category (e.g., all letters of the alphabet). In the present study, synaesthesia is represented by involuntary and abstract linguistic-colour associations that could be either stronger or weaker. Common connotations and associations are linked with the intentional and concrete dimension, while cross-modal associations probably constitute a chain linking the involuntary and concrete dimension.

The strength of linguistic-colour associations will be assessed here by two quantitative indicators: consistency and range. In addition, qualitative differences between abstract and concrete associations may be placed within a dimension represented by various types of inducer. Some inducers were stipulated as more concrete, some as more abstract, and some as a mixture of both. Concrete word-colour connotations are based on experience and memory with regard to common links between a word and its denotation. Colour is an attribute of a denoted object (e.g., grass/green, sun/yellow). The concrete association reflects the relationship between the object and its attributes (i.e., fruits, colour terms) known from experience rather than abstract reasoning. On the other hand, abstract associations are related to symbols (e.g., numbers and letters of the alphabet) and abstract concepts (e.g., forenames and days of the week), well known to be synaesthetic inducers. The other categories of words within a test, such as months and seasons of the year, verbs, adjectives, and pseudowords, may involve either connotations or synaesthetic associations. It is assumed here that common and concrete associations of colours with colour terms and fruits will be consistent over time for all participants, and this should be reflected in less variance. Because of individual differences in synaesthesia, more abstract word-colour associations should reveal a higher variance in the total sample, but a lower one in strong synaesthetes.

The finding that linguistic-colour synaesthetes use principles common to other sensory and cognitive domains seems to support the view that synaesthesia builds on normal mechanisms (Simner *et al.*, 2005; Barnett, Foxe, *et al.*, 2008). If this hypothesis is plausible, and there is a common mechanism for weak and strong word-colour associations, it should be mirrored in their homogeneous structure in the present study. Both abstract and concrete linguistic-colour associations should be loaded in a one-factor solution by exploratory factor analysis (EFA). The linguistic-colour associations measurement will be validated here by way of multidimensional data analysis, such as factor and cluster analyses.

1.3 Linguistic-colour association assessment

The Linguistic-Colour Association Test (L-CAT) was used to examine linguistic synaesthesia and common associations. The first version of the test comprised 134 linguistic items in the Polish language (on scales: *Alphabet*, *Nouns*, *Adjectives*, *Colour terms*, *Fruits*, *Forenames*, *Days of the week*, *Numbers*, and *Pseudowords*), and 57 musical items (on scales: *Pitches*, *Minor and major keys*, and *Timbres of musical instruments*) demonstrated aurally in random order within each category with the use of headphones. The participants (125 high-school students, aged 16–19 years, $M = 17.72$) were to choose one colour that they associated most with a given item from a palette of 72 colours (9 hues for each of 8 basic colours: brown, red, orange, yellow, green, blue, purple, and grey) shown on the computer screen during the examination (Rogowska, 2007). The retest was carried out 2 months after the test, and the consistency of test–retest colours was the measure of synaesthesia. Unfortunately, some of

Table 1.1 *List of items within L-CAT scales*

Categories of the test	Particular items of the L-CAT
1. Colour terms	red, blue, green, yellow, orange, brown, white, grey, turquoise, purple
2. Fruits (nouns)	lemon, orange, raspberry, gooseberry, banana, plum, blueberry, cherry, apple, strawberry
3. Verbs	work, ride, swim, throw, carry, go out, take, speak, sleep, lie
4. Adjectives	painful, sour, sweet, bitter, rough, salty, loud, soft, sharp, edgy
5. Months and Seasons of the year	January, February, March, April, May, June, July, August, September, October, November, December, spring, summer, autumn, winter
6. Days	Monday, Tuesday, Wednesday, Thursday, Friday, Saturday, Sunday, yesterday, today, tomorrow
7. Forenames (Polish)	Roman, Mateusz, Tomasz, Piotr, Adam, Ewa, Magdalena, Kasia, Natalia, Iza
8. Pseudowords	gręzibów, korpen, pojke, askungen, flikanu, lelurgia, tepar, hynzido, bromsary, czeliś
9. Numbers	1, 2, 3, 4, 5, 6, 7, 8, 9, 10, 100, 1,000, 54, 328
10. Alphabet (in Polish)	A, ą, B, C, ć, D, E, ę, F, g, H, i, J, k, L, ł, M, N, ń, O, ó, P, Q, r, S, ś, T, u, V, w, X, y, Z, ź, ż

Notes: L-CAT = Linguistic-Colour Association Test.

the synaesthetes complained that the range of colours was too narrow and that they sometimes associated several colours with one item. Thus, they reported that they were confused and uncertain as to which colour to choose.

The revised version of the test comprises many more colours than the original version. The palette of colours was developed from the basic list of X11 colour names distributed with the Windows X System and standardized by SVG[1] user agents. In addition, in comparison with the original test, the revised version excluded musical scales, but included a training subtest, verbs instead of nouns, and an extra scale of words that could induce synaesthesia – that is, months and seasons of the year in Polish (see Table 1.1). In the new version of the test, the linguistic items were presented simultaneously in both forms: acoustically in the headphones, and visually as graphemes in colours selected by participants during the trial.

[1] The Scalable Vector Graphics (SVG) specification is an open standard that has been under development by the World Wide Web Consortium (W3C) since 1999.

Thirty-nine undergraduates (including 14 women) aged 17–58 years took part in a pilot study with an immediate retest procedure. After the pilot test, the students were asked to describe their experiences and any difficulties they might have had in performing the test. Some participants reported technical problems in finding appropriate buttons or colours. For that reason, an L-CAT tutorial was designed. In addition, the software itself was improved, because some important data were missing from the protocols or were inaccurate. After the corrections had been made, those pilot study participants who had previously reported problems retook the L-CAT test in its new version and found it more appropriate with regard to their experiences. The revised version of the L-CAT was used in the further research.

The current version of the test began with the tutorial instruction and 16 trials of the Visual Colour Discrimination (VCD) training subtest, which acquainted the participants with the colour palette (see Plate 1a and b). The main test commenced immediately after the completion of the training subtest. Linguistic inducers were presented in Polish, and all terms refer to a Middle-European culture. The test comprised a total of 135 linguistic inducers (see Table 1.1 for more details), within 10 categories: *Colour Terms*, *Fruits*, *Verbs*, *Adjectives*, *Months and Seasons* (12 months and four seasons), *Days* (seven days of the week, with Monday as the first day; and also 'yesterday', 'today', and 'tomorrow'), *Forenames* (Polish), *Pseudowords*, *Numbers* (Arabic symbols), and *Alphabet* (the 35 letters of the Polish alphabet). Particular items from the L-CAT were presented randomly within each category, except for Alphabet. Letters of the alphabet without any semantic context are perceived by a listener as abstract combinations of consonants and vowels. Letters set in an alphabetical sequence, on the other hand, appear to make the test clearer.

Participants indicated one or more colours (maximum of five) that they most associated with the item, using a palette of eight basic colours (see Plate 1a and c) and 360 additional hues (see Plate 2a and b), including 45 tints for each basic colour (see Plate 1b and d). Each colour selection was confirmed twice: by colouring the grapheme in the centre of the screen, and by colouring a small circle in the top left corner of the computer screen (Plate 1d). A subject could use a maximum of five different colours for each item; thus, a maximum of five circles could represent each selection. After choosing all of the appropriate colours (Plate 1c and d), participants confirmed their choices by clicking the 'correct' button (a green *V*), and continued the test by clicking the 'forward' button (green arrow to the right). They could revise one previous item by choosing the 'backward' button (green arrow to the left), or choose the button signifying the absence of any word-colour association (red *X*).

1.4 Consistency of colour measurement

To examine the types of synaesthesia that reveal colour as a concurrent sensation (e.g., linguistic-colour, music-colour, smell-colour), it is necessary to compare two colours assessed on two occasions for the same item (e.g., word, musical pitch), using a test–retest procedure. For example, music-colour synaesthetes should select exactly the same hue of red (e.g., carmine) among countless tints of various colours every time they hear a C-major chord during the examination. The colours assessed for the item in the test and retest are compared in terms of how much they differ.

Currently, computers seems to be the most useful tools for investigating linguistic and musical types of synaesthesia. Some computer tests use the measurement of distances between RGB (red, green, blue) model colours (e.g., de Thornley Head, 2006; Eagleman, Kagan, Nelson, Sagaram, and Sarma, 2007; Laeng, Hugdahl, and Specht, 2011). Although those techniques can effectively examine the virtual spectrum of lights on a computer screen (spectral colours), they seem insufficient for the examination of the human perception of colours of objects (structural colours). There are significant differences between the principles of mixing subtractive and additive colours (see Plate 4a and b for comparison). For example, there is a relatively greater distance between the two opponent colours, red and green, in the classical RYB (red, yellow, blue) model than in the RGB model. The RGB and RYB models also vary with respect to the proportion of representations of warm (red, orange, yellow) and cold (green, blue, purple) colours and, in particular, to the gamut of neutral colours (grey, white, brown).

Since there is evidence that synaesthesia may be a perceptual phenomenon (e.g., Palmeri, Blake, Marois, Flanery, and Whetsell, 2002; Kim, Blake, and Palmeri, 2006), in the present study, synaesthesia was estimated on the basis of the general principles of perception of colour objects and their structure. Colour perception depends on the observer's individual features related to knowledge, experience, and preferences as well as on current mood and emotional state, and variable environmental conditions (e.g., lighting, surface structure of the coloured object, degree of light absorption, reflection, adjoining colours).

Physically, colour derives from a spectrum of light (in the wavelength range visible to the human eye) interacting with the spectral sensitivities of the light receptors in the eye. The visible spectrum of light is in the wavelength range of 390–750 nm, with different pure spectral colours forming a spectrum (e.g., indigo is between 446 and 464 nm). A common list of the spectral colours identifies six main bands: red, orange, yellow, green, blue, and violet, although how people distinguish colours linguistically is a matter of cultural and historical contingency.

Physiological quantifications of colour may be defined by the degree to which different parts of the spectrum stimulate different types of cone cell in the retina. Whereas the RGB colour model relies on the output of physical devices rather than human visual perception, the CIELAB colour model is designed to approximate human vision. The CIELAB colour space specified by the International Commission on Illumination (CIE – Commission internationale de l'éclairage) is a three-dimensional colour appearance model. The three coordinates of CIELab represent the lightness of the colour – *L*: from 0 (black) to 100 (perfect white), and two dimensions of the chromatic value colour space: the red–green opponent channel (*a* – negative values indicate green while positive values indicate magenta) and the yellow–blue opponent channel (*b* – negative values indicate blue and positive values indicate yellow) that correspond to two types of cone in the human eye. The *a* and *b* axes have no specific numerical limits.

It is assumed here that uniform changes of components in the CIELAB colour space aim to correspond to uniform changes in the perceived colour, so that the relative perceptual differences between any two colours in CIELAB can be approximated by treating each colour as a point in a three-dimensional space (with three components: *L*, *a*, *b*) with the Euclidean distance between them. Thus, in the present study, the values of colours recorded in the L-CAT in the RGB colour space (with a range between 0 and 255 for each dimension) were converted into CIELAB. The differences between two colours selected in the test and retest for each item were calculated according to the Euclidean vector distance:

$$\Delta E = \sqrt{(\Delta L)^2 + (\Delta a)^2 + (\Delta b)^2}$$

The differences between two colours could be interpreted as follows: (a) $0 < \Delta E < 1$ – that is, a standard observer cannot see the difference; (b) $1 < \Delta E < 2$ – that is, only an experienced observer can see the difference; (c) $2 < \Delta E < 3.5$ – that is, an inexperienced observer can see the difference; (d) $3.5 < \Delta E < 5$ – that is, everyone can see the difference clearly; and (e) $5 < \Delta E$ – that is, an observer can see two distinct colours. The results of each L-CAT scale were calculated as mean scores of items in the category of words. The statistical analysis was conducted with the STATISTICA software package.

1.5 Colour consistency and reaction time of linguistic-colour associations

The total of 161 participants was divided into two groups because of the distinct test–retest procedures (for more details see Appendix A). The surprise retest (135 L-CAT items in total) was taken immediately after the test (during the same session) by 82 students in Sample A, and 1 month later by 79 students in Sample B. It is difficult to invite people to retake a laboratory test after some time; thus, a retest immediately following the test seemed much easier to use with a larger sample. Participants were not informed about the retest in order to avoid any interference by the use of mnemonic techniques with the test results. After each participant had completed a total of 270 answers to the test–retest items, the computer recorded the values of the colours in RGB format as well as participants' reaction time. Finally, a protocol was generated for each participant (see excerpts in Plate 3).

An analysis of differences between the two alternative L-CAT test–retest procedures was the first step in the present study. Table B1.1 in Appendix B demonstrates descriptive statistics, such as mean (*M*), standard deviation (*SD*), variance (s^2), Kolmogorov–Smirnov *D* statistic (K–S *D*), and analysis of Student's *t*-test for independent samples, for the consistency of colour-word associations and reaction time (RT) of several L-CAT scales. As indicated by the Kolmogorov–Smirnov *D* statistic, both samples demonstrated a normal shape distribution for individual L-CAT scales and a close to normal distribution for the total mean result in the sample that participated in the retest immediately after the test. Sample B, who took the retest 1 month after the test, revealed significantly higher scores – that is, a greater distance between their test and retest colours – than the participants who took the retest immediately after the test. Because the data in the VCD training subtest demonstrated a strong deviation from normality in both samples, a non-parametric statistic was used for the analysis of intergroup differences. The Mann–Whitney *U* test revealed no differences in colour matching among the participants ($z = 0.10$, $p = .92$).

The mean RT measured in seconds (s) was also different in both groups. In comparison to Sample A, the Sample B group demonstrated a significantly shorter mean RT in most of the scales except for Forenames, Pseudowords, and the initial VCD training subtest (Table B1.1 in Appendix B). As indicated by the *U* test, these patterns of difference also applied to Months *and* Seasons ($z = 3.26$, $p = .001$), but not Alphabet ($z = 0.99$, $p = .323$). Taken together, the differences in the RT and colour consistency of associations over time may suggest that the participants from Sample A tried to recall their associations from the test during the retest that followed immediately, and it is likely that these efforts could have been partially effective. Thus, the sample retested immediately after the test needed more time to attain higher scores in colour consistency of associations than the participants retested 1 month later. In conclusion, the procedure with the longer test–retest interval seems more appropriate for synaesthesia assessment.

Because all of the L-CAT scales revealed a normal distribution in both samples, it was possible to covert the total scores into standard normalized *z*-scores with a mean zero and unit variance (separately for each group). The standardization made it possible to merge both samples for further analysis. Descriptive statistics were then computed for the total sample ($N = 161$). The Kolmogorov–Smirnov *D* statistic showed that all scales of the L-CAT met the criteria of continuity and normality (see Table B1.2 in Appendix B and Figure 1.2 for more details).

The *t*-test did not reveal any significant differences between male and female students with the exception of two scales. Women scored lower than men on the Fruits scale [$M_W = -0.18$, $M_M = 0.18$, $t(159) = -2.35$, $p = .02$], and in the L-CAT total [$M_W = -0.07$, $M_M = 0.15$, $t(159) = -2.25$, $p = .03$], suggesting less distance between test–retest colours for women. However, because the remaining scales displayed no differences between men and women, further analysis was conducted for the total sample.

The reliability coefficient (Cronbach's alpha) indicated an acceptable internal consistency for most L-CAT scales, except for low levels of reliability for Colours and Fruits (Table B1.2 in Appendix B). However, as expected, these two scales showed less variability in both samples (see Table B1.1 in Appendix B) before standardization, and thus were included in the structural analysis. The intercorrelation matrix represented significant relationships between particular scales of the L-CAT, with Pearson's coefficients ranging from .21 to .82.

1.6 Structural analysis for colour consistency of linguistic-colour associations

Factor analysis is applied to reduce the number of variables and to detect a structure in the relationships between variables – that is, to classify variables. An EFA was conducted to examine the structure of linguistic synaesthesia in the wider context of linguistic-colour associations. The objective of EFA is to identify unobserved factors, reveal common traits between variables, and provide further information about them. The typical grapheme-colour synaesthesia may be stimulated by the Alphabet and Numbers items, whereas

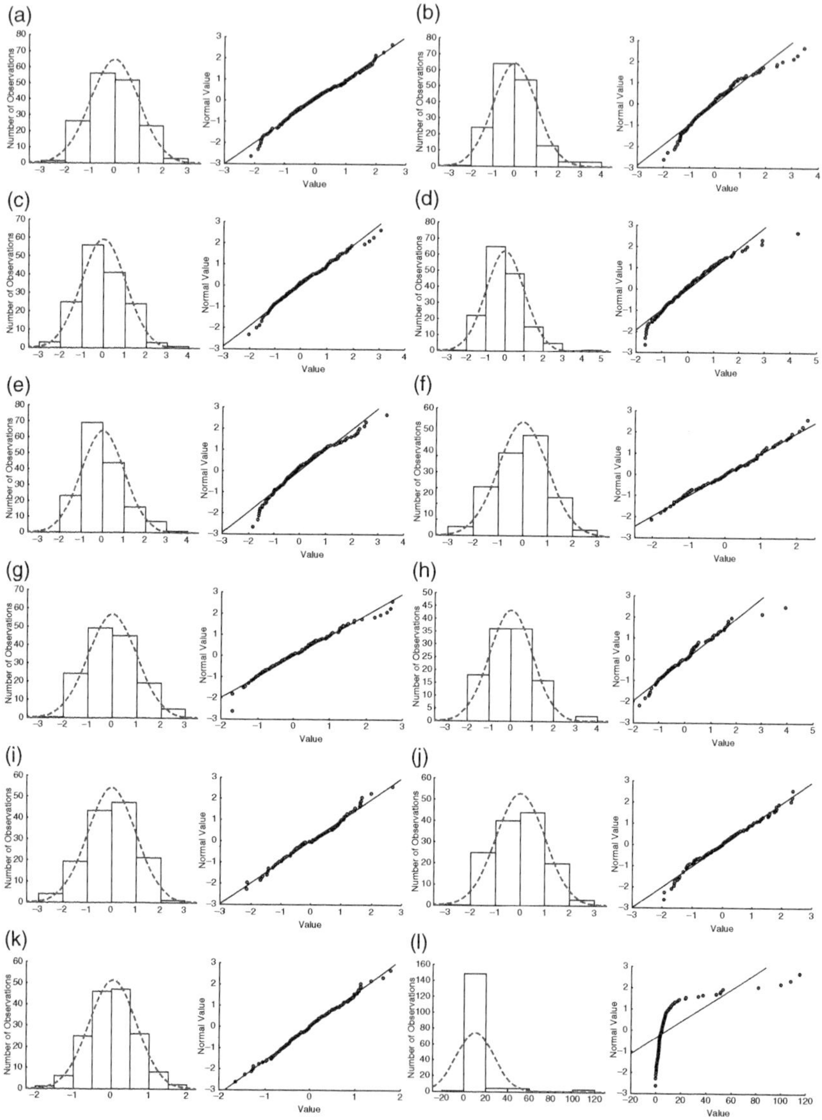

Figure 1.2 Distribution of standardized mean scores for particular L-CAT scales: (a) Colours, (b) Fruits, (c) Verbs, (d) Adjectives, (e) Months and Seasons of the year, (f) Days, (g) Forenames, (h) Pseudowords, (i) Numbers, (j) Alphabet, (k) total L-CAT mean result, and (l) Visual Colour Discrimination (VCD) training subtest. *x*-axis: mean scores of the scale; dashed line: expected normal distribution.

word-colour synaesthesia could be induced by Forenames and Days. Associations common to the general population were included in the Colours and Fruits scales. The other scales – that is, Verbs, Adjectives, Pseudowords, and Months and Seasons of the year – could bring about either word-colour connotations or synaesthetic experiences. Thus, if there are any latent variables within the L-CAT, EFA should be able to identify them.

The initial analysis of the correlation matrix (see Table B1.2 in Appendix B) showed that factor analysis was appropriate for an exploration of the structure of test–retest consistency of linguistic-colour associations. Because all scales had a normal distribution, the maximum likelihood (ML) technique was used as an extraction method in EFA (Cudeck and O'Dell, 1994). The analysis revealed a one-factor solution that accounted for 34% of variance, with goodness of fit amounting to $\chi^2(35) = 51.93$, $p = .033$, $n = 88$ (see Table 1.2 for more details).

An alternative method of extracting factors from the correlation matrix is principal-components analysis (PCA), which usually reduces the number of observed variables to a smaller number of principal components that account for most of the variance of observed variables. PCA with varimax rotation (orthogonal) revealed a two-factor solution, according to the Kaiser criterion (see also the scree test at Figure 1.3a), with eigenvalues accounting together for 53% of variance, $n = 88$ (Table 1.2 and Figure 1.3b).

Higher factor loadings were revealed in the EFA for Alphabet, Numbers, Days, and Forenames. This suggests that synaesthetic abstract

Table 1.2 *Factor loadings for test–retest consistency of linguistic associations with colours from the L-CAT*

	EFA	PCA	
Scales of the L-CAT	1-Factor	Factor 1	Factor 2
Colours	.19	.16	.84
Fruits	.25	.30	.00
Verbs	.61	.69	−.11
Adjectives	.63	.72	−.32
Days	.72	.76	.09
Months and Seasons	.48	.58	−.49
Forenames	.68	.72	.06
Pseudowords	.47	.55	.00
Numbers	.73	.73	.34
Alphabet	.78	.78	.27
Variance accounted	34%	40%	13%

Note: L-CAT = Linguistic-Colour Association Test.

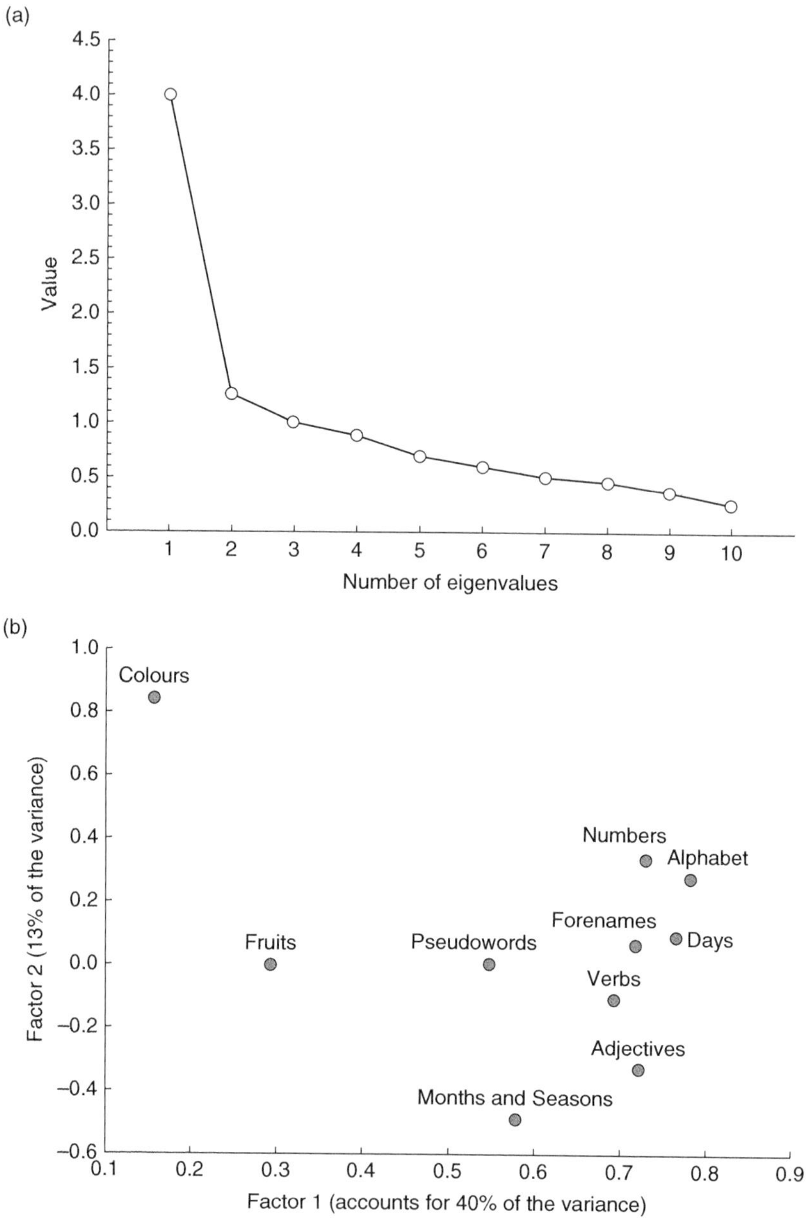

Figure 1.3 Results of PCA analysis with varimax rotation of the consistency of linguistic-colour associations: (a) scree test; (b) scatterplot of factor loadings.

associations with colours are the most representative for this factor, so it seems appropriate to name this factor 'linguistic synaesthesia'. This result confirmed the assumption that all of the L-CAT scales measure the same phenomenon, and that all associations with colour may share a common mechanism with reference to the test–retest consistency of associations. A similar conclusion can be drawn from the PCA, with the exception of Colours, which, as a single variable, constitutes the second factor.

The procedure for factor extraction in the PCA assumes that the number of components extracted is equal to the number of observed variables. These identified components accounted for most of the variance in the data but were not correlated with each other. Indeed, Colours did not correlate significantly with the other L-CAT scales and revealed lower variance and reliability, a finding that may explain these results.

1.7 Range of linguistic-colour associations

A range of linguistic-colour associations, as a second indicator of synaesthesia, was measured here by the number of word-colour associations within various linguistic categories, such as Forenames, Days of the week, etc. Participants could 'pass' on an unlimited number of items within both the test and retest of the L-CAT if they did not associate the word with any colour. Among the total of 21,802 responses derived from 161 participants, 13,996 (64%) linguistic inducers were included in association with colour, and 7,806 (36%) were excluded because participants did not reveal any word-colour associations (Figure 1.4).

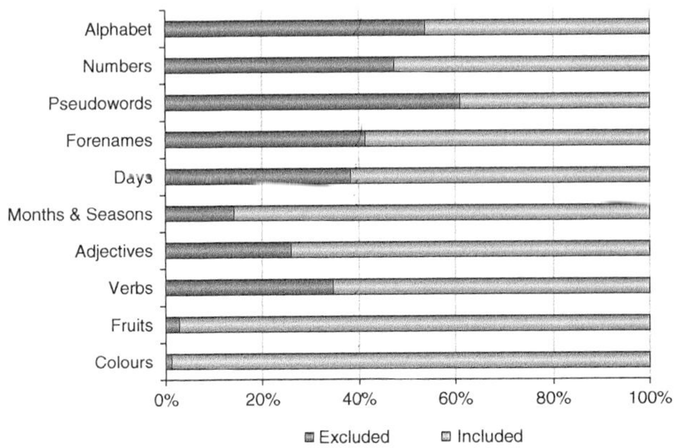

Figure 1.4 Percentage of items within each scale of the L-CAT that participants ($N = 161$) included and excluded from association with colour.

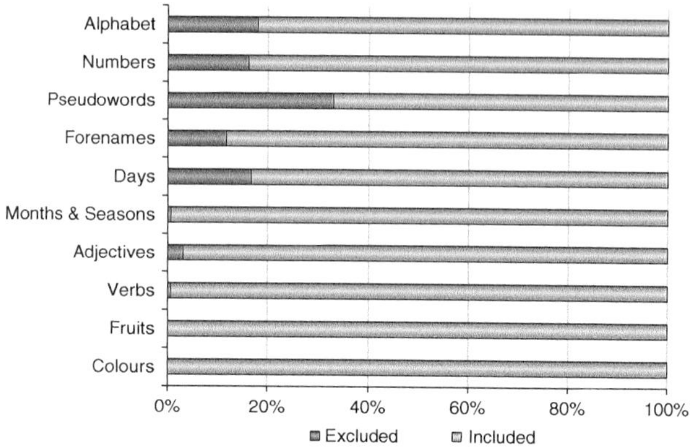

Figure 1.5 Percentage of participants who indicated at least a partial association with colour within the L-CAT scales (Included) or no associations within the scale (Excluded).

The larger and prevailing number of excluded items was noted within the Pseudowords (61%) and Alphabet (54%) scales. In addition, a significant number of excluded inducers of associations with colour were observed within Numbers (47%), Forenames (41%), and Days (38%), which are closely connected with linguistic synaesthesia.

A large number of participants ($n = 73$, 45%) did not select any colour for any of the inducers within at least one L-CAT scale, indicating the absence of any associations with colour in a semantic category. In such a case, the scale was excluded from the analysis of test–retest consistency of associations, because the mean result for the scale could not be calculated. For concrete word-colour associations such as Colours and Fruits, no scale was excluded, and only one person did not select any items for Verbs and Months. However, it should be noted that the majority of participants selected at least several items within the abstract categories of the L-CAT. Fewer than 20% of participants did not select any colour for either Alphabet, Numbers, Forenames, or Days (Figure 1.5).

The best measure of the range of linguistic-colour associations seems to be values calculated for total L-CAT and for each L-CAT scale separately. However, the number of linguistic associations with colour cannot be treated as a good indicator of synaesthesia without the examination of data on the quality of these matches from a test–retest consistency viewpoint. Thus, the range of consistent linguistic associations with colour was computed as a sum of the distances between test–retest colours for each item of the L-CAT. Unfortunately, the best result (identical colours)

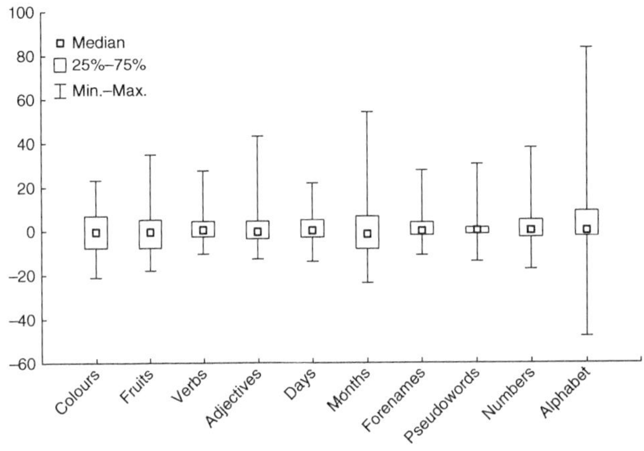

Figure 1.6 Descriptive statistics for the range of linguistic associations with colour in the L-CAT.

was represented by zero, which could have also signified the absence of associations. To eliminate the error, the scores were aggregated after conversion into the standard z scale. The interpretation of the sum then became much easier, since results showing a negative came to indicate strong synaesthesia (the least distance between colours meaning the best test–retest match; for example, a case in which exactly the same colour was selected twice for the item), and results showing a positive suggested connotations or weak synaesthesia (the furthest distance signifying the greatest difference between test–retest colours; for example, when a participant selected for the item acid green in the test and amaranth in the retest).

The Kolmogorov–Smirnov D statistic disproved the assumption of normality for most of the L-CAT scales except for Colours ($D = .05$, $p > .20$) and Fruits ($D = .08$, $p > .20$). The descriptive statistics are demonstrated in Figure 1.6. Unfortunately, these results did not allow the use of parametric statistics in further analysis. The widest range of scores referred to two scales which included most items: the 35 letters of the Alphabet and the 16 items within Months and Seasons of the year.

1.8 Structural analysis of the range of linguistic-colour associations

Cluster analysis involves the task of assigning a set of similar objects to groups. There were two reasons to use cluster analysis in the present

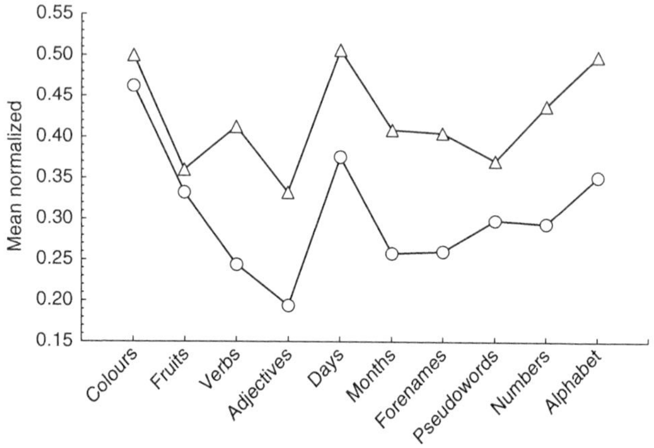

Figure 1.7 The range of linguistic-colour associations in two clusters: Selective Associators (n = 96, black line and circles) and Complete Associators (n = 65, grey line and triangles).

study. First, we intended to check whether the participants deployed distinct strategies for associating the linguistic items of the L-CAT with colours. To answer this question, and in particular to find the correct number of clusters, the expectation-maximization (EM) clustering algorithm was used with a v-fold cross-validation technique. Second, the range of linguistic associations with colours was derived from the analysis of test–retest consistency by way of several earlier transformations (RGB → CIELAB → standard Z → sum of z-scores). As such, it was highly probable that the final values demonstrated a normal distribution. The goal of EM clustering is to estimate the means and standard deviations for each cluster in order to maximize the likelihood of observed data (distribution). In other words, the EM algorithm attempts to approximate the observed distributions of values based on mixtures of different distributions in different clusters (Witten, Frank, and Hall, 2011). Indeed, the analysis indicated the existence of two clusters of participants (Figure 1.7) that could be described as *Complete Associators* (CA) ($n = 65$) and *Selective Associators* (SA) ($n = 96$). SA tended to use consistent linguistic-colour associations in selected scales of the L-CAT, whereas CA demonstrated more consistent linguistic-colour associations in all L-CAT scales.

The CA cluster attained relatively higher scores than SA with respect to the majority of the scales, except for Colours and Fruits (see Figure 1.8 and Table B1.3 in Appendix B for more details). The differences between

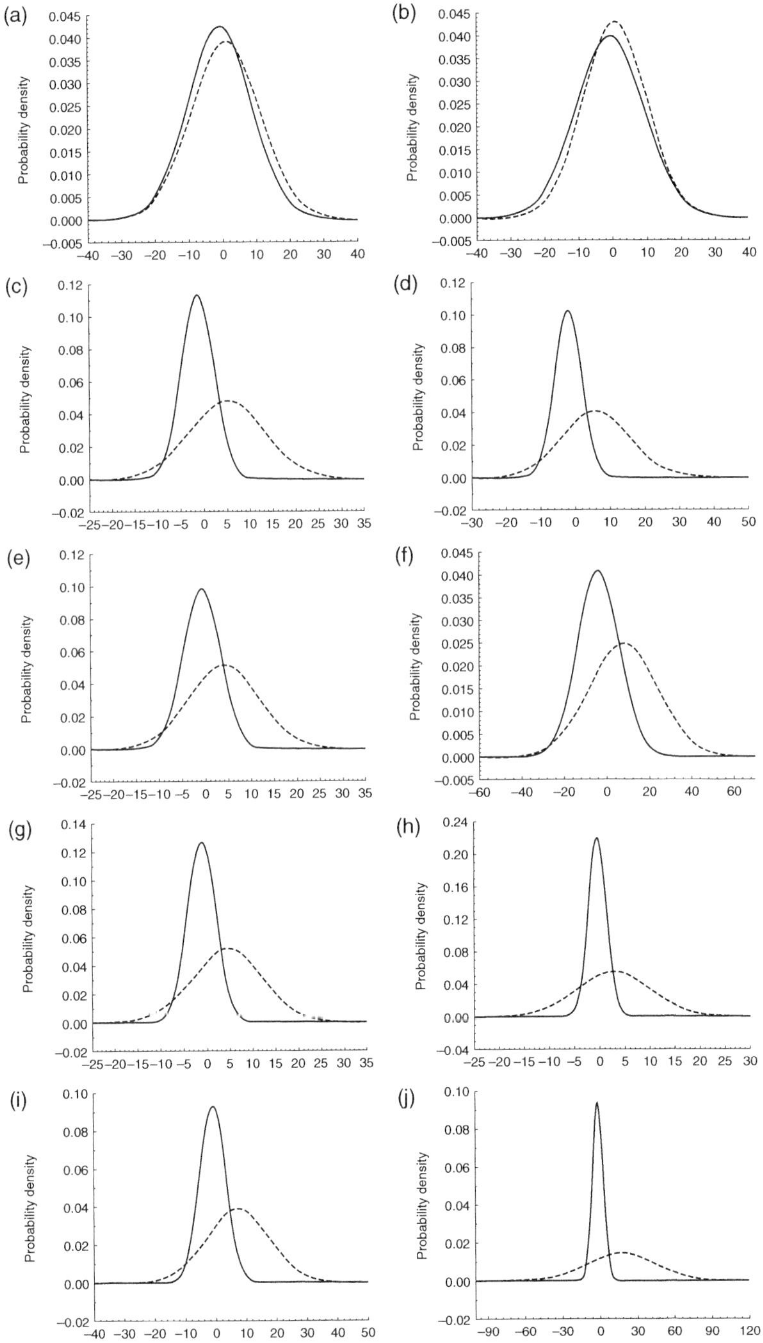

Figure 1.8 Distribution probability of two cluster groups. The result of the EM algorithm with v-fold cross-validation technique consisted of

the clusters followed a kurtosis rather than skewness distribution. The distribution was platykurtic for CA, and leptokurtic for SA. The distribution shape in the SA cluster seems to fit the multivariate Laplace distribution appropriate for representing the statistics of speech signals in various domains (Gazor and Zhang, 2003).

It is important to note that both groups (i.e., CA and SA) used associations between colours and the most concrete words (included within the scales of Fruits and Colours) in the same way (see Plate 3). For example, 'lemon' was yellow for all participants, even for grapheme-colour synaesthetes, who should have more abstract associations with colours (e.g., related to the dominant vowel or the first letter of the word). It can also be confirmed that all associations may have a common base. Because the participants associated months with the dominant (for the season of the year) colours of nature and environmental phenomena (e.g., flowers, grass, leaves on trees, snow, sea, sky), their associations can be classified more as concrete than abstract. The most abstract (synaesthetic) inducers were numbers and letters of the alphabet. Further research is necessary to explain the nature of the concrete–abstract connections.

1.9 The nature of linguistic-colour associations

The present study seems to support the assumption that linguistic-colour synaesthesia is not an anomalous phenomenon but an extremely strong involuntary and abstract form of association (Figure 1.1). The concrete–abstract dimension refers to the quality of associations, while the weak–strong dimension applies to the quantity (intensity) of these associations. Synaesthesia seems to be an abstract type of association that may characterize people with a hypersensitive colour perceptual system (Yaro and Ward, 2007; Banissy, Walsh, and Ward, 2009; Brang *et al.*, 2010). Synaesthetic (abstract) linguistic-colour associations could be as intense and consistent over time as concrete connotations (e.g., the connection between fruits and their colours). Moreover, there are neither qualitative nor quantitative differences between synaesthetes and non-synaesthetes in terms of concrete common associations.

Figure 1.8 (cont.)

two clusters: Cluster 1, a continuous line as the Selective Associators group ($n = 96$), and Cluster 2, a dashed line as the Complete Associators group ($n = 65$). The plots show EM clustering for the L-CAT scales: (a) Colours, (b) Fruits, (c) Verbs, (d) Adjectives, (e) Days, (f) Months, (g) Forenames, (h) Pseudowords, (i) Numbers, and (j) Alphabet.

A concrete word-colour association refers to the colour of an object that denotes the word in the closer nodes in the semantic network (Collins and Quillian, 1969), and can be described as typical, conventional, and unoriginal. This kind of association is not creative, but is based on convergent thinking (Guilford, 1967), and not on remote associations (Mednick, 1962; Mednick and Mednick, 1967). In the present study, colours were matched with words denoting fruits, colour terms, and months and seasons of the year. It was not surprising that the participants, independently of any synaesthetic traits, revealed common associations derived from the learning process of enculturation. The same rule may relate to the origin of synaesthetic colour-word association for numbers, letters of the alphabet, and days of the week. Witthoft and Winawer (2006, 2013) demonstrated that the particular colours seen by a grapheme-colour synaesthete were learned from a set of refrigerator magnets. Thus, synaesthesia could be much more related to both cross-modal and common concrete association than was previously expected. Current research suggests that synaesthesia and cross-modal matching may be a kind of tacit knowledge. Generally, the boundaries between synaesthetic and non-synaesthetic associations are hard to establish. This issue should be more widely explored in the future.

Most earlier studies examined synaesthesia in its strongest form and as a dichotomous phenomenon. Although such procedures are safe because of the high level of confidence of synaesthesia measurement, they limit the possibility of discovering the real nature of this kind of association. The present study proposes to consider synaesthesia as a trait with weaker and stronger dimensions. The normal distribution of consistency of linguistic-colour associations seems to confirm this assumption. This approach creates a new possibility for examining synaesthesia in a general population with the use of parametric statistics. The wide range of consistent linguistic-colour associations increases the probability of the assessment of synaesthesia.

The normal distribution of linguistic-colour associations suggests that synaesthesia may be determined by an almost infinite number of factors such as the learning process (Cohen Kadosh, Henik, and Walsh, 2009; Makioka, 2009; Mroczko *et al.*, 2009), cross-modal interactions (Marks, 1975; Evans and Treisman, 2010), metaphor-based connotations (Seitz, 2005; Keith, 2009), cognitive processing level (Ramachandran and Hubbard, 2001a; Ward, Li, Salih, and Sagiv, 2007), emotion (Ward, 2004; Hochel *et al.*, 2009), or an unknown number of cognitive skills, personality traits, and environmental variables. In view of the need to redefine synaesthesia (Simner, 2012a), it is necessary to explain the term 'synaesthetic trait', understood here as a strong tendency to use involuntarily abstract associations between particular features of intra-modal or cross-modal mental representations, which pertain to both the sensory and the semantic levels of cognitive processing. A general synaesthetic trait may be inherited (Tomson *et al.*, 2011), but a particular type of synaesthesia could crystallize into an idiosyncratic form at some stage of life and remain relatively constant over time. The results of the current study may open up many new possibilities for exploring other forms, types, and categories of synaesthetic association (Rogowska, 2011). The nature of association with synaesthesia in its strongest abstract form poses a fundamental question for the better understanding of human perception, intelligence, and creativity (Ramachandran and Hubbard, 2001b) as well as of sensory, mental, and cognitive disabilities (Ward, 2007; Murray, 2010).

2 Reconciling objective and subjective assessments of linguistic-colour associations: exploring the relationships between linguistic-colour synaesthesia and self-related sensing, body lateralization, and gender

2.1 Reconciling objective and subjective methods for synaesthesia examination

2.1.1 Linguistic-colour synaesthesia assessment

One of the most important methodological problems in synaesthesia research is to reconcile first-person subjective reports of synaesthetic experiences with objective third-person experimental investigations. Harrison and Baron-Cohen (1995) postulated that the diagnosis of synaesthesia requires a combination of subjective self-report methods and objective experimental testing. In addition, Smilek and Dixon (2002) argued that a complete understanding of synaesthesia requires a combination of experimental investigations of synaesthesia and synaesthetes' subjective reports.

Among psychological methods, synaesthesia research has traditionally used variants of the Stroop paradigm as an objective correlate of subjective synaesthetic reports (e.g., Mills, Boteler, and Oliver, 1999; Dixon, Smilek, Cudahy, and Merikle, 2000; Mattingley, Rich, Yelland, and Bradshaw, 2001, Berteletti, Hubbard, and Zorzi, 2010). The other 'gold standard' used in synaesthesia research is the test of consistency of synaesthetic associations (e.g., Baron-Cohen, Harrison, Goldstein, and Wyke, 1993; Baron-Cohen *et al.*, 1996; Asher *et al.*, 2006). Novich *et al.* (2011) used the test–retest consistency method to examine synaesthesia among 19,133 participants who completed the Synaesthesia Battery (Eagleman *et al.*, 2007). They revealed five distinct groupings of forms of synaesthesia: spatial sequence, coloured sequence, coloured music, coloured sensation, and non-visual sequel synaesthesias.

Subjective psychological methods of synaesthesia examination include interviews and questionnaire surveys. Interview-based reports on synaesthesia were predominant at the turn of the nineteenth and twentieth centuries (Marks, 1975). Cytowic (2002) diagnosed synaesthesia according to five criteria:

1. synaesthesia is involuntary but elicited;
2. synaesthesia is spatially extended;
3. synaesthetic precepts are consistent and discrete;
4. synaesthesia is memorable;
5. synaesthesia is emotional.

Interviews seem to be used most frequently in single-case examinations of developmental synaesthesia (e.g., Devereux, 1966; Luria, 1968; Baron-Cohen, Wyke, and Binnie, 1987; Cytowic, 1993; Ward and Simner, 2003), as well as for investigations of acquired synaesthesia (e.g., Armel and Ramachandran, 1999; Jacome, 1999; Podoll and Robinson, 2002; Ward, 2007).

Dixon, Smilek, and Merikle (2004) showed that synaesthetes, who were divided into projectors and associators on the basis of their subjective reports, revealed distinct patterns of the Stroop effect. Individual differences in synaesthetic experiences were also examined by questionnaires. Skelton, Ludwig, and Mohr (2009) compared two questionnaire forms to distinguish between projector and associator synaesthetes: an illustrated form that presented the synaesthetic experience in a visual illustrated format, and a standard form to ascertain these differences through the self-reported rating of statements. In both questionnaires, participants utilized Likert scales to indicate the degree that reflected their own experience. The results of these studies indicated that only the illustrated questionnaire was sufficient to make an accurate and reliable categorization of synaesthetes into projectors and associators.

Most likely, the first synaesthesia questionnaire was systematically developed by Jones (1976, as cited by Wicker and Holahan, 1978). Wicker and Holahan (1978) used the Synaesthesia Questionnaire (SQ) to examine relationships between synaesthesia, verbal analogies, and intersensory alignments. The cover page of the SQ contained a careful definition of synaesthesia and a full description of the phenomenon, along with a number of examples of responses judged as acceptable and unacceptable indicators of synaesthetic experiences. Participants were asked to evaluate the presence, spontaneity, consistency, frequency, vividness, and intensity of their synaesthetic experiences on a 5-point scale. They were also able to describe synaesthetic experiences in an open-ended, unstructured form. A revised version of this questionnaire was developed by Domino (1989).

Smilek and Dixon (2002) argued that identification of synaesthetes on the basis of subjective symptoms rather than objective signs may increase the likelihood of making false-positive declarations. On the other hand, using a test–retest consistency of associations may also result in a false diagnosis, since there are wide similarities between synaesthetes and non-synaesthetes in cross-modal associations. Non-synaesthetes may use mnemotechniques to remember these associations. In these individuals, high consistency scores may be the effect of either excellent memory skills or the learning process, rather than synaesthesia. Elias *et al.*'s (2003) study showed that the behaviour of individuals with explicitly learned associations is virtually identical to that seen in synaesthesia on these tasks. Moreover, neuroimaging data revealed that synaesthetes did not differ from these non-synaesthetes in their patterns of brain activation when both groups were performing a Stroop task. Thus, the distinction between synaesthesia and synaesthesia-like associations (pseudosynaesthesia) should depend primarily on the presence of subjective reports that are validated by objective measures (Dixon *et al.*, 2004; Berteletti *et al.*, 2010). A combination of well-designed experimental studies and subjective reports of synaesthetes has been demonstrated in many studies (e.g., Baron-Cohen *et al.*, 1993; Rich *et al.*, 2005; Ward, Simner, and Auyeung, 2005; Eagleman *et al.*, 2007; Berteletti *et al.*, 2010).

In the present study, the Synaesthetic Association Questionnaire (SAQ) was used for describing some aspects of both cross-modal associations and linguistic-colour synaesthesias. Identification of synaesthetes was assessed by both methods: the SAQ and the Linguistic-Colour Association Test (L-CAT). The aim in using the L-CAT was to examine the test–retest consistency of linguistic-colour associations. Lower and negative (below zero) scores indicated more consistent linguistic-colour associations, whereas higher and positive (above zero) scores showed greater variability in associations (see Section 1.7 for more details). The SAQ was used to describe synaesthetic experiences and reveal some potential factors that may determine the occurrence of synaesthesia. A demographic information form was used to assess each participant's age and gender. Respondents were asked to indicate their dominant (left or right) hand, foot, and eye, with regard to strength, skill, and endurance. They were also asked to rate on a 5-point scale (from *Never* to *Very often*) their frequency of health problems during the last year and to choose on a dichotomous response scale any vision defect (i.e., long- or near-sightedness, astigmatism, squint, and colour-blindness) they might have.

The main section of the SAQ consisted of nine questions (with several items each) related to self-rated perception, memory, and imagery with regard to five modalities; and eight questions analysing linguistic-colour associations in detail (e.g., type of synaesthesia depending on category of words involved as well as on the intensity, vividness, changeability, and usability of associations). Respondents rated each item on a 5-point scale with various options for responses to particular questions, depending on the category of a statement. Most questions also included an item with an open-ended response, 'Other', where participants could describe subjective experiences not reported in previous options. The result was calculated as a total and separately for each category.

A total of 141 subjects, including 74 women (52%), completed both the L-CAT and the SAQ (for details, see Appendix A). Among the participants, four individuals estimated their own vision as bad (3%), 26 as poor (18%), 68 as good (48%), and 43 as excellent (31%). Common vision defects were found in 63 participants (45%), including 48 cases of short-sightedness (34%), 11 of long-sightedness (8%), 20 of astigmatism (14%), and one of squint (1%). None of the participants declared colour blindness. Participants were mostly right-handed (n = 134, 95%); only six (4%) were left-handed and one was ambidextrous (1%). Body lateralization, referring to either the dominant hand, foot, or eye, was found in 44 participants (31% of the total); among them, 28 (20%) declared only handedness-footedness lateralization (e.g., right-handed and left-footed).

Participants were requested to tick an appropriate box representing their associations with various sensory experiences. Table 2.1 shows the number of answers selected by participants (N = 141). Colour was associated with either hearing, smell, or touch in one case, and with

Table 2.1 *Number of self-reported associations between sensory experiences (*N *= 141)*

	Concurrent				
Inducer	Vision	Hearing	Taste	Smell	Touch
Colour	139	1	5	1	1
Shape	113	0	0	0	46
Inscription	137	14	0	0	4
Picture	135	9	1	4	10
Musical sound	13	137	0	0	14
Environmental sound	22	136	0	1	9
Timbre of voice	14	138	1	2	2
Speak	18	132	4	0	5
Food	19	0	135	57	3
Smell	9	2	14	133	0
Touch	34	5	3	6	124
Pain	20	9	3	1	123
Movement	57	19	2	2	123

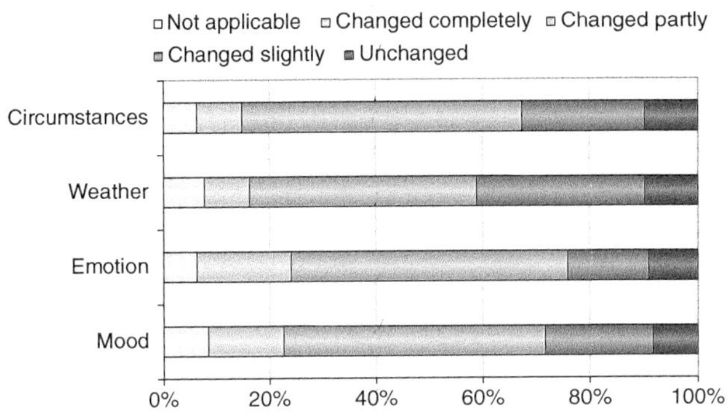

Figure 2.1 Changeability of intramodal and cross-modal associations ($N = 141$).

taste in five cases; whereas image was matched with hearing in nine cases. The next question of the SAQ concerned the changeability of both intramodal and cross-modal associations (Figure 2.1). Depending on circumstances, weather, emotions, or mood, these associations changed completely in 12–25 individuals, whereas in 12–14 participants, these associations were stable and unchanged.

Participants in the present study seemed to experience cross-modal and intramodal associations quite frequently. The configuration of these associations seems to suggest that they may play an integrative role in cognitive processes. Moreover, the changeability of these associations, depending on both internal (states of emotions and mood) and external factors (circumstances and weather), seems more adaptive for 90% of participants. However, 10% of participants declared consistent intra- and cross-modal associations, which can be an indicator of a sensory type of synaesthesia (Rogowska, 2011).

In the next question of the SAQ, participants indicated whether they associated words in selected semantic categories (i.e., forenames, days of the week, months, numbers, alphabet, words in the native language, and words in a foreign language) with particular visual attributes of objects (i.e., colour, shape, inscription, and movement). This question pertained to typical associations within linguistic-colour synaesthesia. As shown in Figure 2.2, colour was mostly associated with months, shape with numbers, movement with days, and inscription with the alphabet. Among colour-word associations, 56 referred to months, 16 to days, 15 to forenames, nine to numbers, seven to either native or foreign language, and six to the alphabet.

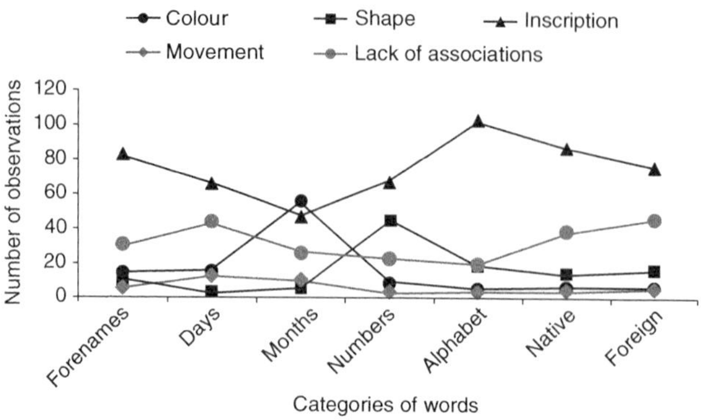

Figure 2.2 Associations between selected categories of linguistic inducers (forenames, days, months, numbers, alphabet, and native and foreign words) and visual attributes of objects (colour, shape, inscription, and movement).

Linguistic-visual associations seem to mostly represent close connections between words and their denotations (such as in month-colour synaesthesia), or between visual features of the conception (such as shape-number, and inscription-alphabet association). The movement-day association reported by 15 participants seems to represent time-space synaesthesia. The most controversial were the revealed month-colour associations. Almost 40% of respondents declared month-colour associations, but the analysis of the colour selections in L-CAT (see Chapter 1 for more details) showed that months were mostly associated with the dominant colours of nature (grass, flowers, and leaves). This kind of association occurs so often that it seems highly uncertain whether it actually represents month-colour synaesthesia or is a common semantic type of association. Thus, in the present study, month-colour associations were excluded from linguistic-colour synaesthesia. In this context, month-colour associations should be examined by a battery of psychological and neuroscience methods (both quantitative and qualitative) for better confirmation of either their genuine synaesthetic or common non-synaesthetic nature.

The total sample (N = 141) was divided into groups on the basis of linguistic-colour associations within particular semantic categories. The aim of the comparison was to examine whether participants who claimed to possess linguistic-colour associations in the SAQ also demonstrated lower scores in the range of consistent linguistic-colour

Table 2.2 *Comparison of mean scores in particular scales of the L-CAT in groups that selected either positive or negative responses in the SAQ indicating linguistic-colour associations in particular categories, respectively (N = 141)*

	Linguistic-colour associations in the SAQ					
Linguistic-colour	Negative		Positive			
associations in the L-CAT	*n*	*M*	*n*	*M*	*z*	*p*
Forename-colour	126	1.63	15	−0.85	1.51	.13
Day-colour	125	1.73	16	−1.13	1.22	.22
Months-colour	85	1.36	56	1.12	−0.05	.96
Number-colour	132	2.32	9	3.18	−0.25	.80
Alphabet-colour	135	6.46	6	−11.83	2.06*	.04
Total linguistic-colour	134	17.40	7	7.05	0.04	.97

Notes: L-CAT = Linguistic-Colour Association Test; SAQ = Synaesthetic Association Questionnaire.

associations in particular scales of the L-CAT, respectively (Table 2.2). For example, mean scores in the Forenames scale in the L-CAT were compared between two groups of participants who selected either a positive or a negative response in the SAQ with regard to forename-colour associations. The Mann–Whitney *U* test was used to detect the differences between the two samples (reported positive and negative declarations in the SAQ) in the range of consistent linguistic-colour associations of the L-CAT, and separately for the particular five scales that are ordinarily related to synaesthesia (i.e., Forenames, Days, Months, Numbers, and Alphabet). Generally, the groups of participants who declared themselves to possess linguistic-colour associations in particular categories of the SAQ also demonstrated lower scores than other groups in the range of linguistic-colour associations of the L-CAT, respectively (except for Numbers). However, significant differences were found only in the Alphabet scale of the L-CAT (see Table 2.2).

Moreover, Spearman's coefficient of correlations between linguistic-colour associations derived from the self-report method (the SAQ) and examined with the L-CAT test revealed that only the range of alphabet-colour associations of the L-CAT was negatively related to alphabet-colour associations of the SAQ; $r_s = -.17$, $p = .039$. This suggests that stronger grapheme-colour associators (derived from the L-CAT) demonstrated more frequently conscious alphabet-colour associations (in the SAQ). No relationships were found between the self-reported and tested methods of assessment of forename-colour, day-colour, and number-colour associations.

Finally, in order to reconcile the objective and subjective methods, a group of linguistic-colour synaesthetes was selected on the basis of both the SAQ and the L-CAT. Synaesthesia proper was confirmed in those participants who claimed to experience linguistic-colour associations in particular synaesthetic categories of the SAQ (i.e., forenames, days, numbers, and alphabet), and who simultaneously demonstrated a negative score (below zero) in the range of linguistic-colour associations within abstract scales of the L-CAT, respectively (i.e., Forenames, Days, Numbers, and Alphabet). Table 2.3 presents age, gender, body-sidedness, and subtype of linguistic-colour synaesthesia for subjects

Table 2.3 *Linguistic-colour synaesthetes selected on the basis of the SAQ and L-CAT*

					Subtypes of linguistic-colour synaesthesia			
Initials	Age	Gender	Body-sidedness	Sample	FC	DC	NC	GC
R. A.	23	W	O	A	√			
P. D.	25	W	O	A	√			
Z. K.	22	W	O	A	√			
Z. Ba.	22	W	O	A	√			
P. T.	22	M	O	B	√			
W. P.	22	M	O	B	√			
Z. Be.	22	W	L	B	√			
Z. A.	22	W	O	A		√		
K. E.	22	W	O	A		√		
S. J.	25	M	O	B		√		
K. K.	22	W	O	B		√		
Se. P.	22	M	L	B		√		
M. M.	22	W	O	A			√	
C. K.	23	W	O	A			√	
K. M.	22	W	O	A	√			√
D. L.	22	M	L	A	√	√		
M. K	23	M	L	A			√	√
H. A.	20	W	O	B		√		√
Sp. P	22	M	L	B	√	√	√	√

Notes: Gender – W = women; M = men. Body-sidedness – O = one-sided; L = lateralized. Sample A: test–retest immediately (*n* = 82). Sample B: test–retest after 1 month (*n* = 79). Subtypes of linguistic-colour synaesthesia – FC = forename-colour; DC = day-colour; NC = number-colour; GC = grapheme-colour. L-CAT = Linguistic-Colour Association Test; SAQ = Synaesthetic Association Questionnaire.

appraised as synaesthetes in both samples: A (students of physiotherapy) and B (students of physical education).

Among 19 participants classified here as linguistic-colour synaesthetes (14% of the total 141 students), 14 had a single subtype: seven – forename-colour, five – day-colour, and two – number-colour (see Table 2.3). Moreover, four synaesthetes represented two subtypes each: grapheme-colour appeared together with day-colour, forename-colour, or number-colour; in one case, forename-colour occurred with day-colour. One person (Sp. P.) was a multiple linguistic-colour synaesthete, representing all subtypes – that is, grapheme-colour, number-colour, day-colour, and forename-colour.

Although grapheme-colour synaesthesia was most frequently reported (69%) among 572 synaesthetes examined by Day (2005), many synaesthetes demonstrate cross-modal and multimodal synaesthetic associations between particular features of the five senses. For example, mirror-touch synaesthetes outperformed non-synaesthetic participants on measures of facial expression recognition (Banissy *et al.*, 2011). Moreover, some types of synaesthesia may co-occur in multiple synaesthetes. Novich *et al.* (2011) analysed reports of 19,133 participants who completed the online Synaesthesia Battery, which mainly examines the consistency of synaesthetic associations in repeated tests, and separately for 22 types of synaesthesia. The results of that study indicated that different types of synaesthesia tended to co-occur within five clusters: coloured sequence synaesthesias (CSSs), coloured music synaesthesias, non-visual sequel synaesthesias, spatial sequence synaesthesia (SSSs), and coloured sensation synaesthesias. This seems to confirm the assumption that the strength of synaesthesia may be measured by the number of types co-occurring in the synaesthete (Rogowska, 2011), and that this strength may be related to the size of global hyperconnectivity. The majority of synaesthetes in the present study (14 out of 19) were single types. The strongest linguistic-colour synaesthete (Sp. P.) was a multiple type, who associated all linguistic inducers (i.e., forenames, days, digits, and letters) with colours.

Reconciling a subjective self-report questionnaire method (the SAQ) with an objective test for consistency of linguistic-colour associations (the L-CAT) seems to guarantee reliable results for diagnosing synaesthesia. In the present research, first-person subjective reports were used to validate the results derived by the experimental test–retest method (L-CAT). Indeed, relying on test–retest consistency of linguistic-colour associations would be very inaccurate, since common cross-modal and individual linguistic-colour associations may be consistent because of the use of mnemotechniques or other close and typical links between words (conception) and colours of denoted objects (closely related to abstract conception). Because synaesthetic and non-synaesthetic associations are both qualitatively and quantitatively similar (e.g., Elias *et al.*, 2003), there is no consensus as to whether the results of the experimental test refer to synaesthesia, excellent memory skills, or a learning process.

Moreover, since the L-CAT demonstrated continuous and normal distribution for consistency of linguistic-colour associations, the main question is this: where are the boundaries between synaesthetic and non-synaesthetic responses? Any scheme for how to classify people as synaesthetes – for example, a statistical strategy (e.g., using means and standard deviations to categorize participants into synaesthetes and non-synaesthetes) – is an arbitrary decision that may result in errors of either the first or second kind. Until scientists have found more reliable methods of synaesthesia identification, the combination of first-person reports with experimental third-person methods remains the best choice (Smilek and Dixon, 2002) for synaesthesia identification.

The results of the present study seem to suggest that individuals who demonstrated linguistic-colour associations in the SAQ, in fact, differed significantly from non-associators only in the Alphabet scale of the L-CAT. Thus, this may suggest that many individuals who did not claim to experience forename-colour, number-colour, and day-colour synaesthetic associations were not aware of their synaesthesia, so that there are many more synaesthetes than is indicated by the SAQ. An alternative explanation could be the opposite – that is, that many individuals who claimed to possess synaesthetic associations in the SAQ experienced inconsistent associations with the test–retest method, so that there are many fewer synaesthetes than are revealed by the self-report method.

On the other hand, it is not certain whether the consistency of linguistic-colour associations over time is a necessary condition for the occurrence of linguistic synaesthesia. Therefore, it is also likely that there are more synaesthetes than we could find by using the self-report and test of consistency methods together. Indeed, consistency seems to be characteristic of non-synaesthetic associations, such as common cross-modal associations or associations between objects and their attributes (e.g., colour, smell, sound). Nevertheless, among four types of linguistic-colour synaesthetic inducers (forenames, days, numbers, and letters), the alphabet seems to be the best category for the measurement of grapheme-colour synaesthesia that is conscious and consistent over time.

2.1.2 *Variability of synaesthetic associations*

Although consistency of associations remains one of the best measures of synaesthesia, it is unclear whether these synaesthetic associations are dependent, at least to some degree, on other variables (such as environment, circumstances, current mental state of consciousness, mood, age, etc.) that may affect their outputs. Synaesthetes usually report having experienced synaesthetic associations as far back as they can remember. However, there is some evidence that synaesthesia is sometimes experienced as stronger or weaker, and that in some circumstances, it may disappear altogether (Spalding and Zangwill, 1950; Sacks *et al.*, 1988; Simner, Mayo, and Spiller, 2009). Simner (2012a) points out that some participants in her numerous studies did not demonstrate a consistency of synaesthetic associations measured by tests, although they felt strongly that they experienced synaesthesia and they showed a slight tendency to repeat the same descriptions over time. The other participants reported synaesthesia but claimed from the start that their sensations may never be consistent.

A study conducted on a large group of synaesthetes revealed that, at least in some instances, synaesthetic experiences can change over time (Rich *et al.*, 2005). For example, in this study, some synaesthetes reported that synaesthesia became weaker with age; many synaesthetes first became aware of their synaesthesia when they were learning the alphabet, counting, or reading; seven respondents (3%) did not recall having experienced synaesthesia in early childhood, and three of them recalled their first synaesthetic experiences from adolescence. Moreover, 6% of synaesthetes in this study (Rich *et al.*, 2005) reported that the frequency or intensity of their synaesthetic experiences had diminished with age, and 7% of synaesthetes reported that synaesthesia did not occur regularly. In addition, for many synaesthetes, attention had a strong influence on the intensity of synaesthetic experience (increasing or decreasing the vividness of concurrents). Moreover, fatigue, emotional state or stress level, and the consumption of alcohol or other psychoactive substances modulated synaesthesia in 28% of respondents, by either attenuating or enhancing the experience.

The present study explored the issue of consistency over time versus changeability, using the self-report questionnaire method. In this context, the collected data refer to meta-knowledge about linguistic-colour associations. A comparison of the responses of synaesthetes and non-synaesthetes may be helpful for the identification of synaesthesia in the future.

One of the questions of the SAQ referred to several aspects of the consistency of linguistic-visual associations over time such as the period of experience and changeability. Among the 141 participants, 26 (18% of all, including five synaesthetes) claimed to have always experienced identical linguistic-visual associations; in 62 (44%, including eight synaesthetes), these associations changed slightly; in 40 (28%, including five synaesthetes), these associations were slightly similar; in three (2%), they were completely different; and 10 participants (7%) stated that they had not experienced any linguistic-visual associations. However, there was not a significant correlation between the consistency of linguistic-visual associations self-reported in the SAQ and the consistency of linguistic-colour associations examined with the L-CAT. The Mann–Whitney *U* test showed that linguistic-colour synaesthetes (n = 19) declared their associations to be more consistent over time than the non-synaesthetes (n = 122), $z = -1.99$, $p = .047$.

Among the 141 participants, 39 (28% of all, including eight linguistic-colour synaesthetes) stated in the SAQ that the associations did not change over the lifespan; according to 17 (12%, including one synaesthete), they changed depending on emotions; 63 participants (45%, including five synaesthetes) maintained that these associations changed depending on circumstances; 13 (9%, including one synaesthete) were convinced that the intensity of these associations decreased over time; and 13 (9%, including one synaesthete) claimed that these associations become more intensive over the lifetime.

When these answers were ranged from 0 (associations *remain unchanged*) to 4 (*increase in intensity*), a positive correlation of these items was revealed with a range in the following L-CAT scales: Colours ($r_s = .17$, $p = .045$, $N = 141$) and Forenames ($r_s = .20$, $p = .018$, $N = 141$). This suggests that the more consistent linguistic-colour associations revealed by the L-CAT were correlated with self-reported invariability of linguistic-visual associations. In addition, the sample of linguistic-colour synaesthetes (n = 19) revealed significantly more unchanged associations than the group of non-synaesthetes (n = 122), $z = 2.83$, $p = .005$.

In their answers to the question, 'How long have you experienced these associations?', 97 participants (69% of all, including 16 synaesthetes) claimed that they had had them as far back as they could remember; 14 (10%, including one synaesthete) had had them since primary school; 11 (8%, including two synaesthetes) had had them since secondary school; five (4%) had had them for some time; and 14 (10%) were convinced that they did not have any associations. When these answers were ranged from 4 (*Always*) to 0 (*I never experience them*), a negative correlation of these questions appeared with the range of linguistic-colour associations in Days ($r_s = -.18$, $p = .036$, $N = 141$). This shows that stronger associations between Colours and Days may be connected with an earlier emergence of linguistic-visual associations. Interestingly, the Mann–Whitney *U* test did not reveal significant differences in these questions between linguistic-colour synaesthetes ($n = 19$) and non-synaesthetes ($n = 122$), $z = -1.04$, $p = .30$. This may suggest that synaesthetic associations and non-synaesthetic cross-modal associations arise at the same stages of life.

The other question of the SAQ referred to the possibility of using linguistic-visual associations in daily activity. Among 141 participants, 53 subjects (37%, including 12 linguistic-colour synaesthetes) claimed that these associations may be helpful; one linguistic-colour synaesthete (1%) maintained that they may be slightly harmful; and for 87 (62%, including six synaesthetes), these associations were neutral. When these answers were ranged (4 – *very helpful*, 3 – *slightly helpful*, 2 – *neutral*, 1 – *slightly harmful*, 0 – *very harmful*), a positive correlation was found with the range of Forenames ($r_s = .17$, $p = .044$). This suggests that these associations are useful for weaker linguistic-colour associators. However, no significant differences in the answers to this question between linguistic-colour synaesthetes ($n = 19$) and non-synaesthetes ($n = 122$) were found with the Mann–Whitney *U* test, $z = -0.33$, $p = .75$.

Participants used these linguistic-visual associations on several occasions, mostly for identification, differentiation, and remembering (see Figure 2.3). When the answers were ranged from 0 (*Never*) to 4 (*Always*), there was a positive correlation between the use of linguistic-visual associations in learning foreign languages and the consistency of the Adjectives scale of the L-CAT ($r_s = .17$, $p = .047$), between using them in mathematics and the consistency of the Alphabet scale ($r_s = .23$,

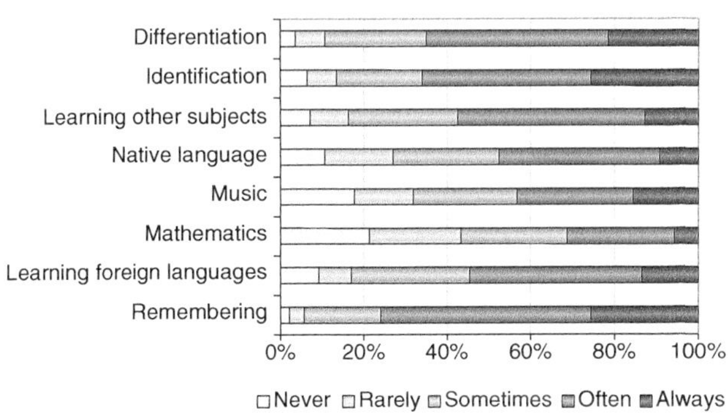

Figure 2.3 Usage of word-colour associations in cognitive activity.

$p = .015$), and between using them for differentiation and the consistency of Pseudowords ($r_s = .24$, $p = .024$).

To summarize the present results, linguistic-colour associations revealed a useful strategy for identification, differentiation, and remembering in the majority of both synaesthetes and non-synaesthetes. Synaesthetes often use their synaesthetic associations to help them complete memory tasks (Linssen, 2011). A recent study seemed to indicate that synaesthetes may learn more initially, rather than forgetting less over time (Gross, Neargarderô, Caldwell-Harris, and Cronin-Golomb, 2011). However, the present study seems to show that weaker linguistic-colour associators use visual features of words as a mnemotechnique more frequently than stronger synaesthetes. On the other hand, because there were no correlations between other scales of the L-CAT and particular strategies in using linguistic-visual associations, it is also possible that associations between words and their visual features are not limited to synaesthesia but, rather, are applied in common daily activities as mnemotechniques. Indeed, Gross *et al.* (2011) found that synaesthetes used similar strategies to non-synaesthetes, and suggested that grapheme-colour synaesthetes used conventional methods of verbal organization.

Although, in general, synaesthetes declared in the SAQ more consistent linguistic-colour associations than non-synaesthetes, the majority of synaesthetic experiences changed slightly, mostly depending on circumstances. These synaesthetic associations increase over the lifetime in some synaesthetes and decrease in others. In the study, most synaesthetes, as well as most non-synaesthetes, were convinced that they had always experienced their linguistic-colour associations. Only three individuals stated that they had become synaesthetes during their school years. Thus, the early stage of linguistic-colour associations is not the best criterion of synaesthesia.

Perhaps the strength and consistency of synaesthesia depends to some degree on the conscious usage of synaesthesia in daily activities. In their study, Rich *et al.* (2005) showed that most synaesthetes (71%) reported the usefulness of synaesthetic experiences for remembering information (e.g., car licence plates, telephone numbers), organizing files (e.g., matching the colour of a folder or label with a topic), creativity, mathematics (e.g., mental arithmetic), and learning languages. Indeed, grapheme-colour synaesthetes often report using synaesthetic colours as a memorizing technique (e.g., Smilek, Dixon, Cudahy, and Merikle, 2002; Yaro and Ward, 2007; Radvansky, Gibson, and McNerney, 2011).

On the other hand, 30% of synaesthetes in Rich *et al.*'s study (2005) reported that synaesthesia could be a disadvantage (e.g., confusing words that elicited similar synaesthetic colours or word meanings). Some synaesthetes (19%) experienced specific emotions as part of their synaesthesia, such as feeling negatively disposed towards people with names that elicited unpleasant colours, or being irritated by road signs that appeared in the 'wrong' colour (Rich *et al.*, 2005). Moreover, Ramachandran and Hubbard (2001b) reported that synaesthetes in their study demonstrated strong averse responses to 'discordant' sensory inputs.

It seems probable that the consistency of synaesthetic experiences may depend on emotion. Thus, if synaesthetic experiences are felt as pleasant, and are often and willingly used for daily activities, they become more stable over time or even increase, whereas disagreeable synaesthetic experiences may be less consistent over time or decrease. Indeed, emotional synaesthetes (proposed by Emrich, Schneider, and Zedler as a subtype of synaesthesia, as cited in Sinke *et al.*, 2012) seem to demonstrate a generally low consistency over time in synaesthetic associations. Their inducer-concurrent pairing changes (leading to a high intrapersonal variance) are due to the constant modulation of their current affective state. Moreover, in drug-induced synaesthesia, the visual concurrent is mainly modulated by the affective state of the intoxicated person (Sinke *et al.*, 2012).

There is no consensus as to whether lexical-colour synaesthesia could arise at any stage of ontogenesis. Rather, depending on an integrative or compensatory function, different types of synaesthesia could appear during various periods of human life that are critical for the development of perception (Rogowska, 2011). Indeed, a study of a large, randomized population of children aged 6–8 years revealed that grapheme-colour synaesthesia emerges along a developmental path and evolves over time following environmental exposure to learned linguistic units (Simner, Harrold, *et al.*, 2009; Simner, 2012a). Furthermore, studies comparing the prevalence in children (Simner, Harrold, *et al.*, 2009) and the adult population (Simner, Mulvenna, *et al.*, 2006) showed that grapheme-colour synaesthesia expands from childhood (1.3% of synaesthetes) to achieve more consistent inducer-concurrent mappings in adulthood through stages of incremental acquisition (2.2% of synaesthetes). In those studies, synaesthetes were conservatively identified on the basis of test–retest consistency of grapheme-colour associations and quantitative questionnaire data.

Because grapheme-colour synaesthesia is connected with knowledge of culturally acquired symbols and concepts (Simner, 2007; Nikolić, 2009), it cannot emerge at birth. Similarly, such types of cognitive-based synaesthesia as lexical-colour (Simner, 2007; Mroczko *et al.*, 2009; Simner, Harrold, *et al.*, 2009), musical notation-colour (Ward,

Tsakanikos, and Bray, 2006), time-space (Brang, Teuscher, Miller, Ramachandran, and Coulson, 2011), ordinal-linguistic personification (Simner and Hubbard, 2006; Simner and Holenstein, 2007; Amin *et al.*, 2011; Simner *et al.*, 2011), personality-colour (Day, 2005), personally familiar names-colour (Weiss, Shah, Toni, Zilles, and Fink, 2001), and orgasm-colour (Novich *et al.*, 2011) are expected at later stages of child development or in adolescence.

In addition, emotionally mediated synaesthesia (Ward, 2004; Hochel *et al.*, 2009), mirror-touch (Blakemore, Bristow, Bird, Frith, and Ward, 2005; Banissy and Ward, 2007; Banissy, Cohen Kadosh, *et al.*, 2009; Banissy *et al.*, 2011; Holle, Banissy, Wright, Bowling, and Ward, 2011), mirror-pain (Fitzgibbon, Giummarra, Georgiou-Karistianis, Enticott, and Bradshaw, 2010; Fitzgibbon, Enticott, Bradshaw, *et al.*, 2012), and tactile-emotion (Ramachandran and Brang, 2008) are dependent on the development of emotion, empathy, and social cognitive processes (Fitzgibbon *et al.*, 2010; Fitzgibbon, Enticott, Rich, *et al.*, 2012) that could not have existed as such in infancy. Nevertheless, the developmental basis of synaesthesia is unknown because of the absence of longitudinal and cross-sectional studies on the prevalence of particular types and kinds of synaesthesia across the lifespan. Further developmental research is necessary to fully explain the nature of synaesthesia.

2.2 Relationships between linguistic-colour synaesthesia and self-rated sensing, gender, lateralization, and psychopathology

2.2.1 Relationships between self-rated sensing and linguistic-colour synaesthesia

According to the compensatory hypothesis (Rogowska, 2011), linguistic-colour synaesthesia may be a specific compensatory strategy of mind used when a cognitive problem exceeds the developmental capability of a child in the process of language acquisition (Cohen Kadosh, Henik, and Walsh, 2009). In this view, a linguistic inducer may correspond to a cognitive limitation or deficit of language processing (e.g., in speech recognition or comprehension) as well as to a cognitive limitation at the semantic level, depending on the stage of cognitive development. For example, number-colour synaesthesia may be related to the problem of classification of a sequence of digits (Green and Goswami, 2008), time-space synaesthesia may be connected to the sequence of time understanding, and grapheme-colour synaesthesia may be an effect of the alphabet-learning sequence.

As such, a synaesthetic concurrent may be an internally produced concrete cue (such as a colour or shape) that is included in a mental representation of an abstract concept for its better understanding and recognition within a cognitive system. Thus, a synaesthetic concurrent may be seen as one of the attributes of the concept that appear automatically as implicit knowledge. Indeed, researchers (e.g., Myles, Dixon, Smilek, and Merikle, 2003; Bargary, Barnett, Mitchell, and Newell, 2009; Barnett, Feeney, Gormley, and Newell, 2009; Nikolić, Jürgens, Rothen, Meier, and Mroczko, 2011; van Leeuwen, den Ouden, and Hagoort, 2011) suggest that the meaning of the inducer plays an important role in experiencing linguistic-colour synaesthesia.

On the other hand, instead of compensatory processes, developmental linguistic-colour synaesthesia may rely mostly on integrative processes. In this alternative explanation, there is no impairment of the cognitive system required for compensation, but, on the contrary, a colour concurrent can demonstrate excellent functioning related to hypersensitivity (Banissy, Walsh, *et al.*, 2009; Hänggi *et al.*, 2011). If the integrative hypothesis is appropriate, a person with linguistic-colour synaesthesia may display extraordinary cognitive abilities in visual perception, but speech-colour synaesthetes may display ordinary hearing abilities; and, consequently, grapheme-colour synaesthetes can reveal extraordinary colour perception but ordinary shape perception. According to the compensatory hypothesis, synaesthetes may demonstrate a very low (below ordinary) level of hearing or shape recognition, respectively, to give rise to the speech-colour or grapheme-colour type of synaesthesia.

To explore these hypotheses, the sample of synaesthetes ($n = 19$) was compared with the sample of non-synaesthetes ($n = 122$) with regard to self-rated sensing. Descriptive statistics for the self-rated sensing in the SAQ and total range of linguistic-colour associations examined with the L-CAT are shown in Table B2.1 in Appendix B. Higher scores in particular SAQ scales mean that individuals estimated their own sensory ability better, with reference to perception, memory, and imagination. Lower total L-CAT scores suggest a greater consistency over time and stronger linguistic-colour associations. Because most variables were ordinal scales, the analysis of differences between synaesthetes and non-synaesthetes was performed with the Mann–Whitney U test with standardized z-values. Moreover, the non-parametric Spearman's rank test was used to examine correlations between total L-CAT and scales of the SAQ.

Analysis of differences between linguistic-colour synaesthetes ($n = 19$) and non-synaesthetes ($n = 122$) revealed that the groups differed from each other significantly in terms of self-related taste ($z = -2.31$, $p = .021$)

and colour perception ($z = 2.26$, $p = .024$) in the SAQ, and also in the L-CAT total range ($z = -3.76$, $p < .001$). Synaesthetes demonstrated lower scores in self-rated taste perception but higher scores in colour perception than non-synaesthetes. However, after the Bonferroni correction ($p < .003$), only one difference met the expected criteria of p value – namely, total L-CAT. As expected, synaesthetes showed significantly stronger linguistic-colour associations than non-synaesthetes.

As the correlation analysis revealed, the strength of linguistic-colour associations increased with decreasing touch ($r_s = .23$, $p = .007$) and sidedness scores ($r_s = -.23$, $p = .006$). It can be concluded that stronger linguistic-colour associators are more lateralized, and they declared worse touch perception than weaker associators. However, after the Bonferroni correction ($p < .004$), none of these relations demonstrated a sufficient level of significance.

In the present study, linguistic-colour synaesthetes revealed a tendency to estimate their own perception as better for colour but worse for taste, compared to non-synaesthetes. These results seem to be more related to the integrative hypothesis, since taste tends not to be involved in language processes. However, analysis of the correlation suggests that the strength of linguistic-colour synaesthesia is only slightly associated with body lateralization and with weakness of touch perception. Because both body/brain lateralization and the somatosensory cortex are related to language processing and production, it may be possible that the compensatory hypothesis is valid. Unfortunately, the present evidence is extremely weak. Thus, in order to draw a final conclusion, it would be necessary to repeat the research with a much larger number of synaesthetes.

2.2.2 *Relationships between demographic variables and linguistic-colour synaesthesia*

Gender differences could shed light on the genetic and neurocognitive bases of linguistic-colour synaesthesia. Synaesthesia is often reported to be more common in women, and with widely variable outcomes, the female to male ratio is estimated to range from 6:1 (e.g., Baron-Cohen *et al.*, 1996; Rich *et al.*, 2005) to 1:1 (Simner, Mulvenna, *et al.*, 2006). Unfortunately, the majority of early studies focused on spectacularly strong cases of synaesthesia, and divided subjects into two groups: experimental groups with synaesthesia and control groups without synaesthesia. Participants recognized as synaesthetes were conscious of their synaesthetic ability, were interested in synaesthesia, were enlisted via the internet or newspaper announcements, and were usually members of a synaesthesia association (e.g., the American Synesthesia Association, the UK Synaesthesia Association).

On the other hand, in a more recent study using opportunistic samples (with participants recruited from university communities), no single significant gender asymmetry was found (Simner, Mulvenna, *et al.*, 2006). Some investigators have suspected genetic sources of synaesthesia related to an X-linked chromosome on the basis of the higher prevalence of women among synaesthetes (Bailey and Johnson, 1997; Barnett, Finucane, *et al.*, 2008). However, a study on the genetics sources of synaesthesia did not find any support for the X-linkage hypothesis (Asher *et al.*, 2009). Moreover, current findings indicate that genetic heterogeneity characterizes synaesthesia (Brang and Ramachandran, 2011; Tomson *et al.*, 2011).

In the present study, of linguistic-colour synaesthetes (n = 19), 12 were women and seven were men, whereas, of the group of non-synaesthetes (n = 122), 62 were women and 60 were men. There were no significant associations between linguistic-colour synaesthesia and gender, when tested for independence in a 2 (Synaesthetes, Non-synaesthetes) × 2 (Men, Women) contingency table (Pearson's $\chi^2(1) = 1.00$, $p = .32$, $\varphi = .08$).

A non-parametric Mann–Whitney U test was performed to analyse differences between men (n = 67) and women (n = 74) in sidedness, and also in several SAQ scales concerning self-related perceptual abilities (such as vision defect, sight, hearing, taste, smell, touch, movement, total sensing, language, face, colour, inscription, and shape), and in the total L-CAT. Women scored significantly higher than men in sidedness ($z = 2.82$, $p = .005$), sight ($z = 2.57$, $p = .010$), face ($z = 2.74$, $p = .006$), and colour ($z = 4.12$, $p = .00004$); and lower in the total L-CAT ($z = -2.56$, $p = .011$). However, with the Bonferroni correction ($p < .003$), only one difference met the expected criteria of p value – that is, colour perception of the SAQ.

Although the present study did not show significant gender differences in the prevalence of linguistic-colour synaesthesia (recognized on the basis of both objective and subjective methods simultaneously), women revealed a tendency to experience more consistent linguistic-colour associations than men (as a range of consistent linguistic-colour associations of the L-CAT). Moreover, women seemed more one-sided than men, and they estimated their face perception, sight, and especially colour vision higher.

Synaesthesia may be connected to a specific brain configuration manifested by the interaction between gender and lateralization rather than to simple gender differences (Springer and Deutsch, 1997). Because of their different cerebral organization, women are known to be better at language processing (e.g., verbal fluency, grammatical skills, speed of articulation), manual precision, mathematical calculating, and perceptual speed, whereas men are found to be better in spatial imagery, and constructive and technical skills (e.g., Halpern, 1992). Research shows that the male brain is more lateralized than the female brain (e.g., Voyer, 1996; Kansaku and Kitazawa, 2001). Woman may commonly have better access to both hemispheres of the brain, whereas men often demonstrate an asymmetric specialization of either the left or the right hemisphere. However, right-handed women are more left-brained, whereas men are more right-brained, except for left-handers.

Morton and Rafto (2010) reviewed the results of numerous studies on brain lateralization, and showed the left cerebral hemisphere to be specialized in top-down, deductive, cognitive dissection of local detail, and that most right-handed individuals manifest facilities for language, orientation to local detail, and object abstraction-identification abilities. The left hemisphere also appears to possess a hypothesis-generating event 'interpreter'. In contrast, the right hemisphere is specialized in bottom-up, inductive, perceptual synthesis of global structure, and has been demonstrated to excel in general global analysis, object localization, facial recognition, and spatial construction (Morton and Rafto, 2010).

Not only gender but also handedness and footedness are related to brain specialization in language processing and cognitive functioning (Springer and Deutsch, 1997). Arteaga and Poblano (2008) revealed that eye and facial movements are related to left- or right-hand preference and specialization in language development as well as visual, haptic perception, and recognition in an age-dependent fashion in a complex process. Left-handed children have been shown to take more time to recognize non-sensory monosyllabic words. Lateralization of the language function may be even better predicted on the basis of footedness than handedness (Elias and Bryden, 1998). Left-footed persons demonstrated a slight dominance of the left ear, whereas right-footed individuals showed a significant dominance of the right ear. Moreover, postural asymmetry, besides footedness, may also make some contribution to language lateralization (Day and MacNeilage, 1996).

Cytowic (1997) suggested that synaesthetes tend to be female, left-handed, often poor at mathematics and direction-finding, and prone to 'precognitive' experiences such as predictive dreams and *déjà vu*. However, investigations of these issues did not reveal any higher frequency of precognitive experiences or left-handedness in synaesthetes (Baron-Cohen *et al.*, 1996; Rich *et al.*, 2005). Synaesthetes as a group are more likely to be artistic, but worse at mathematics and navigation, than non-synaesthetes (Rich *et al.*, 2005). Moreover, significantly more synaesthetes than non-synaesthetes reported in one study that they had strengths in the areas of verbal and written communication, languages, and memory, but poor hand–eye coordination or balance, poor sense of direction, difficulty with map reading, and problems distinguishing left from right (Rich *et al.*, 2005).

A case study by Brang and Ramachandran (2010) seemed to indicate that some relationships between laterality and synaesthesia do exist, since a right-handed bidirectional grapheme-colour synaesthete (J. S.) experienced a colour concurrent mostly in the left visual field and in the central vision of peripheral space. He also claimed to possess eidetic imagery, and this was confirmed experimentally. These results support the cross-activation hypothesis and suggest a relatively early stage of visual processing in grapheme-colour synaesthesia. Furthermore, because the V4 area in the visual cortex mostly processes information from the contralateral visual field, this finding also suggests a right-hemisphere bias in J. S.'s colour response.

Moreover, another synaesthete (J. C.) described by Ramachandran and Hubbard (2001a) demonstrated laterality, and a more recent study by Brang, Teuscher, *et al.* (2011) has provided evidence that handedness is related to time-space synaesthesia. Left-handed time-space synaesthetes tended to report anticlockwise arrangements of time sequences. In that study non-synaesthetes revealed a similar pattern of associations to synaesthetes. This may suggest that the implicit biases noted in controls are mediated by similar mechanisms as in synaesthesia, highlighting the graded nature of synaesthetic associations. Thus, the present study examined gender and self-report body-sidedness in relation to linguistic-colour associations in synaesthetes as well as in non-synaesthetes.

In analysis of the results of the present study by the Mann–Whitney *U* test, there were no significant differences between one-sided ($n = 97$) and lateralized ($n = 44$) samples, either in the total L-CAT, or in any of the SAQ scales. The chi-square test using a 2 (Synaesthesia: Synaesthetes, Non-synaesthetes) × 2 (Sidedness: One-sided, Lateralized) contingency table did not reveal any significant relationships between linguistic-colour synaesthesia and body lateralization, since among one-sided participants there were 14 synaesthetes and 83 non-synaesthetes, and the lateralized sample contained five synaesthetes and 39 non-synaesthetes (Yates' $\chi^2(1) = 0.05, p = .82, \varphi = .04$).

The chi-square test of independence was conducted separately for synaesthetes ($n = 19$) and non-synaesthetes ($n = 122$), with a 2 (Gender: Men, Women) × 2 (Sidedness: One-sided, Lateralized) contingency table (see Figure 2.4). Within the group of synaesthetes, men ($n = 4$)

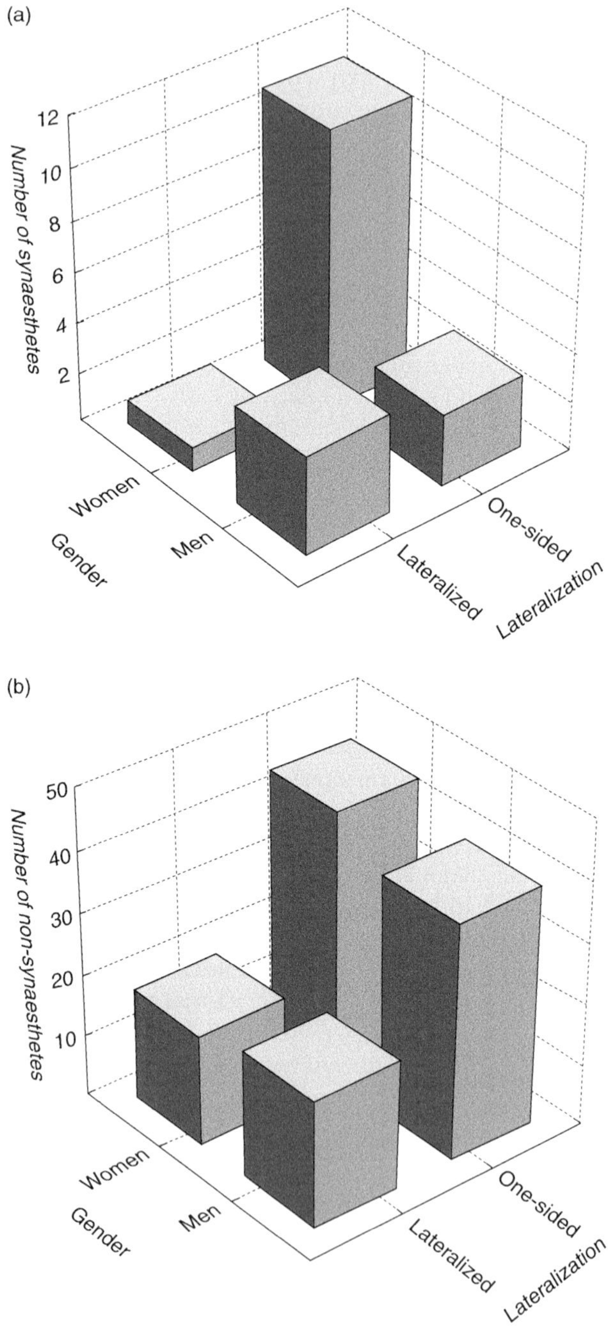

Figure 2.4 Association between sidedness and gender in (a) synaesthetes and (b) non-synaesthetes.

demonstrated more frequent body lateralization than women (n = 1), whereas one-sided women (n = 11) significantly predominated over one-sided men (n = 3) (Fisher's exact test, p = .038, two-tailed). The association between gender and sidedness was not found in the non-synaesthetes (n = 122), since 21 men and 18 women were included in their lateralized group, whereas the one-sided sample contained 39 men and 44 women, Pearson's $\chi^2(1) = 0.50$, $p = .48$, $\varphi = .06$.

The present study seems to suggest that synaesthesia occurs in relation to an interaction between lateralization and gender. As such, synaesthesia may be found more frequently among lateralized men and one-sided women. Among lateralized synaesthetes, two participants declared right-handedness and left-eyedness (one man: D. L., and one woman: Z. Be.), one man was right-handed and left-footed (M. K.), one man was right-handed but left-footed and left-eyed (Se. P.), and one man (the strongest synaesthete in the present sample) was left-handed and left-eyed, but right-footed (Sp. P.).

A study using functional magnetic resonance imaging (fMRI, Clements *et al.*, 2006) indicated that males were more left-lateralized during a phonological task and showed greater bilateral activity during the visuospatial task, whereas females showed greater bilateral activity during the phonological task and were more right-lateralized during the visuospatial task. More recently, an electroencephalography (EEG) study of gender-related differences in brain function (Koles, Lind, and Flor-Henry, 2010) has provided further evidence that verbal and spatial challenges are more lateralized in males than in females, and that females are more verbal and verbalize more interpretively than males, whereas males are more spatial and verbalize more consequentially than females.

Generally, the right hemisphere is responsible for judging the position of objects in space, understanding body position, comprehending and remembering visual objects and performing actions, putting pieces of information together to make an entire picture, and motor control of the left side of the body. The right hemisphere also specializes in intuition and holistic perception, feelings, and sensitivity; first impressions and emotions; daydreaming, imagination, and visualization; creativity; mysticism; colour perception; motor skills; spatial awareness; impulsiveness; and introversion.

Functions related to the left hemisphere include the understanding and use of language (i.e., listening, reading, speaking, and writing), memory for spoken and written language, detailed analysis of information, and motor control of the right side of the body. The left hemisphere also specializes in logic and rationality, deductive reasoning, knowledge, definitions, details and analytical thought, abstractions, structure of objects, discipline and rules, planning and goals, time sequences, mathematics, categorizing, productivity and efficiency, stability, and extraversion.

Rich *et al.* (2006) used fMRI to compare patterns of cortical activity for the perception of external-coloured stimuli and internally generated colours in a group of grapheme-colour synaesthetes and matched non-synaesthetic controls. In both synaesthetes and non-synaesthetes, a voluntary colour imagery task activated the colour-selective area, V4, in the right hemisphere. In contrast, the synaesthetic colour task resulted in unique activity for synaesthetes in the left medial lingual gyrus, an area previously implicated in tasks involving colour knowledge. Thus, it seems most probable that linguistic-colour synaesthesia is related to the equal functioning of both hemispheres in language processing.

Generally, left-handed individuals reveal less brain asymmetry than their right-handed counterparts (Peters, 1995). For example, language processing is localized in the left hemisphere in 95% of right-handed and 70% of left-handed persons (Loring *et al.*, 1990). However, most of the remaining 30% of left-handed individuals demonstrate bilateral language processing, instead of dominance of the right hemisphere of the brain.

Perhaps linguistic-colour synaesthesia occurs in those one-sided women who demonstrate less lateralization of language in the left hemisphere (instead, language is represented symmetrically in both hemispheres). Furthermore, synaesthesia may be more prone to occur in those lateralized men who also demonstrate a bilateral representation of language. This hypothesis may be examined in the future by functional resonance techniques, together with tests for language skills and body lateralization.

Powell, Kemp, and García-Finaña (2012) explored the interaction between language and spatial laterality and their association with cognitive ability in working memory, verbal comprehension, and perceptual organization, using the Wechsler Adult Intelligence Scale (WAIS). They found lower working memory scores in left-handers than in right-handers. Moreover, when language and spatial processing were associated with the same hemisphere (i.e., both lateralized to the right hemisphere or both lateralized to the left), cognitive ability in verbal comprehension and perceptual organization decreased. This interaction seems to confirm a 'hemispheric crowding' hypothesis, which proposes increased cognitive ability when language and spatial laterality are dissociated. In this context, linguistic-colour synaesthesia may be involved in a compensatory mechanism (Rogowska, 2011) in those individuals who demonstrated decreased cognitive ability affecting bilateral brain organization in language processing. Because of the higher activity of the right hemisphere, coloured words may be easily projected into a space in the projected type of synaesthete.

On the other hand, delays in lateralization can affect many cognitive and behavioural skills, especially language and social skills. For example, language deficits including those in articulation or understanding, fluency, grammar, vocabulary, and the literal meaning of words may originate from difficulties with the development of the left hemisphere. Deficits in right-hemisphere language development can lead to difficulties in reading, and processing of non-literal language and metaphors as well as difficulties with non-verbal social abilities such as understanding of facial cues or body language. Hernaandez, Camacho-Rosales, Nieto, and Barroso (1997) showed that children with language and control of the preferred hand lateralized to the same hemisphere were superior in reading speed, accuracy, and comprehension to children with a non-convergent cerebral organization.

Cytowic (2002) suggested that non-right-handed individuals and females predominate among synaesthetes. Moreover, Cytowic (1997, 2002) also indicated that synaesthetes attained higher scores in the non-stereotypical male–female scale of the Minnesota Multiphasic Personality Inventory (MMPI), and that some of them demonstrated dyscalculia, dyslexia, autism, and attention deficit, whereas the majority demonstrated subtle mathematical deficiencies (such as lexical-to-digit transcoding), right–left confusion, and poor sense of direction. Cytowic (1997) assumed that these findings were consistent with anomalous cerebral dominance.

Indeed, extraordinary cerebral organization and functioning may affect learning deficits in reading, writing, and spelling, related to either dyslexia, dysgraphia, or dyscalculia (Galaburda, Sherman, Rosen, Aboitiz, and Geschwind, 1985). Dyslectics demonstrate impaired phonological processing (producing and interpreting language sound patterns) and weak alphabetic skills (written symbols representing speech). More recent neuroimaging studies have shown that dyslexic brains are more symmetrical in the planum temporale, whereas, in most individuals without dyslexia, the planum temporale is larger on the left side of the brain (Shaywitz *et al.*, 1998, 2002; Heim and Keil, 2004). The planum temporale is an auditory region which is a part of the language network. The symmetry of this area may interfere with learning to read and write. Moreover, Simos, Breier, Fletcher, Bergman, and Papanicolaou (2000) showed that reading difficulties in developmental dyslexia are associated with an aberrant pattern of functional connectivity between brain areas normally involved in reading – namely, the ventral visual association cortex and temporoparietal areas in the left hemisphere. Habib (2000) proposed the 'temporal processing impairment' theory, in which dyslexia is understood as a multisystem deficit possibly based on a fundamental incapacity of the brain in performing tasks requiring processing of brief stimuli in rapid temporal succession.

A multiple case study (Ramus *et al.*, 2003) revealed that a significant proportion of dyslexics suffered from additional auditory, visual, or motor disorders. These results seem to support the phonological deficit theory of developmental dyslexia, while acknowledging the presence of additional sensory and motor disorders in certain individuals (Ramus *et al.*, 2003). Indeed, recent results of the ERP longitudinal study (Stefanics *et al.*, 2011) suggest that the neuronal responses underlying some aspects of auditory sensory processing may be impaired in dyslexia. Moreover, Díaz, Hintz, Kiebel, and von Kriegstein (2012) have indicated that phonological difficulties in adult dyslexics are associated with dysfunction of the auditory sensory thalamus, and more specifically of the medial geniculate body (MGB), when the task required attending to phonemes compared with other speech features.

However, Pernet, Poline, Demonet, and Rousselet (2009) found the occurrence of various subtypes of dyslexia to be characterized by different brain phenotypes related to different deficits of the automatization of language-based processes such as grapheme-phoneme correspondence or rapid access to lexicon entries. Nevertheless, an understanding of brain organization in linguistic-colour synaesthesia may be helpful in distinguishing this phenomenon from dyslexia. Does synaesthesia arise as a defensive mechanism against dyslexia? This speculation requires verification by numerous studies in the fields of neuroscience, psycholinguistics, and psychology.

2.2.3 Synaesthesia and psychopathology

Strong synaesthetic projections seem to be similar to hallucinations produced in schizophrenia or caused by hallucinogenic drugs. Cytowic (1997) has suggested that synaesthetes seem more prone to unusual experiences, such as *déjà vu*, clairvoyance, precognitive dreams, and a sense of portentousness. Indeed, there is some evidence that synaesthesia is related to absorption, aura vision, lucid dreams, and both mystical and out-of-body experiences, all of which are also related to dissociation and schizophrenia (e.g., Glicksohn, Salinger, and Roychman, 1992; Glicksohn, Alon, Perlmutter, and Purisman, 2001; Thalbourne, Houran, Alias, and Grugger, 2001; Terhune, 2009; Zingrone, Alvarado, and Agee, 2009; Studerus, Gamma, Kometer, and Vollenweider, 2012).

Moreover, there is evidence that synaesthesia may be evoked or obstructed by psychoactive substances (e.g., Kafka, 1997; Cytowic, 2002; Brang and Ramachandran, 2008; Ahmadi *et al.*, 2011; Sinke *et al.*, 2012). Narcotic synaesthesia may be encountered in substance-induced psychedelic states, such as those evoked by LSD (Ramachandran and Hubbard, 2001b) or dimethyltryptamine (DMT) (Luke, 2011). Brang and Ramachandran (2008) proposed that narcotic synaesthesia may be related to the activity of serotonin S2a receptors, which can be modulated by various drugs (or indeed by meditation).

There are also cases of acquired and post-accidental synaesthesia, which occurs independently and unwittingly during adulthood as a result of biochemical brain changes, neurological dysfunctions, or permanent damage to the nerve as the result of an accident or disease such as cancer, multiple sclerosis, or migraine (Nold, 1997; Armel and Ramachandran, 1999; Jacome, 1999; Podoll and Robinson, 2002; Villemure, Wassimi, Bennett, Shir, and Bushnell, 2006; Rao, Nobre, Alexander, and Ceowy, 2007; Ro *et al.*, 2007; Afra *et al.*, 2009; Alstadhaug and Benjaminsen, 2010; Niccolai, van Leeuwen, Blakemore, and Stoerig, 2012). If there is a general relationship between psychopathological states and synaesthesia, this should be confirmed in the present study.

The prevalence of self-reported psychopathological states was explored in the present study by using the SAQ. Among participants, 109 persons had had during the last year a headache or migraine (77% of all), 12 (8%) had had other pain (e.g., stomach ache, backache), one had suffered epilepsy (1%), eight had become unconscious (6%), 90 were under the influence of alcohol (64%), eight experienced narcotics (6%), none took psychotropic drugs, and one survived brain damage (1%). Gender differences in psychopathological experiences were examined with the Mann–Whitney U test. Women suffered both migraine ($z = 3.31, p < .001$) and loss of consciousness ($z = 2.00, p = .045$) more frequently than men, but they were under the influence of alcohol ($z = -4.19, p < .001$) and narcotics ($z = -2.33, p = .020$) less frequently than men.

The sample of synaesthetes ($n = 19$) was compared with the group of non-synaesthetes ($n = 122$) with respect to self-reported frequency of psychopathological experiences, such as brain damage, headache, or migraine; other pain (e.g., stomach ache, backache); epilepsy; and loss of consciousness and intoxication under alcohol, narcotics, or psychotropic drugs. The Mann–Whitney U test did not reveal significant differences between synaesthetes and non-synaesthetes in terms of the frequency of psychopathological experiences on particular scales.

However, when the chi-square test of independence was conducted separately for each psychopathological condition, a significant relationship

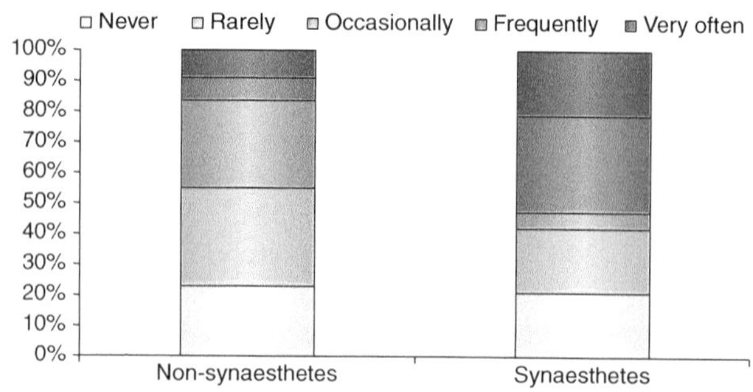

Figure 2.5 Frequency of migraine experiences (%) in non-synaesthetes (n = 122) and synaesthetes (n = 19).

was found between synaesthesia and migraine experiences: Pearson's $\chi^2(4) = 15.495$, $p = .004$, $\varphi = .33$. Synaesthetes more frequently experienced headache or migraine than non-synaesthetes (see Figure 2.5). No other significant relationships were found.

The present study seems to reveal that linguistic-colour synaesthetes more frequently experienced headache or migraine than non-synaesthetes. Indeed, there is some evidence that synaesthesia may be related to migraine and aura vision (Zingrone *et al.*, 2009). In the case report described by Alstadhaug and Benjaminsen (2010), a 40-year-old woman with a cyclic mood disorder had suffered from migraine with several episodes of visual-taste synaesthesia experiences during the visual aura phase. In addition, Podoll and Robinson (2002) reported the occurrence of auditory-visual acquired synaesthesia in a 66-year-old art teacher who suffered from attacks of basilar migraine with aura. In these women, an alarm clock could induce a coloured optical pattern in the centre of the field of vision, pulsing in correspondence with the sound. Podoll and Robinson (2002) mentioned two other case reports of auditory-visual synaesthetic episodes which co-occurred with migraine. One explanation for these connections is that headache leads to an alteration of neuro-processes and changes of perception, which may cause synaesthesia.

On the other hand, synaesthesia may be related generally to pain experience. Among 572 synaesthetes recorded by Day (2005), 36 (6.3%) reported pain-colour synaesthesia. The cases of pain-colour synaesthesia seem to suggest that the state of pathological pain may influence metabolic changes in the brain, leading to synaesthesia. This seems consistent with numerous studies (e.g., Ramachandran, Rogers-Ramachandran, and Cobb, 1995; Ramachandran and Rogers-Ramachandran, 1996, 2000;

Mon-Williams, Wann, Jenkinson, and Rushton, 1997) that have demonstrated phantom synaesthesia, in which a patient could feel sensations in an amputated arm, or could experience pain in a phantom limb, during visual feedback, using a special mirror box ('virtual reality box'). However, further research is necessary to confirm these relationships between synaesthesia and both migraine and other types of pain.

2.3 Structural analysis of the data

A hierarchical cluster analysis was performed as a preliminary investigation of interrelations between the self-reported variables of the SAQ and the total range of consistent linguistic-colour associations of the L-CAT. In the agglomerative strategy of the hierarchical clustering method, each observation starts in its own cluster, and pairs of clusters are merged as one moves up the hierarchy. The weighted pair-group method with the centroid average (WPGMC) and Euclidean distance were used for the present data. The WPGMC method is preferable when considerable differences are expected in cluster sizes, since the distance between two clusters is determined as the difference between centroids relative to cluster sizes (Sneath and Sokal, 1973). The present study involved the total L-CAT and those variables of the SAQ that might be correlated with synaesthesia (Figure 2.6).

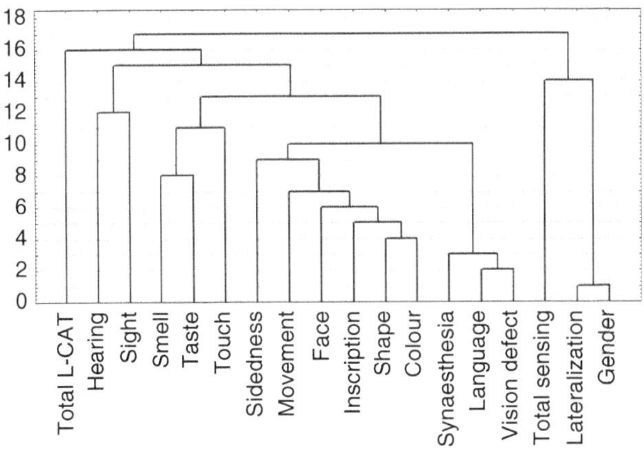

Figure 2.6 The vertical hierarchical tree plot as a result of hierarchical cluster analysis with Euclidean distance and the weighted pair-group centroid (median) method ($N = 141$).

The range of consistent linguistic-colour associations of total L-CAT is mostly related to self-rated hearing and sight on the highest level of cluster hierarchy. The second cluster consisted of three other senses (touch is related to both smell and taste) at the higher level and two subclusters at the lower level: the first subcluster included sidedness, movement, and perception of face, inscription, shape, and colour; and the second subcluster included synaesthesia classification (using both the SAQ and the L-CAT methods) together with self-rated language skills and self-related vision defects. The other cluster comprised a self-rated total sensing, and belonged to a sample depending on gender (women and men) and body-sidedness (lateralized and one-sided).

The cluster analysis seems to indicate that the set of variables was classified into the following categories: linguistic-colour associations (outcome of the L-CAT), senses (smell, taste, touch, sight, and hearing), perceptual features of objects (colour, shape, movement, face perception, and inscription, as well as body-sidedness, which can be related to space orientation), language processing (linguistic skills, being a linguistic-colour synaesthete, and vision defects that may be related to the written form of language), and psychosomatic features related to brain organization (gender, lateralization, and total sensing). A stronger relationship was found between gender and lateralization, while the weakest relation was demonstrated between the range of linguistic-colour associations measured with the L-CAT and other variables.

Belonging to a sample of linguistic-colour synaesthetes (on the bases of both the SAQ and L-CAT methods) was revealed to be most closely related to self-rated linguistic skills and vision defects, and this may be consistent with the compensatory hypothesis (Rogowska, 2011). Vision defects may affect difficulty with written language processing; thus, linguistic-colour synaesthesia (which relies on imagined colours) may arise to compensate visual deficiencies and improve linguistic skills. However, the linguistic-colour associations assessed with the L-CAT seem to be rather poorly related to any other variable included in the cluster analysis. These weak relationships between the linguistic-colour associations and other variables may depend on distinct scales of measurement (the continuous scale of the L-CAT in comparison to the 'yes/no' answers or 5-point Likert scale of the SAQ). Further structural analysis by stronger methods of measurement of sensory abilities (e.g., experimental methods and tests instead of self-report questionnaires) and stronger statistical methods of analysis (e.g., factor analysis or structural equation modelling, instead of cluster analysis) may be helpful in the future exploration of these issues, particularly in examining how synaesthesia is configured with many other cognitive variables.

The hierarchical structure of interrelated variables detected with a preliminary hierarchical clustering method was compared to an alternative structural model of regression. Regression by means of projections to latent structures (partial least squares (PLS)) is a useful alternative to the linear multiple-regression model when predictor-variables are correlated with each other and the number of these variables is relatively high compared with the number of observations (Abdi, 2010). The PLS method extracts orthogonal linear combinations of predictors (factors) from the predictor data that explain variance in both the predictor variables and the response variable.

The goal of PLS regression was to predict linguistic-colour associations of the L-CAT (response variable) from a large number of cognitive-related predictor variables of the SAQ, and also to describe the structure of the present data. The model of regression included the following SAQ scales as predictor variables: vision defect, sight, hearing, smell, taste, touch, total sensing, movement, perception of colour, shape, inscription and face, language skills, handedness, body lateralization, gender, and synaesthesia dichotomous classification.

Because the PLS was used here for an exploratory analysis, there was no assumption regarding the number of extracted factors. Thus, the number of factors to be included in a fitted model was determined by calculating a prediction accuracy estimate based on cross-validation and the non-linear iterative partial least squares (NIPALS) algorithm, the one most commonly used for computing the first few components in PLS regression.

The analysis conducted on the total sample (N = 141) extracted one factor as a latent variable that accounted for 20% of the variance of linguistic-colour associations of the L-CAT and for 14% of the variance of self-related cognitive variables of the SAQ (see Table 2.4). The value of Q^2 determines the optimal number of latent variables to keep the quality of prediction for a random model of PLS regression (Abdi, 2010). In the present study, Q^2 is larger than the threshold 0 (Q^2= 0.3), indicating sufficient value for the one latent variable solution. The most significant

Table 2.4 *Variance of* X *and* Y *explained by the latent vectors and* Q^2 *in total sample* (N = *141)*

Latent vector	R^2X	Eigenvalue	R^2Y	Q^2	Boundary	Significance	Iteracy
1	.14	2.70	.20	0.03	.00	Yes	1

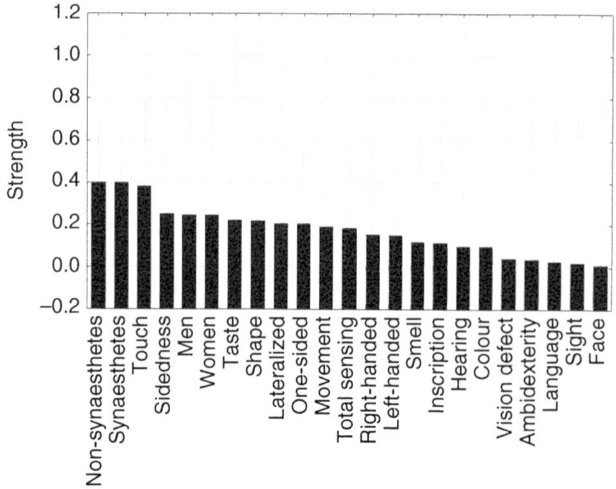

Figure 2.7 Significance of variables for the PLS regression model.

variables for the PLS regression model included synaesthesia and self-related variables of the SAQ such as touch, sidedness, gender, taste, shape, lateralization, movement, and total sensing (see Figures 2.7 and 2.8). The unobserved latent variable is mostly related to positive scores in touch, movement, total sensing, and shape perception in lateralized and male non-synaesthetes, and it is also connected to negative scores in body-sidedness in one-sided and female synaesthetes (Figure 2.8).

The results of the cluster analysis indicated that closer relationships were noted between body lateralization and gender. Particular features of objects such as colour, shape, inscription, face, and movement, together with sidedness, were included in the next cluster, nearest to synaesthesia. Furthermore, higher-level clusters were related to the perception of touch, taste, and smell. Subsequent clusters referred to sight and hearing, which together were linked with consistency of linguistic-colour associations.

Linguistic-colour synaesthesia as a categorical variable (non-synaesthetes, synaesthetes) was mostly associated with self-related language capacity and vision defects. On the other hand, the consistency of linguistic-colour associations of the L-CAT revealed the weakest relationship as that with the cluster that concerned total sensing, body lateralization, and gender. The structure of clusters indicates that linguistic-colour synaesthesia as a quality variable is more related to features of objects and analytical-type cognitive processes, whereas the

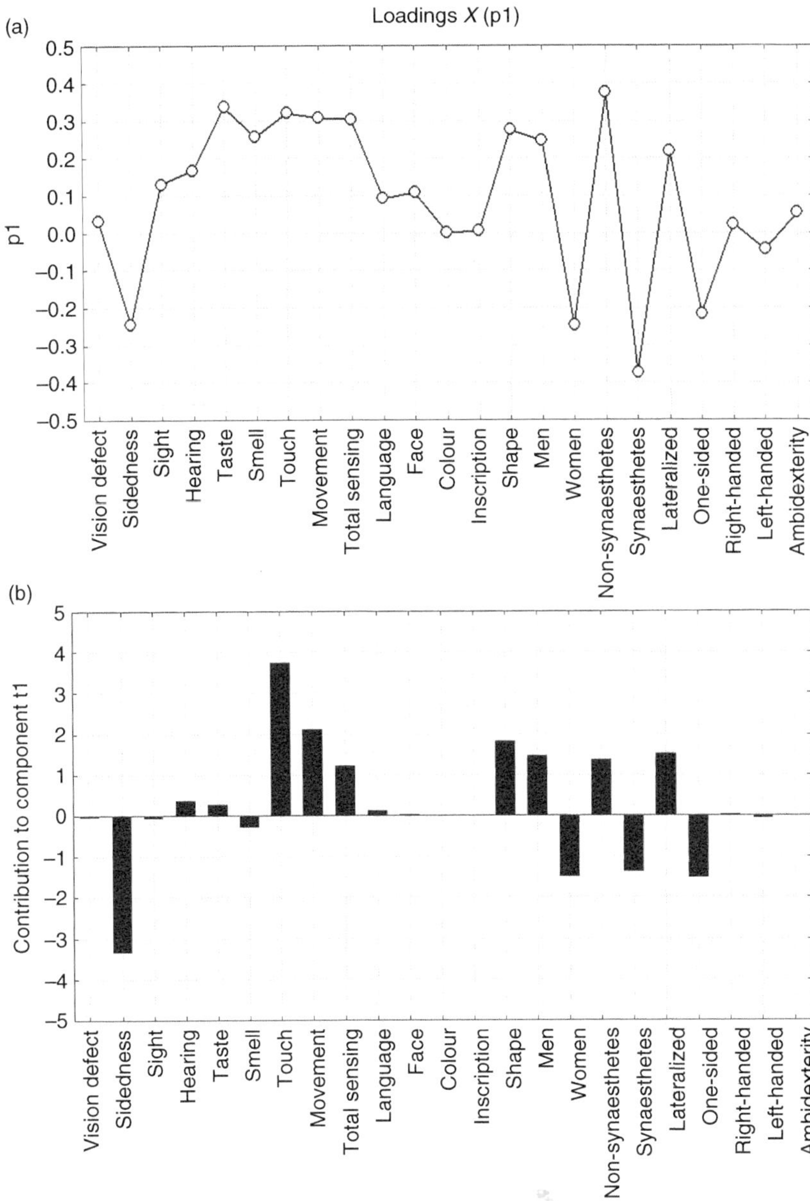

Figure 2.8 The PLS regression model: (a) p1 factor loadings of *X*; (b) contribution to component. p1 = loading vector; t1 = score vector.

consistency of linguistic-colour associations as a quantity indicator of synaesthesia is more connected to synthetic-type general sensory information processing.

In the present study, estimation of the relationships among variables was conducted by PLS regression analysis. Consistency of linguistic-colour associations of the L-CAT was a dependent variable, whereas the SAQ scales were independent variables. The most important predictors within the unobserved latent variable (explaining 20% of the consistency of linguistic-colour associations) were as follows: touch, body-sidedness, gender, perception of taste and shape, body lateralization, movement, and total sensing, respectively. This configuration of predictor variables seems to correspond with sensory integration processes at an early stage of cognitive development.

According to Piaget (1952), during the sensorimotor stage (the first 2 years of life) infants explore relationships between their bodies and the environment on the basis of informal experimentation with objects by using multisensory perceptions (e.g., seeing, touching, smelling, tasting and sucking) and motor activities. The understanding of objects begins during the substage of *coordination of reactions* (8–12 months of life), when children begin to recognize certain objects as having specific qualities. During the substage of *early representational thought* (18–24 months), children begin to develop symbols to represent events or objects. During this period, a child creates mental representations of objects with the dominant participation of sensory integration processes, which are crucial for forming symbolic thoughts in later stages of intelligence development. Due to the evolution of language and cognitive abilities in memory, imagination, and attention, concrete operations are replaced by abstract thinking in later years of life.

But what happens when the integration process is not harmonious, because of poor development of the somatosensory system related to either biological factors (e.g., strong lateralization, retarded brain maturation, insufficient myelination, brain infection, effect of medicines) or environmental factors (e.g., sensory deprivation)? Perhaps in such cases synaesthesia plays a compensatory role (Rogowska, 2011), similar to other types of synaesthesia (e.g., phantom, artificial, virtual, narcotic, or post-hypnotic synaesthesia).

The somatosensory association cortex receives synthesized connections from the primary and secondary sensory cortices that are involved in complex associations. Damage to this region of the brain can affect the ability to recognize objects, even when the objects can be felt (Swenson, 2006). Thus, it seems possible that linguistic-colour synaesthesia is related to some kind of deficit in the somatosensory association cortex.

Cortical injury in the somatosensory system can lead to a loss of thermal sensation and inability to distinguish pain, aura vision during migraine (involving thermal and painful sensations), and sensory Jacksonian seizure (which involves an abnormal, localizable, cutaneous sensation but without apparent stimuli). Some investigations suggest that synaesthesia may also be related to pain sensations in many ways.

Synaesthesia was found to be associated with migraine (Podoll and Robinson, 2002; Alstadhaug and Benjaminsen, 2010), aura vision (Zingrone *et al.*, 2009), and phantom pains (e.g., Ramachandran and Rogers-Ramachandran, 2000; Holmes and Spence, 2005). Mirror-touch synaesthetes experience tactile sensations on their own bodies when observing someone else being touched (Banissy and Ward, 2007; Banissy, Cohen Kadosh, *et al.*, 2009). Blakemore *et al.* (2005) found that the mirror system for touch is overactive in the somatosensory cortex of mirror-touch synaesthetes, above the threshold for conscious tactile perception. Synaesthetes experienced observed or imagined pain as if it were their own (Fitzgibbon *et al.*, 2010). Moreover, pain-colour synaesthesia was recorded in 6.3% of 572 synaesthetes by Day (2005; see also Steen, 2001).

Linguistic-colour synaesthesia may be an effect of compensation for some deficit in the somatosensory cortex. Thus, detection of a specific configuration of neurocognitive features in vision, hearing, and motor control, as well as a language process, may be crucial in explaining both the linguistic type of synaesthesia and linguistic deficit in dyslexia. In synaesthesia, a better functioning sensory modality at the present stage of cognitive development may share in forming an additional attribute for mental representation of either concrete objects or abstract concepts. For example, if colour perception is better developed than any other sense perception, it is likely that colour will be a synaesthetic concurrent. Indeed, there is some evidence (Banissy, Walsh, *et al.*, 2009) that synaesthetes who have experienced concurrent colour sensation demonstrate enhanced colour sensitivity. Moreover, in the present study, synaesthetes claimed better colour perception than non-synaesthetes, a finding that seems to confirm this observation.

The results of the present study seem to correspond to the hyperconnectivity conception of synaesthesia. An examination of hyperconnectivity between grapheme and colour areas revealed globally altered network architecture within grapheme-colour synaesthetes' brains (Hänggi *et al.*, 2011). This globally altered structural network topology was reflected in reduced small-worldness, increased clustering, increased degree, and decreased betweenness centrality, and it also increased intramodular and intermodular connectivity of the fusiform gyrus (FuG) and intraparietal sulcus (IPS). However, connectivity alterations were widespread and not restricted to the FuG and IPS. This global hyperconnectivity may suggest that there are numerous relationships between modalities in synaesthetes' brains (Bargary and Mitchell, 2008; Hänggi *et al.*, 2011).

In conclusion, linguistic-colour synaesthesia seems to be related to a specific brain organization that relies on a more symmetrical representation of language (instead of the left hemispheric dominance) in one-sided women and lateralized men, and also in poor functioning of the somatosensory system. Due to the compensatory hypothesis (Rogowska, 2011), some deficit in touch perception may be compensated for by colour in linguistic-colour synaesthesia during the sensorimotor stage of development. However, further investigation using neuroscientific, psycholinguistic, and psychological methods is necessary for the examination of all these hypotheses.

In the present study, among 141 participants, 19 (13%) subjects were arbitrarily recognized as linguistic-colour synaesthetes on the basis of both self-report and test–retest methods. However, it is important to note that many more participants declared synaesthetic associations between linguistic inducers and the colour concurrent, and also many more participants demonstrated very high scores in their consistency test (of the L-CAT). Thus, it seems highly probable that there were many more weaker linguistic-colour synaesthetes in the present sample. The problem is how to distinguish weak linguistic-colour synaesthetes from strong linguistic-colour associators. The L-CAT demonstrated the consistency of linguistic-colour associations as a continuous and normally distributed variable. The question remains as to where the boundary lies between ordinary association and unusual synaesthesia. Since synaesthetes in the present study demonstrated similar tendencies to non-synaesthetes in many phenomenological aspects of linguistic-colour associations, synaesthesia may be simply yet another type of common association, rather than a mysterious and extraordinary phenomenon.

Moreover, we may all be some kind of synaesthete, but each of us demonstrates a unique pattern of mixed senses, similar to our unique epidermal ridges. This specific synaesthetic pattern may reflect an individual history of interaction between cognitive development and the environment, but also between our cognitive abilities and dysfunctions at particular stages of our development. This kind of information could be very useful for cognitive, developmental, and clinical psychologists as well as for neuroscientists.

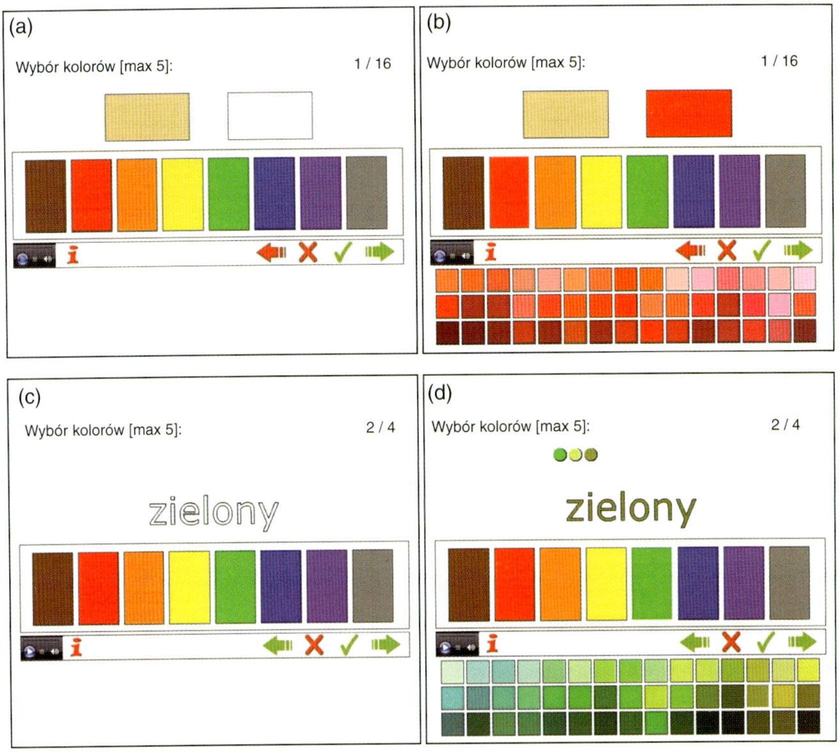

Plate 1 The Linguistic-Colour Association Test (L-CAT) started with instructions presented as a screencast, containing audio and video narration on how to use the software features. Next, the Visual Colour Discrimination (VCD) training subtest began automatically (a)–(b). The purpose of the VCD was to examine the ability of colour discrimination, as well as to recognize where particular colours were placed on the palette, before running the main test. (a) Participants were presented with two rectangles at the top of the computer screen and the palette of the basic eight colours (brown, red, orange, yellow, green, blue, purple, and grey) at the bottom. The rectangle on the left-hand side was presented in a random colour in each of 16 trials. Participants were asked to select a colour for the rectangle on the right-hand side of the computer screen that most closely matched the colour of the rectangle on the left-hand side. (b) Navigating with their mouse, participants chose one of eight basic colours and then selected one of 45 different hues of the chosen basic colour. If the appropriate colour was found, participants clicked the green 'V' (tick) button to confirm the selection, and then clicked the green 'right arrow' button to go further. The screencast with instructions was available constantly during the test, accessed by clicking the 'Play' button on the left-hand side of the middle bar of the computer screen. The main test of the L-CAT (c)–(d) started with instructions in the screencast, which was available constantly until the end of the test. Participants were presented with randomly ordered words within each of 10 categories (total 135 trials; see Table 1.1) in

Plate 1 (cont.)

both forms at the same time: aurally as phonemes (using the headphones) and visually as graphemes (on the computer screen). (c) Using a colour palette, participants selected the colour that best matched their synaesthetic percept for the item. (d) The colour chosen by the participant was displayed both on the graphemes and in the circle in the top left corner of the computer screen. Participants could choose a maximum of five distinct colours for each item. When they had completed selecting the colour(s), the participants clicked the green 'V' button to confirm this, and then clicked the green 'right arrow' button to continue. If participants did not report any colour association for the item, they clicked the red 'X' button, and then the green 'right arrow' button to continue.

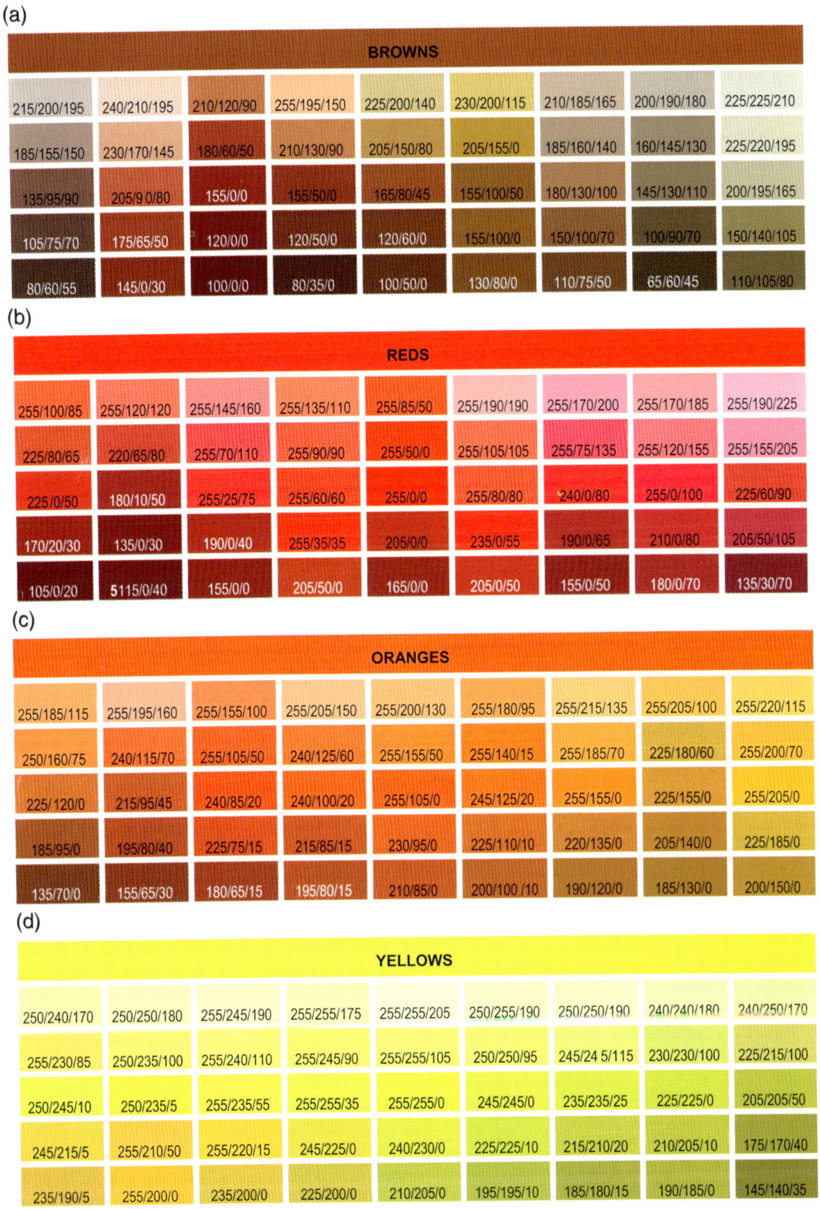

Plate 2a Palette of warm colours used in the computer L-CAT (RGB).

(e)

GREENS								
205/255/205	155/255/205	100/255/155	195/255/165	155/255/155	215/255/100	205/255/100	210/225/130	230/255/60
125/250/220	50/255/205	0/235/145	155/255/100	100/255/100	195/255/30	155/205/0	185/200/60	205/205/0
0/215/195	0/205/155	0/205/100	50/205/50	0/255/0	100/255 /50	100/155/0	150/165/45	130/130/0
0/175/165	50/155/100	0/155/100	0/155/0	0/130/0	0/205/0	70/105/0	85/95/25	100/100/50
0/130/120	30/100/65	0/115/75	30/115/30	0/100/0	20/100/0	0/60/0	30/50/0	50/50/0

(f)

BLUES								
200/200/225	205/205/2 55	155/205/255	100/205/255	180/220/225	205/235/25 5	150/235/255	120/220/ 225	205/255/255
150/150/255	100/100/255	100/155/255	0/155/255	50/100/255	50/155/255	0/205/255	0/220/255	100/255/255
100/100/155	75/75/215	80/130/215	0/100/255	0/0/255	0/100/205	0/155/205	0/220/225	0/255/255
80/70/170	50/50/155	50/100/155	50/50/205	0/0/155	50/50/255	0/100/155	55/175/190	50/205/205
100/50/255	30/30/100	0/50/100	0/50/155	0/0/100	0/50/205	0/75/115	95/155/150	0/130/130

(g)

PURPLES								
205/205/255	190/170/235	205/155/205	255/205/255	205/155/255	255/155/255	255/0/255	255/155/205	255/100/255
155/155/205	155/125/225	155/100/205	205/100/255	170/90/255	205/85/230	200/0/200	215/90/170	255/80/215
135/110/180	130/90/215	130/60/90	175/90/255	155/0/255	205/0/255	155/0/155	205/50/155	255/50/205
125/65/255	100/50/205	105/50/150	155/50/255	100/50/155	175/50/215	130/0/130	205/0/155	255/50/155
100/0/255	100/0/205	80/40/115	135/0/255	100/0/155	155/0/205	100/0/100	155/50/100	205/0/100

(h)

GREYS (BLACK & WHITES)								
220/220/220	225/225/225	230/230/230	245/245/245	255/255/255	240/245/240	240/250/255	255/240/250	255/255/240
175/175/175	180/180/180	190/190/190	205/205/205	215/215/215	215/220/215	220/225/225	255/245/240	245/245/205
130/130/130	140/140/140	150/150/150	160/160/160	165/165/165	150/170/150	175/190/190	240/235/230	240/240/210
80/80/80	90/90/90	100/100/100	115/115/115	125/125/125	125/135/125	125/140/150	225/220/195	230/230/200
0/0/0	40/40/40	50/50/50	65/65/65	75/75/75	80/90/80	80/85/95	200/195/165	230/230/185

Plate 2b Palette of cold colours used in the computer L-CAT (RGB).

(a)

L.p.	Słowo	Odpowiedzi punktowe	
1	biały	255,255,240	255,255,240
2	brązowy	120,50,0	120,50,0
3	czerwony	255,5,0	255,5,0
4	fioletowy	0,0,250	100,0,205
5	niebieski	0,0,250 0,100,225 50,50,255	0,0,250 brak brak
6	pomarańczowy	255,254,0 255,155,50	245,245,0 255,105,0
7	szary	115,115,115	115,115,115
8	turkusowy	255,5,0	255,5,0
9	zielony	0,155,0 155,80,45	30,115,30 brak
10	żółty	255,254,0	255,254,0
11	agrest	150,165,45 brak	50,205,50 180,180,180
12	banan	250,250,95	255,254,0
13	cytryna	255,254,0 250,235,5 250,245,10	255,254,0 brak brak
14	jabłko	240,210,195	50,205,50
15	jagoda	100,0,100 brak	100,0,205 0,0,250
16	malina	225,60,90	255,5,0
17	pomarańcza	255,155,0 brak	255,105,0 255,254,0
18	poziomka	255,5,0	255,5,0
19	śliwka	100,0,100 brak	100,0,205 0,0,155
20	wiśnia	100,0,100 brak	0,0,0 255,5,0
21	jechać	175,175,175	180,180,180
22	leżeć	250,160,75	180,180,180
23	mówić	0,100,225	0,0,250
24	pływać	100,155,255	0,0,250
25	pracować	255,230,85 brak	255,254,0 255,105,0
26	przenosić	255,235,55	255,254,0
27	rzucać	225,0,50	255,5,0
28	spać	0,100,225	0,0,250
29	wychodzić	brak	180,180,180
30	zabierać	250,160,75	0,0,0
31	bolesny	255,205,150	255,155,50
32	głośny	175,175,175	brak
33	gorzki	175,175,175	180,180,180
34	kanciasty	250,160,75 brak	0,0,0 180,180,180
35	kwaśny	255,5,0	brak
36	miękki	175,175,175 255,255,240	180,180,180 0,0,250
37	ostry	0,0,250 255,5,0	180,180,180 brak
38	słodki	255,254,0 brak	255,254,0 255,105,0
39	słony	175,175,175	180,180,180
40	szorstki	175,175,175	180,180,180
41	czwartek	255,155,0	255,155,50
42	niedziela	0,0,100	0,0,155
43	piątek	255,255,240 0,0,250	255,255,240 0,100,225
44	poniedziałek	255,255,240 0,0,250	255,255,240 0,0,255
45	sobota	185,95,0	120,50,0
46	środa	255,5,0	255,5,0
47	wtorek	255,105,0	255,105,0
48	dzisiaj	255,140,15	245,225,0
49	jesień	240,100,20	255,140,15
50	jutro	255,50,0	255,140,15
51	lato	245,225,0	255,254,0
52	wczoraj	255,105,0	255,140,15
53	wiosna	0,250,0 255,254,0	0,155,0 brak
54	zima	255,255,240 0,0,0	255,255,240 140,140,140
55	czerwiec	225,0,50	255,50,0
56	grudzień	115,115,115 255,255,240	115,115,115 brak
57	kwiecień	100,155,0 brak	0,130,0 20,100,0

Plate 3 Excerpts from the L-CAT protocols. (a)–(b), Stronger synaesthetes among Complete Associators (total of 135 items of the test) were associated with colours with a relatively high degree of test–retest consistency. (c)–(d), However, weaker synaesthetes among Selective Associators (selected categories of items and selected items within a category) were also associated with colours with a high degree of test–retest consistency.

(a)

58	lipiec	20,100,0	20,100,0
59	listopad	100,90,70	135,70,0
60	luty	255,255,240 brak	255,255,240 50,50,255
61	maj	255,254,0	255,254,0
62	marzec	235,235,25 brak brak	175,170,40 0,130,0 250,235,5
63	październik	255,255,240 brak	255,255,240 180,180,180
64	sierpień	170,20,30	255,5,0
65	styczeń	255,140,15	255,155,50
66	wrzesień	145,130,110	80,80,80
67	Adam	0,100,205	50,50,255
68	Ewa	0,155,0	0,155,0
69	Iza	255,254,0 brak	255,254,0 255,155,50
70	Kasia	100,155,0	20,100,0
71	Magda	0,100,205	0,0,250
72	Mateusz	50,155,255	80,130,215
73	Natalia	255,254,0	255,230,85
74	Piotrek	255,254,0	255,254,0
75	Roman	255,105,0	255,5,0
76	Tomasz	0,155,205	0,100,225
77	askungen	brak	255,155,50
78	bromsary	130,80,0	255,155,50
79	czeliś	255,140,15	255,5,0
80	flikanu	100,0,100	125,65,255
81	gręzibów	130,80,0	180,180,180
82	hynzido	128,128,128	180,180,180
83	korpen	255,140,15 brak	0,0,0 180,180,180
84	lelurgia	255,155,0	255,155,50
85	pojke	245,245,0	255,254,0
86	tepar	0,0,0	0,0,0
87	1	255,255,240 brak	255,255,240 180,180,180
88	10	115,115,115	180,180,180
89	100	0,0,0	0,0,0
90	1000	150,150,150 255,255,240 255,255,255	180,180,180 brak brak
91	2	120,60,0	20,100,0
92	3	0,0,255	0,130,0
93	328	0,0,255	0,130,0
94	4	255,5,0	255,5,0
95	5	255,254,0	255,254,0

96	54	255,254,0 255,5,0	255,255,105 255,155,50
97	6	0,0,0	0,0,0
98	7	128,64,0	0,155,0
99	8	0,50,205	180,180,180
100	9	255,128,0	255,160,205
101	A	0,0,250	brak
102	ą	0,155,0	0,0,0
103	B	255,254,0	255,155,50
104	C	255,0,0	255,5,0
105	ć	255,0,0	255,5,0
106	D	128,64,0 brak	120,50,0 155,100,0
107	E	0,155,0	0,130,0
108	ę	0,155,0	20,100,0
109	F	140,140,140	165,165,165
110	g	240,100,20 brak	255,155,50 165,165,165
111	H	115,115,115	165,165,165
112	i	165,165,165 brak	165,165,165 255,255,240
113	J	215,220,215	165,165,165
114	k	255,140,15	255,140,15
115	L	255,140,15	255,140,15
116	ł	220,135,0	220,135,0
117	M	0,0,250	0,0,250
118	N	0,50,205	50,100,255
119	ń	0,50,205	50,100,255
120	O	128,128,128	128,128,128
121	ó	128,128,128 brak	128,128,128 255,255,240
122	P	255,254,0	255,254,0
123	Q	128,128,128	180,180,180
124	r	255,5,0	255,5,0
125	S	255,0,0	255,5,0
126	ś	255,5,0	255,5,0
127	T	0,0,0	0,0,0
128	u	128,128,128	180,180,180
129	V	128,128,128 brak	0,0,0 205,205,205
130	w	128,128,128	0,0,0
131	X	0,0,0	0,0,0
132	y	128,128,128	255,155,50
133	Z	0,0,0	0,0,0
134	ź	0,0,0	180,180,180
135	ż	0,0,0	0,0,0

Plate 3 (cont.)

(b)

1	biały	255,255,240	255,255,240
2	brązowy	120,50,0	128,64,0
3	czerwony	255,5,0	255,5,0
4	fioletowy	128,0,255	128,0,255
5	niebieski	0,0,250	0,0,255
6	pomarańczowy	255,128,0	255,128,0
7	szary	128,128,128	128,128,128
8	turkusowy	0,205,255	0,205,255
9	zielony	0,255,0 20,100,0	0,255,0 brak
10	żółty	255,255,0	255,255,0
11	agrest	0,60,0 brak	70,105,0 100,0,155
12	banan	185,180,15 215,210,20	225,225,0 brak
13	cytryna	215,210,20	225,225,0
14	jabłko	100,155,0 170,20,30 brak	0,255,0 70,105,0 0,130,0
15	jagoda	100,0,205	100,0,155
16	malina	255,25,75	255,25,75
17	pomarańcza	225,75,15	240,85,20
18	poziomka	170,20,30	255,25,75
19	śliwka	80,40,115	100,0,205
20	wiśnia	150,0,0	150,0,0
21	jechać	128,128,128	128,128,128
22	leżeć	255,255,240	255,255,240
23	mówić	90,90,90 255,240,250	0,0,0 255,255,240
24	pływać	0,205,255 50,100,255	0,205,255 50,100,255
25	pracować	128,128,128	80,85,95
26	przenosić	80,90,80 80,35,0 0,0,0	80,90,80 120,50,0 brak
27	rzucać	195,195,10	225,225,10
28	spać	0,0,0	0,0,0
29	wychodzić	80,35,0	100,50,0
30	zabierać	205,0,0	165,0,0
31	bolesny	100,50,155	130,0,130
32	głośny	50,50,50	65,65,65
33	gorzki	128,64,0	128,64,0
34	kanciasty	100,0,100	128,0,255
35	kwaśny	0,205,0	70,105,0
36	miękki	0,220,225 0,130,0	205,235,255 brak
37	ostry	125,125,125	100,0,155
38	słodki	255,145,160 255,254,0	255,145,160 brak
39	słony	145,140,35	175,170,40
40	szorstki	150,0,0 80,85,95	150,0,0 115,115,115
41	czwartek	255,105,0 brak	255,128,0 255,155,0
42	niedziela	255,0,0	255,0,0
43	piątek	0,0,255	0,0,255
44	poniedziałek	128,0,255	128,0,255
45	sobota	20,100,0	0,255,0
46	środa	255,255,0	255,255,0
47	wtorek	255,128,0	255,128,0
48	dzisiaj	128,128,128 brak	128,128,128 175,190,190
49	jesień	155,50,0 215,85,15	128,64,0 brak
50	jutro	50,50,255	0,205,255
51	lato	255,0,0 255,128,0	255,0,0 255,128,0
52	wczoraj	105,50,150	190,190,190
53	wiosna	255,254,0 195,255,30	255,254,0 195,255,30
54	zima	200,195,165 80,90,80 240,235,230 brak	200,195,165 80,85,95 225,220,195 245,245,205
55	czerwiec	255,0,0	255,0,0
56	grudzień	255,0,0 70,105,0	205,0,0 brak
57	kwiecień	0,115,75	70,105,0
58	lipiec	0,205,255	0,205,255
59	listopad	128,0,255	100,50,205
60	luty	70,105,0	0,255,0

Plate 3 (cont.)

(b)

61	maj	0,0,250	0,0,255
62	marzec	255,128,0	30,50,0
63	październik	135,70,0	255,128,0
64	sierpień	255,128,0	150,100,70
65	styczeń	125,135,125	150,150,150
66	wrzesień	128,0,255	128,64,0
67	Adam	255,0,0	255,0,0
68	Ewa	255,255,0	255,255,0
69	Iza	255,255,0	255,255,0
70	Kasia	0,255,0	0,255,0
71	Magda	0,0,255	0,0,255
72	Mateusz	200,100,10	255,128,0
73	Natalia	128,128,128	128,128,128
74	Piotrek	128,64,0	128,64,0
75	Roman	0,60,0	100,155,0
76	Tomasz	128,0,255	128,0,255
77	askungen	255,128,0	155,50,255
78	bromsary	255,255,0	215,210,20
79	czeliś	70,105,0	255,80,80
80	flikanu	128,0,255	100,0,155
81	gręzibów	128,64,0	128,64,0
82	hynzido	128,128,128	128,128,128
83	korpen	70,105,0	100,155,0
84	lelurgia	128,128,128	150,170,150
85	pojke	100,0,100	100,0,100
86	tepar	255,128,0	120,50,0
87	1	255,255,240	255,255,240
88	10	0,0,255	0,0,255
89	100	0,0,0	0,0,0
90	1000	125,125,125	128,128,128
91	2	70,105,0	70,105,0
92	3	255,255,0	215,210,20
93	328	0,0,255	0,0,255
94	4	255,0,0	255,0,0
95	5	0,0,255	0,0,255
96	54	50,50,205	0,100,225
97	6	128,0,255	85,95,25
98	7	0,255,0	0,255,0

99	8	128,0,255	128,0,255
100	9	255,0,0	255,0,0
101	A	255,0,0	255,0,0
102	ą	255,128,0	255,5,0
103	B	0,205,255 0,0,250	0,205,255 brak
104	C	255,255,0	255,255,0
105	ć	255,240,110	215,210,20
106	D	205,0,255	255,5,0
107	E	189,185,0	255,255,0
108	ę	185,95,0	255,128,0
109	F	130,0,130	128,0,255
110	g	255,128,0	255,128,0
111	H	0,0,0	0,0,0
112	i	255,240,250	255,255,240
113	J	128,0,255	128,0,255
114	k	0,205,155	0,205,100
115	L	100,255,50	0,100,155
116	ł	128,128,128	128,128,128
117	M	0,0,255	0,0,255
118	N	128,128,128	128,128,128
119	ń	165,165,165	150,170,150
120	O	240,0,80	255,145,160
121	ó	128,0,255	150,150,150
122	P	128,64,0	128,64,0
123	Q	100,100,100	128,128,128
124	r	235,235,25	235,235,25
125	S	85,95,25	70,105,0
126	ś	145,140,35	100,100,50
127	T	128,0,255	128,0,255
128	u	0,100,225	128,128,128
129	V	128,128,128	128,128,128
130	w	165,165,165	128,0,255
131	X	0,0,0	0,0,0
132	y	40,40,40 0,0,0	40,40,40 brak
133	Z	70,105,0	30,50,0
134	ź	50,50,0	70,105,0
135	ż	40,40,40	50,50,50

(c)

1	biały	255,255,240	255,255,240
2	brązowy	128,64,0	128,64,0
3	czerwony	255,0,0	255,0,0
4	fioletowy	155,0,255	128,0,255
5	niebieski	0,0,250	0,0,255
6	pomarańczowy	255,128,0	255,128,0
7	szary	128,128,128	128,128,128
8	turkusowy	0,255,255	0,255,255
9	zielony	50,205,50	0,155,0
10	żółty	255,255,0	255,255,0
11	agrest	brak	brak
12	banan	250,245,10	255,230,85
13	cytryna	255,255,0	255,254,0
14	jabłko	205,0,0 0,205,0 230,230,100	170,20,30 50,205,50 230,255,60
15	jagoda	100,0,100	100,0,100
16	malina	190,0,65 180,0,70	205,0,50 brak
17	pomarańcza	255,128,0	240,100,20
18	poziomka	255,50,0 225,0,50	255,25,75 brak
19	śliwka	100,0,155	130,0,130
20	wiśnia	105,0,20	150,0,0
21	jechać	brak	brak
22	leżeć	245,245,205	245,245,205
23	mówić	brak	brak
24	pływać	0,255,255	50,205,205
25	pracować	brak	145,0,30
26	przenosić	110,105,80	brak
27	rzucać	130,80,0	100,50,0
28	spać	155,205,255	80,130,215
29	wychodzić	185,180,15	brak
30	zabierać	0,0,100	brak
31	bolesny	0,0,100	0,0,250
32	głośny	180,220,225	205,255,255
33	gorzki	100,50,155	155,0,0
34	kanciasty	185,95,0	205,155,0
35	kwaśny	230,230,100	245,225,0
36	miękki	235,200,0	155,205,255
37	ostry	255,5,0 brak	150,0,0 255,35,35
38	słodki	255,35,35	255,0,100
39	słony	255,255,240	255,255,240
40	szorstki	160,160,160	100,100,100
41	czwartek	brak	brak
42	niedziela	brak	brak
43	piątek	brak	brak
44	poniedziałek	brak	brak
45	sobota	brak	brak
46	środa	brak	brak
47	wtorek	brak	brak
48	dzisiaj	brak	brak
49	jesień	180,65,15	205,155,0
50	jutro	brak	brak
51	lato	255,254,0	255,254,0
52	wczoraj	brak	brak
53	wiosna	255,50,155	100,255,100
54	zima	50,155,255	0,0,250
55	czerwiec	255,0,0	225,155,0
56	grudzień	0,0,155	0,0,255
57	kwiecień	255,155,205	100,255,50
58	lipiec	250,245,10	230,230,100
59	listopad	230,95,0	255,155,0
60	luty	50,205,205	100,255,255
61	maj	255,70,110	255,70,110
62	marzec	180,65,15	255,155,205
63	październik	165,0,0	155,100,50
64	sierpień	0,155,0	0,155,0
65	styczeń	225,220,195	205,255,255
66	wrzesień	255,205,0	185,95,0

Plate 3 (cont.)

(c)

67	Adam		0,0,100		165,0,0
68	Ewa		0,75,115		80,40,115
69	Iza		145,0,30		128,64,0
70	Kasia		0,60,0		175,170,40
71	Magda		0,220,225		0,220,255
72	Mateusz		128,128,128		0,0,155
73	Natalia		105,0,20		0,130,0
74	Piotrek		145,140,35		100,50,155
75	Roman		165,165,165		80,90,80
76	Tomasz		65,60,45		50,50,50
77	askungen		brak		brak
78	bromsary		brak		brak
79	czeliś		brak		brak
80	flikanu		brak		brak
81	gręzibów		brak		brak
82	hynzido		brak		brak
83	korpen		brak		0,130,120
84	lelurgia		brak		brak
85	pojke		brak		brak
86	tepar		brak		brak
87	1		brak		brak
88	10		brak		brak
89	100		brak		brak
90	1000		brak		brak
91	2		brak		brak
92	3		brak		brak
93	328		brak		brak
94	4		brak		brak
95	5		brak		brak
96	54		brak		brak
97	6		brak		brak
98	7		brak		brak
99	8		brak		brak
100	9		brak		brak
101	A		brak		brak
102	ą		brak		brak
103	B		brak		brak
104	C		brak		brak
105	ć		brak		brak
106	D		brak		brak
107	E		brak		brak
108	ę		brak		brak
109	F		brak		brak
110	g		brak		brak
111	H		brak		brak
112	i		brak		brak
113	J		brak		brak
114	k		brak		brak
115	L		brak		brak
116	ł		brak		brak
117	M		brak		brak
118	N		brak		brak
119	ń		brak		brak
120	O		brak		brak
121	ó		brak		brak
122	P		brak		brak
123	Q		brak		brak
124	r		brak		brak
125	S		brak		brak
126	ś		brak		brak
127	T		brak		brak
128	u		brak		brak
129	V		brak		brak
130	w		brak		brak
131	X		brak		brak
132	y		brak		brak
133	Z		brak		brak
134	ź		brak		brak
135	ż		brak		brak

Plate 3 (cont.)

(d)

1	biały	255,255,240	255,255,240
2	brązowy	128,64,0	128,64,0
3	czerwony	255,0,0	255,0,0
4	fioletowy	128,0,255	175,90,255
5	niebieski	0,0,255	0,0,255
6	pomarańczowy	255,155,0	255,128,0
7	szary	128,128,128	128,128,128
8	turkusowy	30,70,170	175,90,255
9	zielony	0,255,0	0,255,0
10	żółty	255,255,0	255,255,0
11	agrest	70,105,0	0,155,0
12	banan	255,255,0	255,255,0
13	cytryna	255,255,0	255,255,105
14	jabłko	0,255,0	0,255,0
15	jagoda	210,0,80	100,0,100
16	malina	255,25,75	155,0,155
17	pomarańcza	255,155,0	255,155,0
18	poziomka	brak	205,50,155
19	śliwka	100,0,100	100,0,155
20	wiśnia	190,0,40	180,10,50
21	jechać	255,5,0	255,0,0
22	leżeć	brak	brak
23	mówić	brak	brak
24	pływać	50,100,255	0,155,255
25	pracować	brak	brak
26	przenosić	brak	brak
27	rzucać	brak	brak
28	spać	255,255,240	0,0,0
29	wychodzić	brak	brak
30	zabierać	0,0,0	brak
31	bolesny	brak	255,0,0
32	głośny	brak	brak
33	gorzki	brak	128,128,128
34	kanciasty	brak	brak
35	kwaśny	255,255,0	255,255,0
36	miękki	255,255,240	255,255,240
37	ostry	255,0,0	255,0,0
38	słodki	255,255,240	255,255,240
39	słony	255,255,240	255,255,240
40	szorstki	130,130,130	80,80,80
41	czwartek	brak	brak
42	niedziela	brak	brak
43	piątek	brak	brak
44	poniedziałek	brak	brak
45	sobota	brak	brak
46	środa	brak	brak
47	wtorek	brak	brak
48	dzisiaj	brak	brak
49	jesień	210,85,0	128,128,128
50	jutro	brak	brak
51	lato	255,50,0	255,255,0
52	wczoraj	brak	brak
53	wiosna	0,255,0	0,255,0
54	zima	255,255,240	brak
55	czerwiec	255,255,0	brak
56	grudzień	brak	128,128,128
57	kwiecień	brak	brak
58	lipiec	brak	brak
59	listopad	128,128,128	128,128,128
60	luty	brak	brak
61	maj	255,255,0	255,255,0
62	marzec	brak	brak
63	październik	brak	brak
64	sierpień	brak	brak
65	styczeń	brak	brak
66	wrzesień	brak	brak
67	Adam	brak	brak
68	Ewa	brak	brak

Plate 3 (cont.)

(d)

69	Iza	brak	brak
70	Kasia	255,0,0	255,0,0
71	Magda	0,0,0	0,0,0
72	Mateusz	brak	brak
73	Natalia	255,0,0	brak
74	Piotrek	brak	brak
75	Roman	255,255,240	brak
76	Tomasz	brak	brak
77	askungen	brak	brak
78	bromsary	brak	brak
79	czeliś	brak	brak
80	flikanu	brak	brak
81	gręzibów	0,255,0	brak
82	hynzido	brak	brak
83	korpen	brak	brak
84	lelurgia	brak	brak
85	pojke	255,255,0	255,255,0
86	tepar	brak	brak
87	1	brak	brak
88	10	brak	brak
89	100	brak	brak
90	1000	brak	brak
91	2	brak	brak
92	3	brak	brak
93	328	brak	brak
94	4	brak	brak
95	5	brak	brak
96	54	brak	brak
97	6	brak	brak
98	7	brak	255,0,0
99	8	brak	brak
100	9	brak	brak
101	A	brak	brak
102	ą	brak	brak

103	B	brak	brak
104	C	brak	brak
105	ć	brak	brak
106	D	brak	brak
107	E	brak	brak
108	ę	brak	brak
109	F	brak	brak
110	g	brak	brak
111	H	brak	brak
112	i	brak	brak
113	J	brak	brak
114	k	brak	brak
115	L	brak	brak
116	ł	brak	brak
117	M	brak	brak
118	N	brak	brak
119	ń	brak	brak
120	O	brak	brak
121	ó	brak	brak
122	P	brak	brak
123	Q	brak	brak
124	r	brak	brak
125	S	255,0,0	brak
126	ś	brak	brak
127	T	brak	brak
128	u	brak	brak
129	V	255,0,0	brak
130	w	0,0,255	brak
131	X	0,0,0	brak
132	y	brak	brak
133	Z	brak	brak
134	ź	brak	brak
135	ż	brak	brak

Plate 3 (cont.)

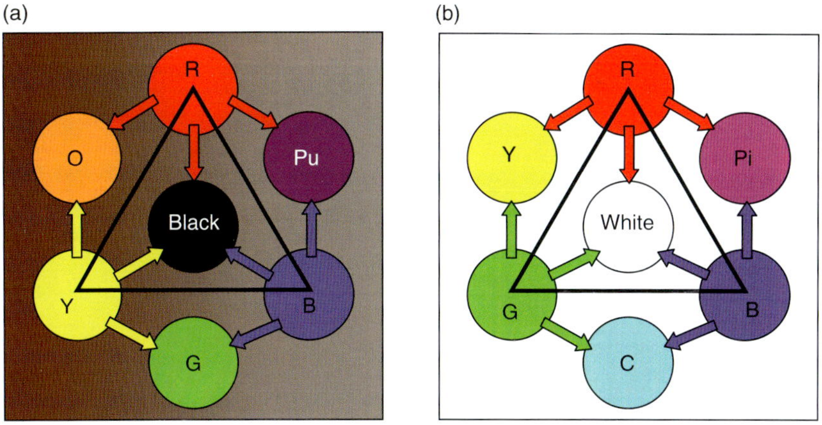

Plate 4 Different principles of colour mixing in the structural RYB and spectral RGB colour models. (a) Secondary colours in subtractive mixing: orange (Y + R), green (Y + B), and purple (B + R). Black results from mixing primary colours (R + Y + B), and the resulting mix of two opponent colours is grey (pairs of complementary colours: R–G, O–B, Y–Pu). Perception of the object's colour depends not only on the absorption of light leaving its surface but also on a host of contextual cues that provide a rich matrix of colours, different hues, saturation, and lightness. (b) Secondary colours in additive mixing: yellow (G + R), pink (B + R), and cyan (B + G). White results from mixing primary colours (R + G + B). The visible spectrum of light comprises only pure and bright colours as in a rainbow (e.g., brown or ochre cannot appear in the spectrum).

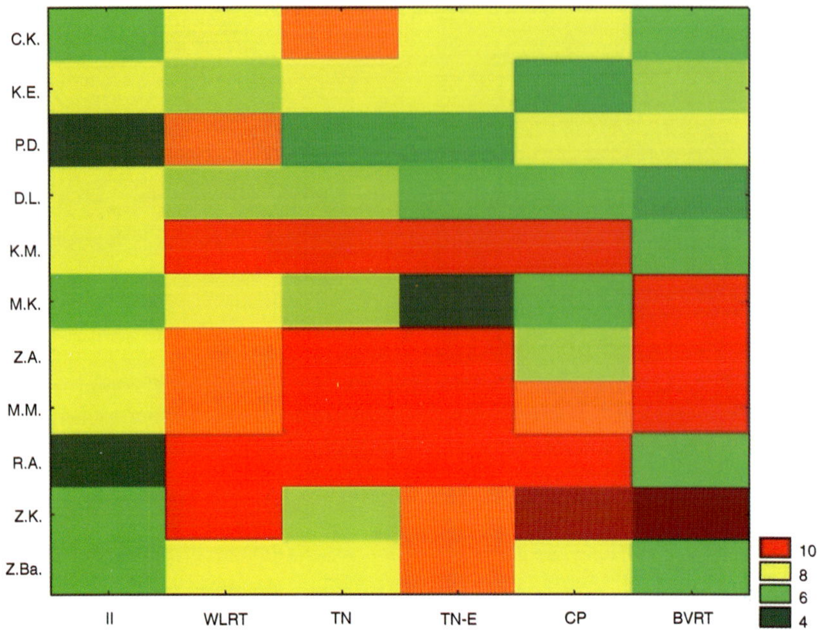

Plate 5 Two-way joining tree clustering for traits of cognitive variables (on *x*-axis) in synaesthetes sample (initials of particular synaesthetes on *y*-axis).

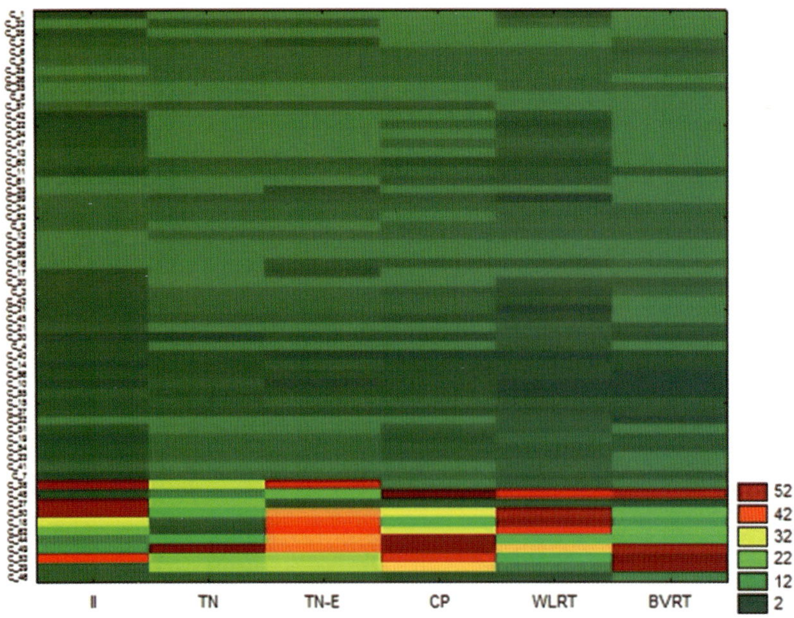

Plate 6 Two-way joining tree clustering for traits of cognitive variables (on *x*-axis) in non-synaesthetes sample (initials of particular synaesthetes on *y*-axis).

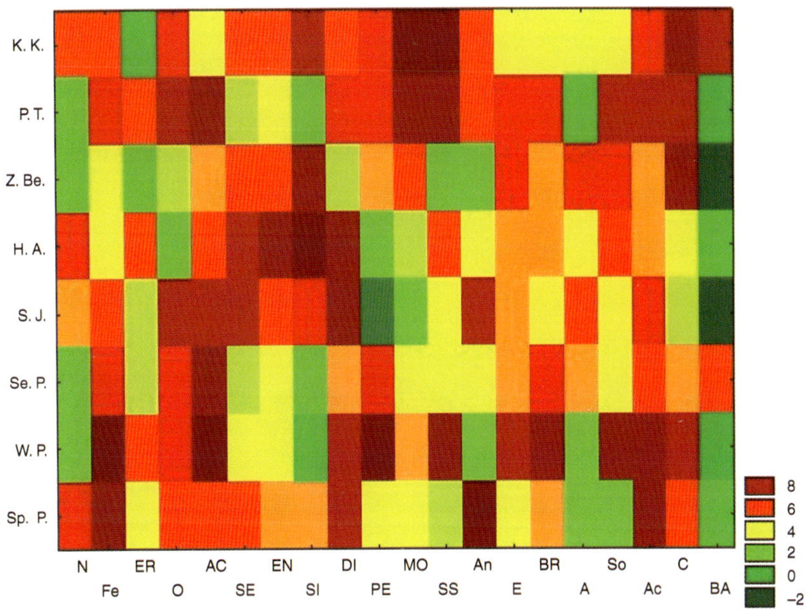

Plate 7 Two-way joining tree clustering for traits of personality and temperament (x-axis) in the sample of synaesthetes (initials of particular synaesthetes on y-axis).

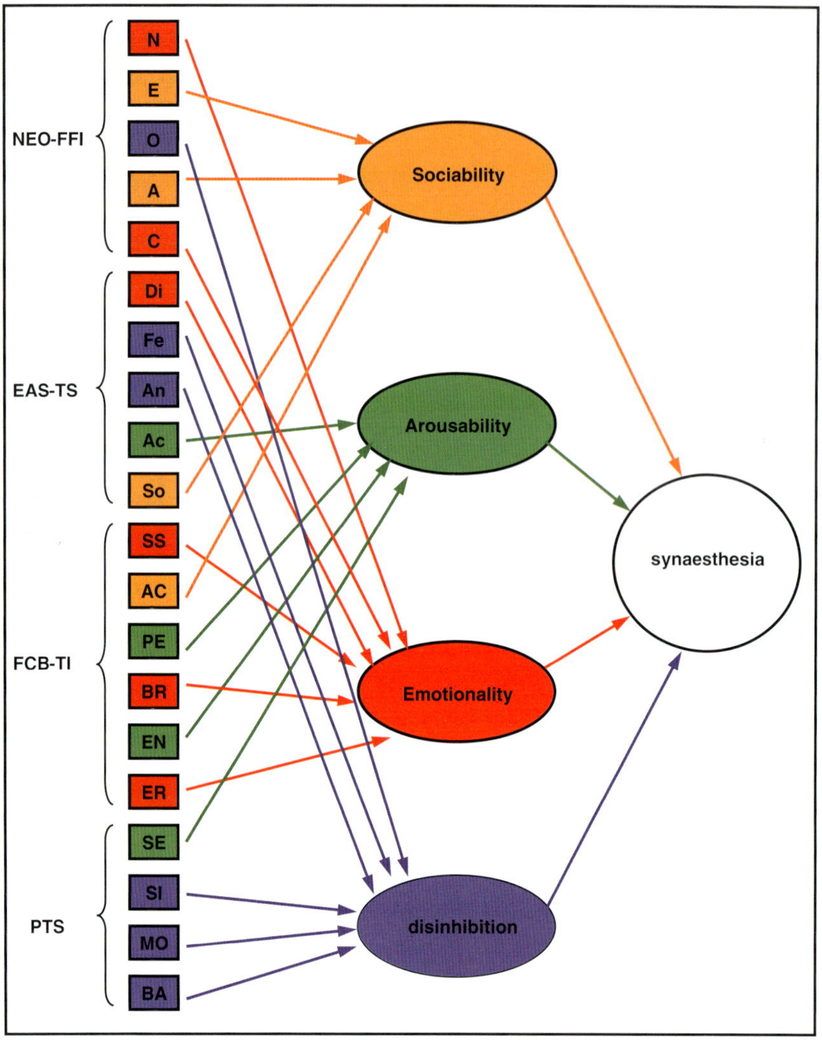

Plate 8 Model of PLS regression analysis that shows the relationships between linguistic-colour synaesthesia and two levels of predictors, the latent and response variables, in the synaesthete sample ($n = 8$).

3 Cognitive determinants of linguistic-colour associations

Linguistic-colour synaesthesia is a cognitive phenomenon. Numerous studies have been conducted on aspects of the cognitive abilities of synaesthetes such as memory (e.g., Luria, 1968; Smilek, Dixon, *et al.*, 2002; Mills, Innis, Westendorf, Owsianiecki, and McDonald, 2006; Yaro and Ward, 2007; Rothen and Meier, 2009), attention (e.g., Smilek, Dixon, and Merikle, 2003; Laeng, Svartdal, and Oelmann, 2004; Rich and Mattingley, 2005; Sagiv and Robertson, 2005; Edquist, Rich, Brinkman, and Mattingley, 2006; Mattingley, Payne, and Rich, 2006; Sagiv, Heer, and Robertson, 2006), imagination (e.g., Barnett and Newell, 2008; Spiller and Jansari, 2008), and consciousness (e.g., Gray, Williams, Nunn, and Baron-Cohen, 1997; Dixon *et al.*, 2000; Grossenbacher and Lovelace, 2001; Mattingley *et al.*, 2001; Smilek, Dixon, Cudahy, and Merikle, 2001; Rich and Mattingley, 2002; Gray, 2005; Dixon, Smilek, Duffy, Zanna, and Merikle, 2006). Some studies have implied that synaesthesia may be correlated with the number and type of senses engaged in it (Day, 2005; Simner and Hubbard, 2006), level of processed information (Ramachandran and Hubbard, 2001b), and type of individual perception (Cohen Kadosh, Cohen Kadosh, and Henik, 2007; Banissy, Walsh, *et al.*, 2009). Moreover, synaesthetic perception may depend on the context and meaning of the stimulus that induces the synaesthesia (Myles *et al.*, 2003; Dixon *et al.*, 2006).

Correlative and comparative studies have also indicated a connection between synaesthesia and absorption (Rader and Tellegen, 1981, 1987; Glicksohn *et al.*, 1992; Rogowska, 2007), physiognomic perception (Dailey, Martindale, and Borkum, 1997), and syncretic perception (Glicksohn *et al.*, 1992). Cognitive research on synaesthesia is crucial for the explanation of synaesthetic experiences as well as 'normal' non-synaesthetic perception, or perceptual disturbances such as hallucinations, out-of-body experiences, aura vision, and many other unusual states of consciousness.

3.1 Memory

The relationship between synaesthesia and memory has been widely explored in cognitive science and neuroscience. Linssen (2011) reviewed a wide range of literature, aiming to assess the present understanding of the relationship between synaesthesia and memory, including neuro-anatomical evidence, case studies, group studies, and possible theoretical explanations. There is evidence of extraordinary memory in synaesthetes, as in the case of the famous synaesthete and mnemonist, Solomon V. Shereshevskii (Luria, 1968), or the mathematical and linguistic savant, Daniel Tammet (2006; Baron-Cohen *et al.*, 2007).

The assumption that synaesthetes have superior memory abilities was examined by Yaro and Ward (2007). Among 46 synaesthetes surveyed by the study, the majority (70%) believed that their memory abilities were better than average. However, when linguistic-colour synaesthetes were examined in several memory tests, they revealed only a slightly better memory performance in recalling words but not in memorizing digits or copying complex figures, in comparison with non-synaesthetes. Furthermore, Rothen and Meier (2010a) tested whether grapheme-colour synaesthesia gives rise to a general memory benefit, using the Wechsler Memory Scale (WMS). Synaesthetes performed better (however, still within the ordinary range) in episodic memory, but not in short-term memory.

Thus, instead of generally extraordinary memory skills, greater memory performance in synaesthetes seems to be limited to the domain or domains specific to the type of synaesthesia. As such, grapheme-colour (or phoneme-colour) synaesthetes may have an advantage in recalling written forms of words (or spoken forms), whereas music-colour synaesthetes may be better than non-synaesthetes at remembering musical sounds.

Indeed, synaesthetes seem to exhibit an advantageous memory performance only for tasks congruent with their synaesthetic percept (Radvansky *et al.*, 2011). There is some evidence that grapheme-colour synaesthetes demonstrate a greater recall ability with verbal material (i.e., digits and written names) than non-synaesthetes (Smilek, Dixon, *et al.*, 2002; Mills *et al.*, 2006), whereas time-space synaesthetes display superior abilities in visual spatial memory and also in memory for events in time (Simner, Mayo, and Spiller, 2009; Brang *et al.*, 2010).

Rothen, Meier, and Ward (2012) suggested that synaesthetes do not appear to have a general advantage in all declarative memory tasks. There is, rather, evidence that grapheme-colour synaesthetes typically outperform age- and education-matched controls in tests involving words, colours, and simple abstract figures, but not number matrices and more complex figures (and possibly memory for faces and scenes). Moreover, these advantages may extend to non-declarative memory involving colour (Meier and Rothen, 2007; Rothen, Nyffeler, von Wartburg, Müri, and Meier, 2010).

However, studies also support the general, rather than domain-specific, advantage of memory. For example, Gross *et al.* (2011) tested nine grapheme-colour synaesthetes with standardized neuropsychological measures that should not trigger grapheme-colour synaesthesia (visual spatial tests) and measures that should trigger grapheme-colour synaesthesia (verbal tasks). They found a synaesthetic advantage in both types of test, primarily in the initial encoding of information. These results indicate that synaesthetes may have enhanced encoding rather than superior recall (Gross *et al.*, 2011).

A study by Rogowska (2007) revealed that hearing-colour synaesthetes (both linguistic and music) demonstrated greater ability in working memory (measured by Sternberg's Short-Term Memory Test), apparently supporting the general advantage and cue-induced encoding hypothesis (Gross *et al.*, 2011). The other findings suggest that the enhanced memory in synaesthetes may be due to differences in neuroanatomical structure. Rouw and Scholte (2007) found significantly more white-matter connections in synaesthete brains, in areas involved in processing working memory, suggesting that synaesthetes may have greater memory abilities than non-synaesthetes.

However, it still remains unclear as to whether synaesthetes' memory is enhanced at encoding, storage, or recall, as suggested by Linssen (2011). Moreover, it is also controversial as to whether the enhanced memory of synaesthetes is related to the type of inducer (e.g., verbal task) or concurrent experience (e.g., synaesthetic colour sensation). Yaro and Ward (2007) suggested that the greater memory performance in synaesthetes is colour-specific, since grapheme-colour synaesthetes reveal significantly better memory performance for colours and for words eliciting synaesthetic colours than non-synaesthetes.

In the present study, these issues were examined with reference to the working memory (Rogowska, 2007; Rouw and Scholte, 2007) and the encoding hypothesis (Gross *et al.*, 2011) in a random sample of university students divided into two groups: linguistic-colour synaesthetes and non-synaesthetes (see Appendix A). Memory performance was measured with both verbal material and non-verbal material.

The Word List Recall Test (WLRT) was used here for verbal memory assessment. The WLRT is a working memory test for verbal span consisting of 20 items, including 10 items within the Concrete Words scale (i.e., *tree, board, pencil, book, lighter, table, newspaper, washer, spectacles,* and *ink*) and 10 items within the Abstract Words scale (i.e., *justice, honour, amity, compassion, indigence, survival, infancy, grace, help,* and *support*). The words were presented together for 2 minutes, displayed visually in two columns on the screen with sequential numbers (from 1 to 20). The MS PowerPoint presentation comprised a list of words and a mini-clock in the top-right corner of the screen that showed time passing backwards from 2 minutes to 0. The participants read the words and tried to remember them with the numbers in order, using any mnemotechniques they could. After 2 minutes of memorization, the list of words disappeared and the projection comprised only the clock that again started displaying time passing backwards from 2 minutes to the end of the test. During this 2-minute period, the participants wrote down the words on an A5 paper sheet that comprised a sequence of numbers in two columns as on the screen. If a word was placed correctly in order, a participant scored 2 points, if a word was in the incorrect place 1 point, and if a word was incorrect or missing 0 points. Thus, the maximal score was 40 for the total result of the WLRT, and 20 for each subscale of Concrete Words (CW) and Abstract Words (AW).[1]

The Benton Visual Retention Test (BVRT) measures non-verbal visual perception, short-term/working visual memory, and visual constructive abilities (Benton, 1992). It can also be used to help identify possible learning disabilities. The MS PowerPoint presentation of the BVRT for Form D and Administration A was used in the present study. The slideshow consisted of 10 items presenting one or more (typically three) two-dimensional line drawings of familiar geometric shapes (circles, rectangles, triangles, etc.). The participants were shown a projection of each of 10 designs for the specified 10-second administration on the screen. Following this, a blank screen automatically appeared, and the participant was required to reproduce the designs on an A5 sheet with a pencil, immediately after the presentation of each item. The Number Correct Score (NCS) and the Number Error Score (NES) are used as measures of visual declarative memory performance. A higher NCS result (maximal score: 10) signifies better performance and is calculated as the sum of the total number of accurately reproduced designs. A higher NES score signifies worse performance, and can include 56 types of error concerning the form, shape, pattern, and arrangement on the paper. The NES comprises six categories of error: omissions, distortions,

[1] In the present study, Cronbach's alpha reliabilities for the total WLRT and for CW and AW were .79, .68, and .64, respectively. The split-half reliability coefficients were .90, .86, and .76, respectively.

perseverations, rotations, misplacements, and size errors. Although the NES has a wide range, the typical protocol usually contains fewer than 24 errors.[2]

Colour performance was assessed with the Visual Colour Discrimination (VCD) training subtest (for more details, see Section 1.3) and the L-CAT (for more details, see Section 1.7) with both of the indices: colour consistency scores and response time (RT). Linguistic-colour synaesthetes scoring significantly higher than non-synaesthetes only in verbal memory tasks may support either the cue-induced encoding or the domain-specific (especially inducer-specific) hypothesis.

It also seems interesting to examine whether synaesthetes differ from non-synaesthetes in either abstract or concrete verbal material. McDougall and Pfeifer (2012) examined a group of 30 non-synaesthetes on their memory performance related to visual imagery; recall was found to be better for unambiguous concrete nouns than for abstract nouns. Contrary to these results, it was expected in the present study that synaesthetes would score higher than non-synaesthetes on an abstract list of words, and that they would present similar scores in concrete lists of words, since synaesthesia seems to be mostly related to abstract conceptions (e.g., digits, letters of the alphabet, days of the week).

Linguistic-colour synaesthetes demonstrating significantly higher scores in both verbal and non-verbal tests may confirm a general advantage of memory in synaesthetes. It may also provide evidence that linguistic-colour synaesthesia is related to an integrative process involving the shape of graphemes. Some authors claim that letters with similar shapes tend to be associated with similar colours (Brang, Rouw, *et al.*, 2011; Jürgens and Nikolić, 2012). Moreover, a recent study (Watson *et al.*, 2012) indicated that synaesthetic associations between colour and letters of the alphabet involve letter shapes, ordinality, and frequency. In addition, Rothen and Meier (2010a) found that grapheme-colour synaesthetes have enhanced abilities of recall (drawing) and recognition of simple visual figures.

[2] The interscorer agreement indicated high reliability for the NCS scale (.94 to .97) and the NES scale (.90 to .97) of the BVRT (Benton, 1992). The Spearman–Brown split-half reliability for the Polish sample in age ranged between 18 and 25 years, and for Form D and Administration A it was rather low for the NCS scale (.26) and the NES scale (.28) of the BVRT (Jaworowska, 2007). However, in a larger age-differentiated sample, between 5 and 75 years, the reliability coefficient ranged from .26 to .74 for the NCS scale, and from .28 to .78 for the NES scale (Jaworowska, 2007). In the present sample, Cronbach's alpha amounted to .35 and .20 for the NCS and the NES, respectively. However, split-half reliability for both scales was slightly higher (.40, and .29, respectively).

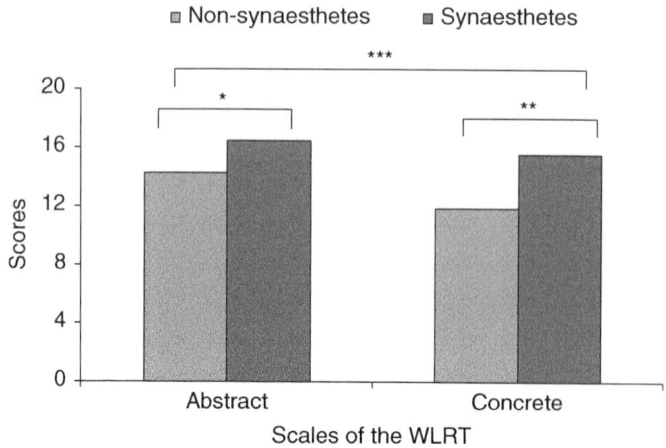

Figure 3.1 Differences between non-synaesthetes and synaesthetes in verbal memory. *Note:* $^*p < .05$, $^{**}p < .01$, $^{***}p < .001$. RT = response time.

The higher VCD scores of linguistic-colour synaesthetes may support the concurrent-specific hypothesis. Rothen and Meier (2010a) claimed that there is a memory advantage for colour that is not directly attributable to synaesthetic associations (either explicit or implicit). If linguistic-colour synaesthetes demonstrate generally better memory for colours, they may display shorter reaction times in the colour discrimination tasks of the VCD, as well as in the linguistic-colour associations of the L-CAT. This could also support the concurrent-specific hypothesis. If linguistic-colour synaesthetes do not differ from non-synaesthetes in any of the tests, this may be evidence against all the hypotheses mentioned above.

A total of 74 students of Sample A participated in the present study (for more details, see Appendix A). Descriptive statistics of both types of memory (visual and verbal) are shown in Table B3.1 in Appendix B. Visual memory (of the BVRT) neither distinguished between synaesthetes and non-synaesthetes nor correlated significantly with the range of consistent linguistic-colour associations. Although verbal memory (of the WLRT) did not correlate significantly with linguistic-colour associations, a significant effect was revealed in the analysis of group differences (see Table B3.1 in Appendix B and Figure 3.1). The synaesthetes scored higher in total WLRT as well as in both subscales of AW and CW.

A one-way ANOVA was then performed in order to examine the relationships between linguistic-colour synaesthesia as a factor and subscales of verbal memory, as measures of responses, in an attempt to determine an effect. The 2 (Synaesthesia: Synaesthetes, Non-synaesthetes) × 2 (Verbal Memory: AW, CW) ANOVA demonstrated a significant main effect: Wilks' $\Lambda = .90$, $F(2, 70) = 3.99$, $p = .023$, $\eta_p^2 = .10$. The synaesthesia effect was significant for AW [$\Delta R^2 = .04$, $F(1, 71) = 4.00$, $p = .049$] and for CW [$\Delta R^2 = .09$, $F(1, 71) = 8.08$, $p = .006$]. It was also interesting to determine whether the types of verbal items (abstract vs. concrete) differed significantly between the groups (synaesthetes and non-synaesthetes). To examine these issues, a one-way repeated-measures analysis of variance (*r*ANOVA) was conducted. The analysis showed a significant intersubjects effect [$F(1, 71) = 7.25$, $p = .009$, $\eta_p^2 = .09$], as well as a within-subjects effect [$F(1, 71) = 10.90$, $p = .002$, $\eta_p^2 = .13$], but without a significant interaction [$F(1, 71) = 2.22$, $p = .141$, $\eta_p^2 = .03$]. Both synaesthetes and non-synaesthetes scored higher marks in recalling abstract words than concrete words; however, this effect was stronger for the non-synaesthete group.

The differences between synaesthetes and non-synaesthetes in colour experiences and RT in the VCD and range of consistent colours in the L-CAT are shown in Table B3.1 in Appendix B. The consistency scores of the L-CAT did not correlate significantly with the VCD. Synaesthetes scored lower than non-synaesthetes in total L-CAT scores and in RT in the VCD. Neither RT in the L-CAT nor total VCD distinguished between synaesthetes and non-synaesthetes. This suggests that synaesthetes scored more consistent linguistic-colour associations than non-synaesthetes, during a relatively similar time. Although synaesthetes had relatively similar scores to non-synaesthetes in distinguishing between the two colours, they needed significantly less time for this (see Figure 3.2).

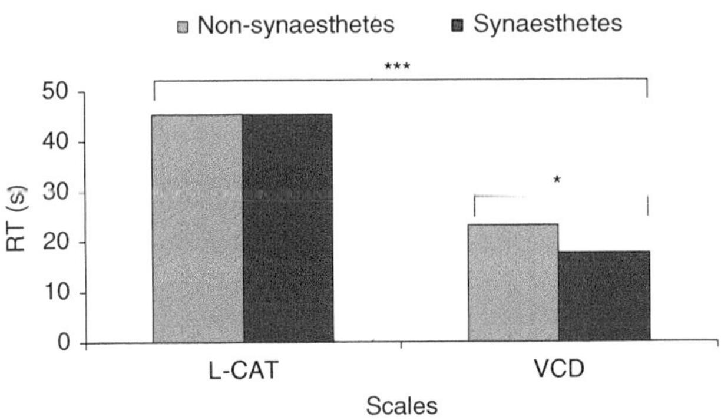

Figure 3.2 Differences between non-synaesthetes and synaesthetes in response time (RT) in the total L-CAT and VCD (*$p < .05$, ***$p < .001$).

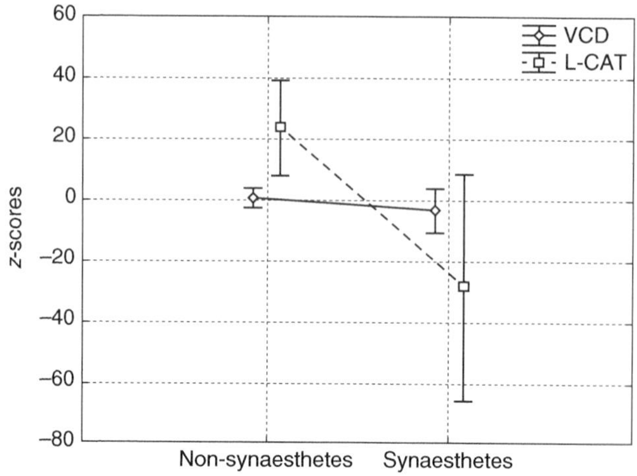

Figure 3.3 Interaction between synaesthesia (non-synaesthetes and synaesthetes) and consistency of colours in the total L-CAT and VCD. *Note:* Error bars show the mean ± 95% confidence interval.

Next, the ANOVA was conducted. The scores of particular items within the VCD scale were converted into normalized *z*-scores and then summarized for comparison with the total L-CAT. Colour consistency concerns two types of colour: (1) perceptual colours available visually and measured on a VCD scale; and (2) imagined colours resulting from the association between verbal items (words, graphemes) and mental representation of colours (assessed in the test–retest procedure by total L-CAT). A 2 (Synaesthesia: Synaesthetes, Non-synaesthetes) × 2 (Colour Consistency: Perceptual, Imagined) one-way *r*ANOVA was conducted to examine the relationships between these variables (see Figure 3.3). The analysis showed a significant intersubject effect [$F(1, 72) = 7.57, p = .008, \eta_p^2 = .10$], as well as an interaction effect [$F(1, 72) = 5.48, p = .022, \eta_p^2 = .07$], but a non-significant within-subject effect [$F(1, 72) = .01, p = .91, \eta_p^2 = .00$]. Synaesthetes demonstrated more consistent colours than non-synaesthetes in both perceptual and imagined types of colour. The interaction effect suggests that the synaesthesia condition influences the consistency of colours, especially the imagined colours of the total L-CAT.

Some case studies have shown that synaesthesia can contribute to extraordinary memory performance (e.g., Luria, 1968; Smilek, Dixon, *et al.*, 2002; Mills *et al.*, 2006; Baron-Cohen *et al.*, 2007; Brang and

Ramachandran, 2010), whereas studies on larger groups of subjects revealed that synaesthetes had just a slight performance advantage and did not usually exceed the average level for a general population (e.g., Yaro and Ward, 2007; Rothen and Meier, 2009). Rothen and Meier (2009) suggested that the superior performance of synaesthetes observed in some case-report studies may be due to individual differences, selection bias, or the use of synaesthesia as a mnemonic strategy. Indeed, synaesthetes have often reported that they employ their synaesthetic percepts to help complete memory tasks (Mills *et al.*, 2006; Yaro and Ward, 2007).

In the present study, linguistic-colour synaesthetes scored slightly higher than non-synaesthetes in the verbal memory test of the WLRT, but not in the visual memory test of the BVRT. This seems consistent with a case study (Mills *et al.*, 2006) in which a multilingual, alphabet-colour synaesthete, a professor of Russian (M. L. S.), displayed an average performance on two visual memory tests: the BVRT-Revised and the Rey Complex Figure Test (RCFT). However, M. L. S. had superior memory performance on a verbal memory test consisting of lists of nouns, the Rey Auditory and Verbal Learning Test (RAVLT). The present study seems to support the assumption that synaesthetes do not exhibit an extraordinary memory, but, rather, enhanced memory performance related to their specific type of synaesthesia (e.g., Ward, Thompson-Lake, Ely, and Kaminski, 2008; Simner, Mayo, and Spiller, 2009).

Moreover, the results of the present study seem consistent with the cue-induced encoding and domain-specific (especially inducer-specific) hypothesis (Smilek, Dixon, *et al.*, 2002; Mills *et al.*, 2006; Yaro and Ward, 2007; Gross *et al.*, 2011; Radvansky *et al.*, 2011; Rothen *et al.*, 2012). The study by Rouw and Scholte (2007) provided further neuroscientific evidence that synaesthetes may have enhanced memory abilities, as reflected by the greater white- and grey-matter connections between areas involved in memory processing and perceptual processing, and adjacent cortical areas. Thus, the enhanced memory performance in synaesthetes may be the result of greater connections between perceptual processing areas and areas involved in processing working memory.

According to the cue-induced encoding conception (Gross *et al.*, 2011), synaesthetic percepts may be consciously adopted as additional cues to memory. Gross *et al.* (2011) suggested that synaesthetes seem to learn more initially rather than forget less over time. The cue-induced encoding-retrieval hypothesis suggests that the cue provided by synaesthetic percepts can be consciously utilized to assist encoding and recall. Synaesthesia seems to provide a richer world of experience, and, as a consequence, additional retrieval cues may be available and beneficial, but not to the point of extraordinary memory ability (Rothen and Meier, 2010a). Rothen *et al.* (2012) suggested that synaesthetes are particularly good at remembering colours, abstract shapes, and visual words (e.g., Yaro and Ward, 2007; Rothen and Meier, 2010a), but perhaps showed less memory advantage for faces and scenes, and for associating objects with spatial positions (e.g., Gross *et al.*, 2011).

Radvansky *et al.* (2011) proposed that grapheme-colour synaesthesia can lead people to place a greater emphasis on item-specific processing, and surface-form characteristics of words in a list (e.g., the letters that make them up) relative to relational processing and more meaning-based processes. Jürgens and Nikolić (2012) found evidence that the synaesthetic concurrent sensation has a true perceptual quality, whereas synaesthetic inducers have a semantic, rather than perceptual, nature. Because of the conception of 'ideaesthesia' (Jürgens and Nikolić, 2012), synaesthesia seems to be better understood in terms of inducing ideas that elicit perceptual concurrents by means of conceptual mechanisms.

In the present study, both synaesthetes and non-synaesthetes demonstrated better recall of abstract words than concrete words, contrary to the results of McDougall and Pfeifer (2012). However, subjects in McDougall and Pfeifer's (2012) study were instructed to use visual imagination for memory performance, and this might have affected their better recalling of concrete nouns. In contrast, the students in the present sample could use their own preferred mnemonics. University students seem to be expert in learning new abstract concepts and foreign words; therefore, better scores in abstract words in the present study may be an effect of years of practice. Thus, the present results seem more related to a specific sample, rather than a specific list of words. Witthoft and Winawer (2006, 2013) postulated that a complete explanation of synaesthesia must incorporate the central role of learning and memory. From this point of view, synaesthesia may be considered an automatic retrieval of highly specific mnemonic associations, in which perceptual contents are brought to mind in a manner akin to mental imagery or the perceptual-reinstatement effects found in memory studies.

Further research on these issues should include more random samples of participants that will represent people of different ages, occupations, and education. Although there were no significant differences between synaesthetes and non-synaesthetes in the visual short-term memory test, this is not strong evidence against the advantage of synaesthetes in visual performance found in other studies (e.g., Rothen and Meier, 2010a; Gross *et al.*, 2011). It is important to note that the BVRT could have been too easy for a sample of students, since almost all of them passed this test very well. Thus, future studies may use modified and more difficult administration of these tests than immediate recall (e.g., shorter time of exposition of figures, lengthened recall duration).

The present study seems (at least partially) to support the concurrent-specific hypothesis. Although synaesthetes do not outperform non-synaesthetes significantly in colour discrimination on the VCD, the mean scores (below 5) of synaesthetes might be interpreted (in view of the CIELAB model) as differences in hues within one colour, whereas non-synaesthetes' mean scores (above 5) refer to differences between various colours. Thus, synaesthetes seem to have passed these tests better. Moreover, the RT of synaesthetes was significantly shorter in the VCD than that of non-synaesthetes. Therefore, even when one assumes that the outcome of the discrimination test did not distinguish synaesthetes from non-synaesthetes, synaesthetes performed this test significantly faster. These findings support the assumption that linguistic--colour synaesthetes demonstrate generally better memory for colours.

The results on the L-CAT in the sample of synaesthetes, in contrast to the VCD, were better for the total range of consistent linguistic-colour association, but were the same as those of the non-synaesthetes for total RT. Thus, the synaesthetes had more consistent linguistic-colour associations than the non-synaesthetes during a relatively similar period of time in the total L-CAT. Again, this supports the previous assumption about enhanced colour perceptual abilities in linguistic-colour synaesthetes. When the ANOVA was conducted, the synaesthetes demonstrated more consistent colours than the non-synaesthetes in both the perceptual and imagined types of colour. In addition, an interaction was found between these variables, possibly indicating that synaesthesia (as a dichotomic variable) can influence the consistency of colours (as a continuous variable), especially imagined colours in the total L-CAT.

The current findings seem to be consistent with other studies (Yaro and Ward, 2007; Rothen and Meier, 2010a) that revealed a general memory advantage for colour in synaesthetes. Colours provide important symbolic and contextual information that is not conveyed by form alone, as suggested by Rich *et al.* (2006). Banissy, Cohen Kadosh, *et al.* (2009) proposed that a hypersensitive concurrent perceptual system is a general property of synaesthesia. According to the compensatory hypothesis (Rogowska, 2011), linguistic-colour synaesthetes may display enhanced colour sensitivity from birth, but some (most likely temporary) deficits during language acquisition at a certain stage of development may elicit synaesthetic representations according to the cue-induced hypothesis. Altogether, the current results appear to indicate that synaesthetes demonstrate enhanced concurrent-specific, as well as inducer-specific, cognitive capacity.

3.2 Imagination

Visual imagery seems to play an important role in linguistic-colour synaesthesia. *Visual imagery* refers to the experience of mentally visualizing the appearance of something, usually without its being present (Allbutt, Ling, Rowley, and Shafiullah, 2011). Synaesthetic concurrent experiences of colour appear to satisfy the criteria of visual mental representation in linguistic-colour synaesthetes. Synaesthetic colour experiences are described as occurring internally in the 'mind's eye' in associator synaesthetes, as well as being reported externally in the 'spatial location' in projector synaesthetes (Dixon *et al.*, 2004). The idiosyncratic schema of colour visualization (e.g., as a path, grapheme, simple geometric figure) in linguistic-colour and hearing-colour synaesthetes may be related to individual differences in imagery abilities (e.g., vividness), to the type of synaesthesia (i.e., associators vs. projectors), or to many other possible factors (e.g., preferred cognitive style: wholist-analytic, verbalizers-imagers, type of sensory integration-deprivation, environmental factors during synaesthesia acquisition, etc.).

Synaesthetic concurrents do not seem to be related only to synaesthesia. There is also some evidence that these synaesthetic experiences may occur without external stimulation but as an effect of imagining an inducer (e.g., Dixon *et al.*, 2000; Elias *et al.*, 2003; Jansari, Spiller, and Redfern, 2006). Spiller and Jansari (2008) explored the synaesthetic experience resulting from a visual mental representation of a grapheme. A sample of six grapheme-colour synaesthetes was faster than the controls at a visual mental imagery task that involved visualizing a letter and making a size-based decision about it. However, significant individual differences were found between synaesthetes, which related to an individual imagery ability (such as its vividness), the type of synaesthesia experienced (projectors vs. associators), or the reported difference in colour experience (imagined vs. written grapheme). Nevertheless, the results of that study (Spiller and Jansari, 2008) suggested that grapheme-colour synaesthetes have stronger imagery abilities than non-synaesthetes, at least in a grapheme-based task.

Barnett and Newell (2008) examined whether synaesthesia was related to the general ability to imagine stimuli, or was, rather, more specifically related to enhanced mental imagery for the set of stimuli that induce or are evoked through synaesthesia. They found evidence that enhanced visual imagery may be a trait common to synaesthetes, since a large group of synaesthetes self-reported more vivid mental images in the Vividness of Visual Imagery Questionnaire (VVIQ) than an age-matched control group.

Price (2009) investigated how general mental imagery might be involved in mediating number-space synaesthesia. Number-space synaesthetes scored higher than controls on visual imagery self-report scales – that is, the Spontaneous Use of Imagery Scale (SUIS) and the visual imagery subscale of the Object-Spatial Imagery Questionnaire (OSIQ) – but not on spatial imagery assessed by the spatial imagery subscale of the OSIQ. Simner, Mayo, and Spiller (2009) examined whether time-space synaesthetes presented an advantage in visual spatial processing. Time-space synaesthetes demonstrated their superior performance in a battery of visual spatial tasks that assessed visual memory recall and the ability to manipulate real or imagined objects in a three-dimensional space. The results of these studies (Price, 2009; Simner, Mayo, and Spiller, 2009) seem to be consistent with the assumption that strong general imagery is a necessary condition to experience synaesthesia (at least for spatial forms).

A high visualization capacity may cause interference between the synaesthetic digit and the background colour (Mattingley *et al.*, 2001). Manipulating the background colour of the search area (i.e., congruent or incongruent with the synaesthetic experience) influences the search efficiency (Smilek *et al.*, 2001). Some authors claim that mental images and perceived stimuli are represented similarly and can be processed in the same way (Borst and Kosslyn, 2008). Rollins (2001) revived Kosslyn's (1994) conception of perception and imagination, which stipulates that the relation between perception and imagination consists of three dimensions: (1) imagery and perception depend on some of the same mechanisms; (2) imagery plays an essential role in perception; and (3) perception generates images. There is evidence that veridical visual perception and visual mental imagery share many neural substrates. Spiller and Jansari (2008) suggested that activating the same early areas of the visual pathway with a mental image may allow a similar progression through the visual areas as a visual perception of that image.

Visual cortex activity may be a promising candidate for an objective index of subjective vividness (Cui, Jeter, Yang, Montague, and Eagleman, 2007). Indeed, a study using fMRI found that non-synaesthetes who reported experiencing vivid visual images showed increased activation in the visual cortex when performing an objective visualization task (Cui *et al.*, 2007). In addition, an fMRI study by Rich *et al.* (2006) on a group of grapheme-colour synaesthetes and matched non-synaesthetic controls revealed that voluntary colour imagery activated the colour-selective area, V4, in the right hemisphere. However, synaesthetic colour resulted in a unique activity for synaesthetes in the left medial lingual gyrus, an area previously implicated in tasks involving colour knowledge.

Grossenbacher and Lovelace (2001) proposed that synaesthesia may occur with incomplete activation of the entire cascade of sensory signalling normally propagated during perception. In linguistic-colour synaesthetes, verbal material may be encoded more as visual objects than as semantic ones. According to the dual-coding theory of memory (Paivio, 1986), synaesthetic experiences may act in a similar way to visual mental images and thus benefit memory performance, as suggested by Rothen *et al.* (2012).

If an advantage in imagery is necessary for synaesthesia occurrence, then synaesthetes may demonstrate heightened general imagery performance not specific to synaesthetic inducers and concurrents. In the present study, individual differences in imagery experience were compared in samples of synaesthetes and non-synaesthetes by using self-reported answers to the Imagination Inventory (II) (Barber and Wilson, 1979). An earlier study by Rogowska (2007) among a random sample of 125 secondary-school students (mean age 18 years) revealed a positive correlation between hearing-colour synaesthetic associations (both linguistic and music) and self-reported imagination assessed with the II. Stronger hearing-colour synaesthetes scored higher in imagery than non-synaesthetes. Thus, it was expected here that a similar pattern would be observed in a sample of university students for linguistic-colour synaesthetes.

The II is a self-reported, brief measure of imagery ability that is primarily used to identify highly hypnotizable subjects (Barber and Wilson, 1979). It consists of 15 items and is divided into three components: five items for Vividness of Sensory Imaginings (VSI) such as the coldness and taste of eaten ice cream, or the sound of an ambulance; two items for the Childhood Imagination (CI) subscale, which characterizes the usage of creative fantasy during play in childhood; and eight items for the Engagement in Experiences (EE) subscale, referring to an extension of engagement in daily activities (e.g., watching a film, reading a book), as well as involvement in emotional, aesthetic, extreme, extraordinary, and transcendental experiences. Participants rated on a 4-degree scale how much they agreed with the sentences describing particular imagined experiences and activities.

Wilson and Barber (1978, 1981, 1983a, 1983b) also developed two other well-known questionnaires for assessing fantasy-prone personality: the Inventory of Childhood Memories and Imaginings (ICMI) and the Creative Imagination Scale (CIS). Although Siuta (1996) found that the rationally derived scales developed by Barber and Wilson (1979) failed to parallel the factor structure derived from an empirical procedure in a Polish sample, the results of the present study were

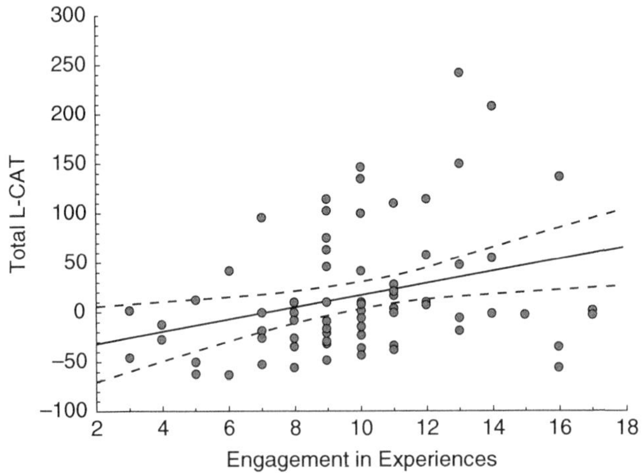

Figure 3.4 Simple linear regression model estimated for Engagement in Experiences (EE) and linguistic-colour associations (L-CAT). *Note:* The fitted regression line is marked by a continuous line, and the confidence intervals by a dashed line.

summarized in three subscales, as in the primary and original version of the II.[3] The cross-cultural validity of the II was supported by low-to-moderate correlations with proneness to hypnosis and fantasy-prone personality (Siuta, 1987, 1996).

Descriptive statistics for the II are shown in Table B3.1 in Appendix B. Linguistic-colour associations correlated significantly with the EE subscale. A positive correlation indicated that stronger linguistic-colour associators demonstrated lower EE scores. A standard regression analysis was conducted in order to explore and model the relationship between the EE subscale of the II as a predictor variable and the linguistic-colour associations of the L-CAT as the response (see scatter plot in Figure 3.4). EE accounted for 8% of the linguistic-colour associations variance, as suggested by regression analysis: $\beta = 0.30$, $B = 6.14$, $SE\ B = 2.27$, $t(72) = 2.71$, $p = .008$, $R^2 = .09$, $\Delta R^2 = .08$, $F(1, 72) = 7.34$, $p < .008$. No other significant relationships between synaesthesia and imagination were found.

[3] The Spearman–Brown split-half reliability was acceptable for the original II (Barber and Wilson, 1979; the coefficient was .76), and also for the Polish version by Siuta (1987) (the coefficient was .67). In the present sample, the split-half reliability was also acceptable for the II (.73), with Cronbach's alpha of .70 for the II total result, and for the three subscales: .65, .58, and .61 for VSI, CI, and EE, respectively.

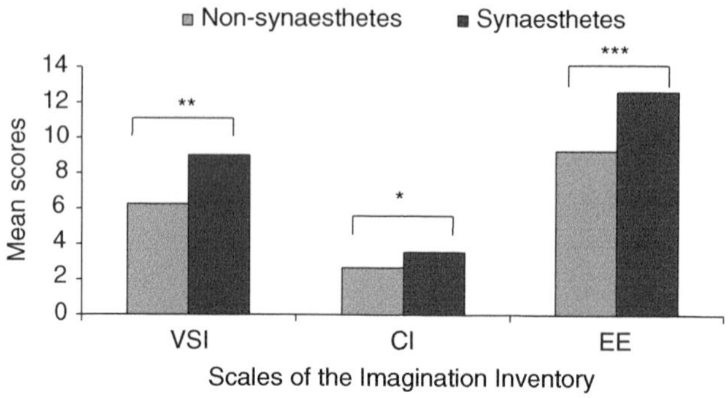

Figure 3.5 Differences between non-synaesthetes and synaesthetes in imagination. *Note:* $^{*}p < .05$, $^{**}p < .01$, $^{***}p < .001$. VSI = Vividness of Sensory Imaginings; CI = Childhood Imagination; EE = Engagement in Experiences.

Synaesthetes scored significantly higher than non-synaesthetes in total II, as well as in the VSI, CI, and EE subscales of the II (see Figure 3.5). Performing multiple two-sample *t*-tests would result in an increased chance of committing a type I error. For this reason, one-way ANOVA was conducted to generalize the *t*-test and to compare the three means of the particular scales of the II. The 2 (Synaesthesia: Synaesthetes, Non-synaesthetes) × 3 (Imagination: VSI, CI, EE) ANOVA revealed a significant main effect: Wilks' $\Lambda = .77$, $F(3, 70) = 6.96$, $p = .0004$, $\eta_p^2 = .23$. The effects of groups were significant for VSI [$\Delta R^2 = .11$, $F(1, 72) = 9.64$, $p = .003$], CI [$\Delta R^2 = .07$, $F(1, 72) = 6.15$, $p = .016$], and EE [$\Delta R^2 = .13$, $F(1, 72) = 12.15$, $p < .001$].

As expected, linguistic-colour synaesthetes scored higher than non-synaesthetes in total II, as well as in all three subscales: VSI, CI, and EE. This seems to support the assumption that synaesthetes demonstrate a general advantage in their imagery capacity (Grossenbacher and Lovelace, 2001; Barnett and Newel, 2008). However, the differences between synaesthetes and non-synaesthetes were greater in reference to the EE subscale. Moreover, stronger linguistic-colour synaesthesia (as measured by the range of consistent linguistic-colour associations in the L-CAT) was related to lower EE and vice versa. It is important to note that the EE subscale of the II mostly corresponds to absorption as a trait. The trait of absorption reflects a motivational readiness to engage in experiential, non-instrumental functioning and distinctive cognitive capacities to efficiently identify and richly elaborate objects of attention (Wild, Kuiken, and Schopflocher, 1995).

Moreover, the pattern of relationships between EE and linguistic-colour synaesthesia seems similar to relationships between absorption and synaesthesia found currently in other studies (see Section 4.2). Absorption was also positively correlated with the range of consistent linguistic-colour associations of the L-CAT, meaning that when the strength of linguistic colour synaesthesia increases, absorption decreases. Similarly, linguistic-colour synaesthetes scored significantly higher on absorption in general than non-synaesthetes. Thus, both results in absorption and EE seem to strongly correspond with each other.

Because the present Sample A also participated in another study on absorption (see Section 4.2), the analysis of correlation between absorption (assessed by the TAS) and imagery (assessed by the II) was conducted here. Indeed, the absorption scale correlated highly with total II ($r = .74, p < .001$), as well as with all three VSI scales ($r = .45, p < .001$), CI ($r_s = .36, p = .003$), and EE ($r = .66, p < .001$) in the total sample ($N = 74$). As expected, among the three subscales of the II, the strongest correlation was found between EE and absorption as a trait. This seems to support the relationship between synaesthesia and absorption, which has been found elsewhere.

The relationship between synaesthesia and absorption was assumed by the authors of the TAS (Rader and Tellegen, 1981, 1987) and confirmed previously in some studies (Zingrone *et al.*, 2009; Studerus, Gamma, and Vollenweider, 2010; Milán *et al.*, 2012; Studerus *et al.*, 2012). Absorption was found to be related to heightened visual imagery (Pekala, Wenger, and Levine, 1985) and proneness to fantasy (Wilson and Barber, 1983b). Glicksohn and Barrett (2003) revealed that the personality trait of absorption is a predisposing factor for hallucinatory experience. This relationship seems be related to the binding potential of the serotonergic receptor 5-HT2A (Ott, Reuter, Hennig, and Vaitl, 2005; Brang and Ramachandran, 2008).

Glicksohn *et al.* (1992, 1999) found that synaesthesia was related to both absorption and eidetic imagery. Moreover, for subjects who scored relatively highly on the absorption scale, there was a negative correlation between structural eidetic imagery and colour-mood synaesthetic differentiation. Thus, the present study seems to confirm to some degree these results. Glicksohn *et al.* (1999) suggested that synaesthesia and eidetics have a common characteristic of cognitive dedifferentiation: synaesthesia entails the dedifferentiation of the sensory modalities, while eidetic imagery entails the dedifferentiation of imagery and perception. Eidetic capacity was also found in a case study of a music-colour synaesthete (Rizzo and Eslinger, 1989) and a number-colour synaesthete (Brang and Ramachandran, 2010). However, it should be noted that eidetic imagery is relatively rare in the adult population. The relationships between eidetic imagery and synaesthesia could be examined more systematically in the future.

The current findings may have important implications for our general understanding of synaesthesia and, in particular, for the explanation of relationships between synaesthesia and individual differences in absorption and imagery. Because visual imagery and absorption are also related to schizophrenia and dissociation (e.g., Glicksohn *et al.*, 1999; Waldo and Merritt, 2000; van de Ven and Merckelbach, 2003), these phenomena may share common mechanisms. Thus, it seems especially interesting to demonstrate the similarities and differences between synaesthesia and psychopathological conditions, as well as to distinguish synaesthetic concurrent visualization from schizophrenic visual hallucination by behavioural and neuroimaging methods.

3.3 Attention

The other aspect of synaesthetic perception is related to attention. Researchers have noticed that attention plays a central role in integrating colour and shape in synaesthesia (Sagiv *et al.*, 2006; Rich and Mattingley, 2010). One study found that synaesthesia was enhanced when the inducing stimulus was near the focus of attention (Sagiv *et al.*, 2006) or when attention was deployed in a perceptually easy versus hard task (Mattingley *et al.*, 2006). Nijboer and van der Stigchel (2009) investigated the extent to which attention was necessary to induce synaesthetic colour experiences. Their findings suggested that attention and hence overt recognition of the inducing stimulus are essential for the synaesthetic colour experience to occur. Reeves, Fuller, and Fine (2005) found evidence in a sample of non-synaesthetes that attention facilitates the creation and maintenance of novel colour-shape bindings in the visual periphery. Without attention, binding was less effective during a task for colour-shape acquisition (Reeves *et al.*, 2005). According to the feature integration theory (Treisman and Gelade, 1980), spatial attention is crucial for binding such features as colour, shape, and other surface features into objects.

Linguistic-colour synaesthetes often report that the colours that they experience in association with graphemes are not under their voluntary control. Automatic occurrence of synaesthetic associations was confirmed by studies demonstrating that synaesthetic colours can interfere with the identification and naming of display colours in modified Stroop interference paradigms (e.g., Mills *et al.*, 1999; Dixon *et al.*, 2000; Lupiáñez and

Callejas, 2006). However, some research on grapheme-colour synaesthesia refers to the extent to which synaesthetic colours arise automatically, without the need for conscious effort or strategic control (e.g., Rich and Mattingley, 2002; Robertson, 2003; Jarick, Dixon, and Smilek, 2011). Some authors have shown that attention plays an important role in modulating synaesthetic colour experience (e.g., Ramachandran and Hubbard, 2001a; Rich and Mattingley, 2002; Mattingley *et al.*, 2006; Jarick, Dixon, Stewart, Maxwell, and Smilek, 2009).

A critical question in understanding the mechanism of synaesthesia has been that of whether synaesthetic colours arise early in visual processing, prior to the allocation of focused attention (e.g., Ramachandran and Hubbard, 2001a; Smilek *et al.*, 2001), or whether they occur at some later stage following explicit recognition of the inducing form. A study using search-related paradigms found support for the presence of a colour congruity bias in synaesthetes' search performance, seeming to demonstrate the impact of synaesthesia on covert attention (e.g., Palmeri *et al.*, 2002; Smilek *et al.*, 2003; Smilek, Callejas, Dixon, and Merikle, 2007; Carriere, Eaton, Reynolds, Dixon, and Smilek, 2008). In contrast, other reports have revealed that synaesthesia does not influence attention during visual search (e.g., Edquist *et al.*, 2006; Sagiv *et al.*, 2006; Gheri, Chopping, and Morgan, 2008). This seems to suggest that synaesthetic colours do not arise early enough in visual processing to guide or attract focal attention, as would be consistent with the hypothesis that inducers must be selectively attended to elicit synaesthetic colours (Robertson, 2003; Laeng *et al.*, 2004; Sagiv and Robertson, 2005; Edquist *et al.*, 2006; Nijboer, Satris, and van der Stigchel, 2011).

However, a more recent study by Carriere *et al.* (2008) found evidence of an interaction between low-level perception and higher-level interpretation of meaning. Furthermore, Chiou *et al.* (2013) revealed that synaesthetic colours appeared to have a stronger influence on performance than synaesthetic shapes when auditory-visual synaesthetes (for whom sounds elicit visual experiences of coloured geometric objects at specific spatial locations) attended to colour, and, vice versa, when they attended to shape. Chiou *et al.* (2013) suggested that visual synaesthetic experience can involve multiple features forming object-like percepts, and that each feature can be selected by attention, despite being internally generated. Therefore, Chiou *et al.* (2013) concluded that the brain mechanisms of synaesthesia may need to incorporate a broader neural network underpinning multiple visual features, perceptual knowledge, and feature integration, rather than solely focusing on colour-sensitive areas.

Another explanation for the discrepancy between the results of research on the role of consciousness and attention in synaesthesia refers to the type of synaesthetic concurrent experiences as either projected externally in space or represented internally in the 'mind's eye'. Synaesthetes classified as projectors may be able to experience synaesthetic colour without attending to (and consciously identifying) the inducing grapheme (e.g., Smilek *et al.* 2001; Dixon and Smilek, 2005). Ward and colleagues (Ward *et al.*, 2007; Ward, Jonas, Dienes, and Seth, 2010) proposed the alternative explanation that all types of projector and associator synaesthetes require attentional mechanisms for accurate grapheme-colour binding. However, projectors are more likely to be aware of the induced colours because they are experienced in the same spatial location as the attended stimuli, whereas associators require the division or shifting of attention between different frames of reference.

Previous research has concerned different aspects of attention in synaesthetes, but has not investigated whether synaesthetes demonstrate a general advantage in attention, or only outperform non-synaesthetes in those tasks that required special synaesthetic perception. The present study investigated these issues in Sample A ($N = 74$) of linguistic-colour synaesthetes and non-synaesthetes by using the d2 Test of Attention (Brickenkamp, 1962). This test measures selective attention in a visual search task, where the target is not related to linguistic-colour synaesthetic perception. A sample of linguistic-colour synaesthetes scoring higher than non-synaesthetes may imply that synaesthesia is related to a general advantage in attention.

The d2 Test of Attention is a standardized refinement of a visual cancellation test (Brickenkamp, 1962). The test items consist of the letters *d* and *p* marked with one to four small dashes, arranged either individually or in pairs above and below the letter. The test consists of 14 lines, each with 47 characters, for a total of 658 items. The subject must scan across each line (20 seconds per line) to identify and cross out each *d* with two dashes. In response to the discrimination of similar visual stimuli, the test measures processing speed, rule compliance, and quality of performance, allowing the estimation of individual attention and concentration performance. The test scores are considered as follows: total number of items processed as an indicator of speed processing; E (raw score of errors) as the sum of all mistakes in two forms: E_1 – errors of omission – and E_2 – errors of commission; percentage of errors within the area of all items processed as an indicator of performance quality; total number of items minus error scores as a general indicator of selective attention; and concentration

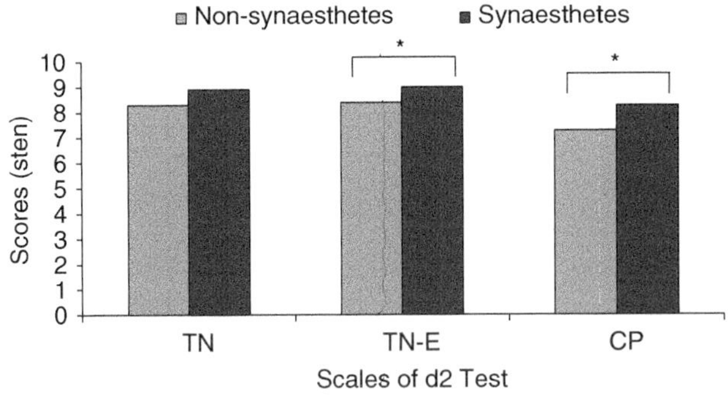

Figure 3.6 Differences between non-synaesthetes and synaesthetes in attention scales. *Note:* $*p < .05$. TN = Total Number of Items Processed; TN-E = Total Number of Items Minus Error Scores; CP = Concentration Performance.

performance derived from the number of correctly crossed-out relevant items (d2) minus the errors of commission (E_2).[4] The d2 Test of Attention correlated positively with Visual Speed and Accuracy, one of the subtests included in the Employee Aptitude Survey, which measures the ability to see details quickly and accurately.

Table B3.1 in Appendix B comprises descriptive statistics for the following scales of the d2 Test of Attention: Total Number of Items Processed (TN), Raw Score of Errors (E), Percentage of Errors (E%), Total Number of Items Minus Error Scores (TN-E), and Concentration Performance (CP). The range of consistent linguistic-colour associations was not correlated significantly with any one of the attention scales. Figure 3.6 demonstrates the differences between synaesthetes and non-synaesthetes in three indices of attention, TN, TN-E, and CP, which were converted into sten scores for comparison. The analysis of differences between synaesthetes and non-synaesthetes revealed a significant effect in both concentration (CP) and general selective attention (TN-E). Synaesthetes scored higher in these variables in comparison to non-synaesthetes (see Table B3.1 in Appendix B for more details).

[4] The reliability is proven to be very high, and the validity of the technique has been documented by a number of research studies. The original German version (Brickenkamp, 1994) has been translated into Polish and standardized in Polish graduate students ($N = 535$) and adults (946) by Dajek (2010), with high Cronbach's alpha reliability coefficients for TN and TN-E of .91 and .92, respectively. In the present study, the alpha reliability was also high for TN and TN-E (.94 and .92, respectively) and ranged from .38 to .95 across the other assessments.

Although the strength of synaesthesia (as measured by the range of consistent linguistic-colour associations in the L-CAT) did not correlate with any one index of attention, some differences between synaesthetes and non-synaesthetes were significant. Thus, synaesthetes scored higher in general selective attention (TN-E) and concentration (CP). These results show that linguistic-colour synaesthetes demonstrated a better ability to pay attention in general, at least with reference to a search-related task. Synaesthesia seems to be a favourable condition for attention, since synaesthetes in the present study revealed a consistent tendency to score higher than non-synaesthetes in all indices of the d2 Test of Attention (however, these differences were not always significantly reliable).

Linguistic-colour synaesthesia seems to require increased resources of attention for the accurate binding of colour to grapheme, and for maintaining synaesthetic concurrent experience (e.g., representation of coloured words) in the focus of attention, together with perceived objects in the external world. Thus, it seems appropriate to assume that synaesthetes need an enhanced attention span for everyday perception, in comparison to non-synaesthetes. Although the present results were not impressive, they support the above hypothesis.

Smilek, Dixon, and Merikle (2006) found that the meanings of the graphemes influenced the efficiency of visual search. They demonstrated that the efficiency of visual search depends on the meaning of an object to the perceiver and the search strategy adopted by the perceiver (Smilek *et al.*, 2006). Since the target in the present study was detection of different number of dashes either above or below the letter *d*, this nonsense stimulus might have hindered the participants' performance. It may explain why synaesthetes did not greatly differ from non-synaesthetes. Nevertheless, more research is necessary to further support the hypothesis of the general advantage of synaesthetes in attention, examining many other types of synaesthesia besides linguistic-colour, as well as using other methods not related specifically to synaesthetic experiences.

3.4 Relationships between linguistic-colour synaesthesia and cognitive variables

Cluster analysis is an explorative method used to divide observations into homogeneous and distinct groups. The groupings are defined by data analysis without any prior knowledge about which elements belong to which clusters. To examine the full complement of relationships between cognitive variables, a two-way joining cluster analysis was conducted in the present study. The objective of this analysis was to detect meaningful patterns of clusters when both cases and variables contribute simultaneously to this effect. The following cognitive variables were selected for analysis: total II as an index of imagination, total WLRT representing verbal memory, NES of the BVRT as a visual memory test, and three scales of attention of the d2 Test of Attention : TN, TN-E, and CP. All of the scores of these variables were converted into sten scores to enable comparison of the results. The two-way joining cluster analysis was performed separately for synaesthetes (see Plate 5) and non-synaesthetes (see Plate 6).

The cluster by feature and by sample was demonstrated by two groups of synaesthetes. The two-way joining cluster analysis seemed to join synaesthetes by attention and memory rather than by imagination. Cluster 1 included five synaesthetes: C. K. (number-colour synaesthete), K. E. (day-colour), P. D. (forename-colour), D. L. (both forename-colour and day-colour), and Z. Ba. (forename-colour). Cluster 2 comprised six synaesthetes Z. K. (forename-colour), R. A. (forename-colour), M. M. (number-colour), Z. A. (day-colour), M. K. (both number-colour and grapheme-colour), and K. M. (both forename-colour and grapheme-colour). All 11 synaesthetes shared similar imagination scores, whereas they were divided into two clusters by a specific connection between memory and attention features.

Among the sample of non-synaesthetes, the two-way joining analysis showed two clusters by a configuration of all cognitive variables involved. Cluster 1 included 52 non-synaesthetes who showed a similar pattern of all variables. Cluster 2 consisted of 11 non-synaesthetes who demonstrated distinguished levels of several cognitive variables that seemed similar to the pattern of Cluster 2 of the synaesthetes. Visual memory (of the BVRT) is most related to concentration of attention (of the CP), whereas verbal memory (of the WRLT) is related to both general attention indices (TN-E) and imagination (of the II).

For further analysis of the present data, a one-way ANOVA was conducted to develop and confirm an explanation for the observed data, as well as to combine multiple comparisons into one model. The main issue examined here was the specification of differences between synaesthetes and non-synaesthetes in cognitive variables.

The total sample ($N = 74$) was divided into four groups due to two-way joining clustering: Synaesthetes 1 (of Cluster 1, $n = 5$), Synaesthetes 2 (of Cluster 2, $n = 6$), Non-synaesthetes 1 (of Cluster 1, $n = 52$), and Non-synaesthetes 2 (of Cluster 2, $n = 11$). A 4 (Clusters: Synaesthetes 1, Synaesthetes 2, Non-synaesthetes 1, Non-synaesthetes 2) × 6 (Cognitive variables: total II, TN, TN-E, CP, WLRT, and BVRT) ANOVA was

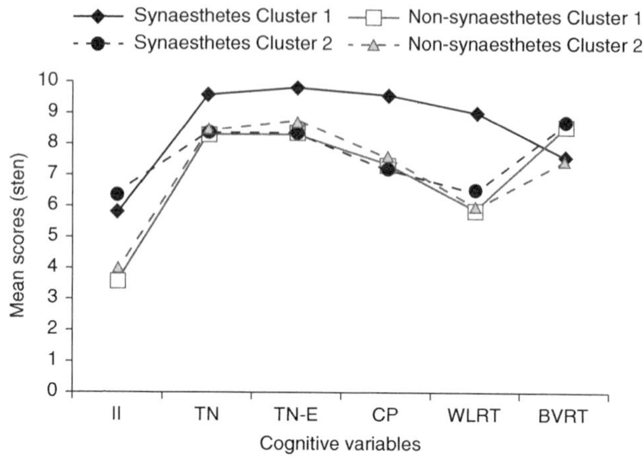

Figure 3.7 Comparison of four samples derived from cluster analysis in mean sten scores of cognitive variables. *Note:* II = the Imagination Inventory; TN = Total Number of Items Processed; TN-E = Total Number of Items Minus Error Scores; CP = Concentration Performance; WLRT = the Word List Recall Test; BVRT = Benton Visual Retention Test.

performed for the examination of interrelationships between these variables (see Figure 3.7).

A significant main effect was found for the model of ANOVA: Wilks' $\Lambda = .53$, $F(18, 182) = 2.54$, $p < .001$, $\eta_p^2 = .20$. The clusters effect was significant for total II [$\Delta R^2 = .24$, $F(3, 69) = 8.600$, $p < .001$] and for total WLRT [$\Delta R^2 = .13$, $F(3, 69) = 4.43$, $p = .007$]. All three indices of attention (TN, TN-E, and CP in the d2 Test of Attention) as well as visual memory (NES of the BVRT) did not satisfy the assumptions of ANOVA by the *F*-test. Fisher's Least Significant Difference (LSD) post hoc test revealed that both clusters of synaesthetes demonstrated significantly higher scores in imagination than non-synaesthetes. Moreover, Cluster 1 of synaesthetes differed significantly from the three other clusters in WLRT, and Cluster 1 of synaesthetes demonstrated significantly higher scores in all three attention scales (TN, TN-E, and CP) than Cluster 1 of non-synaesthetes.

The present study revealed that synaesthesia requires generally increased cognitive resources of attention, imagination, and memory. It is worth noticing that the cluster analysis revealed individual differences for cognitive variables in both linguistic-colour synaesthetes and non-synaesthetes. One cluster of synaesthetes outperformed the other clusters in attention and verbal performances, and the total group of synaesthetes outperformed non-synaesthetes in self-reported imagery. These differences may result from the type of synaesthesia (projectors vs. associators) or may be related to other factors (e.g., preferred learning style, special motivation, opportunities to train cognitive skills). These issues should be clarified by further research. However, it still remains unclear as to whether enhanced cognitive abilities are the basis for the emergence of synaesthesia, or, alternatively, whether synaesthesia is an opportunity that facilitates the development of cognitive skills. This issue must also be investigated in the future.

4 Relationships between linguistic-colour synaesthesia and individual differences in absorption, creative thinking, types of mind, and intelligence

4.1 Examining relationships between linguistic-colour associations and selected aspects of thinking

This chapter examines relationships between linguistic-colour associations and individual differences in absorption, creativity, types of mind, and fluid and emotional intelligence. Rogowska (2007) in her study on a random sample of 125 secondary-school students (mean age 18 years) revealed significant relationships between synaesthetic associations (both linguistic-colour and music-colour) creative behaviour, types of mind, fluid intelligence, working memory, and self-reported absorption and imagination. Synaesthetic associations were measured by a computer test–retest method, which showed a normal distribution of consistent over time auditory-colour associations. The study also found that auditory-colour associations were positively correlated with the Heuristic Behaviour (HS) scale of Popek's (2000) Creative Behaviour Questionnaire, which refers to the cognitive abilities characterizing creative behaviour. Linguistic-colour associations were also related to the absorption and preference of the sensing-thinking types of mind. Predictor variables for the total score of auditory-colour associations (musical and linguistic) included elevated absorption scales of the Tellegen Absorption Scale (TAS) and fluid intelligence of Raven's Standard Progressive Matrices (SPM).

The following study aimed to examine the hypothesis that stronger linguistic-colour synaesthetic associations are related to heightened creativity, absorption, and fluid and emotional intelligence. The preference for sensory-thinking type of mind was also expected as a predictor of synaesthetic associations. In the present study, synaesthesia is understood as a continuous tendency for the involuntary and abstract form of linguistic-colour associations (see Chapter 1). An investigation of the contribution of some aspects of individual differences in synaesthesia could be helpful in predicting this phenomenon on the basis of the configuration of various traits. The connections between linguistic-colour associations were explored here by structural analysis to detect latent variables that may be useful in explaining synaesthesia in a wide context of associations, thinking, and comprehension.

Absorption was measured here by the TAS, which was originally developed to identify personality characteristics related to hypnotic susceptibility (Tellegen and Atkinson, 1974) and was primarily one of 11 factors in Tellegen's Multidimensional Personality Questionnaire (MPQ) (Tellegen, 1982). The scale is a short (10-min) paper-and-pencil test, containing 34 true/false self-report items. The TAS is a widely used measurement of openness to absorbing and self-altering experiences. It assesses individuals' openness to experience, and emotional and cognitive alterations across a variety of situations such as the following: *The sound of a voice can be so fascinating to me that I can just go on listening to it*, or *I can sometimes imagine (or daydream) things so vividly that they hold my attention like a good movie or story does* (Tellegen, 1982; Roche and McConkey, 1990; Patrick, Curtin, and Tellegen, 2002). Because the scale is undimensional, the sum of 'true' responses on the TAS is an indicator of the absorption ability (ranged from 0 to 34).[1]

In the present study, the Test for Creative Thinking-Drawing Production (TCT-DP) was used to evaluate the level of creative thinking (Jellen and Urban, 1989; Urban, 1996, 2005).[2] The TCT-DP is a drawing test developed to measure creativeness, and it is based on a componential model of creativity. On the basis of some given figural fragments, the participant is asked to complete a drawing that has been started but not completed by the artist. The evaluation of drawings is based on the following criteria and uses the gestalt principles: continuations, completion, new elements, connections made with a line, connections made to produce a theme, boundary breaking that is fragment dependent, boundary breaking that is fragment independent, humour and affectivity, unconventionality, and speed.

The Types of Mind Scale (TMS) was administered here to measure the preferred thinking process (Nosal, 1992, 2001) in accordance with Jung's (1921/1971) conception of two dimensions referring to four main

[1] Tellegen (1982) reported high levels of internal reliability (Cronbach's α = .88) and test–retest reliability (.85) in a study sample of college students. The TAS reliability in the present study was also satisfactory (Cronbach's α = .86).

[2] The Polish version of the TCT-DP (Matczak, Jaworowska, and Stańczak, 2000) demonstrated an acceptable reliability for a sample of college students (α = .75), as well as for the sample in the present sample (α = .63).

functions of consciousness: the perceiving function with the sensing (S) and intuition (N) opposition, and the judging function with the thinking (T) and feeling (F) opposition. In the sensing type of perception, information is obtained from the five senses with careful attention to detail and focus on the present concrete reality, whereas intuition involves overall impressions, possibilities, and patterns, often without awareness of the source of knowledge. The thinking function is used to make logical judgements about what has been perceived, while the feeling function is based on personal values. The extent to which individuals prefer particular attitudes and functions over others is theorized to reflect differences in personality (Arnau, Green, Rosen, Gleaves, and Melancon, 2003).

The Myers–Briggs Type Indicator (MBTI) is one of the best-known personality assessments that developed Jung's theory of psychological types (Myers and McCaulley, 1985). The Polish assessment of the TMS (Nosal, 1992) uses a paper-and-pencil, self-report format of 50 forced-choice items, each including four adjectives. For each item, a respondent chooses one adjective that describes his or her own mind best and worst from a set of four adjectives, which constitutes four scales of preference and four scales of aversion to the S–N, and T–F dimensions. The four functions of consciousness are arranged into preference and aversion scales with reference to the following types of mind: ST, SF, NT, and NF.[3]

Raven's SPM[4] was used here to assess intelligence. Its classic form aims to measure the general intellectual abilities (Spearman's *g* factor) of participants (Raven, Raven, and Court, 1998), referring to Cattell's (1971) fluid aspects of intelligence (G_f). The test comprises five sets (A to E) of 12 items each arranged with progressive difficulty. All items are displayed in black ink on a white background, and they consist of a matrix of geometric patterns that are presented as a problem with one design removed from the sequence. The participant's task is to reduce the theme of relations expressed among the designs and choose the missing figure from the alternative set.

In the present study, a sample of students completed the Popular Emotional Intelligence Questionnaire (PEIQ). The PEIQ was created by Matczak, Jaworowska, Ciechanowicz, Stańczak, and Zalewska (Jaworowska

[3] The test–retest reliability of the ST, SF, NT, and NF scales (Nosal, 1992) is acceptable (.73, .77, .83, and .90, respectively). In the present study, the Cronbach's alphas for preference scales were .56, .46, .49, and .75, respectively; and for aversion scales, .55, .54, .43, and .63, respectively.

[4] The psychometric properties of the Polish adaptation of the SPM (Raven *et al.*, 1998; Jaworowska and Szustrowa, 2000) are comparable to its original version, and the Spearman–Brown reliability coefficient is high (above .90) for an adult sample. In the present study, Cronbach's alpha was .79.

and Matczak, 2005) for self-assessment of emotional intelligence (EI) defined as the subset of social intelligence that involves the ability to monitor one's own and others' feelings and emotions, to discriminate among them, and to use this information to guide one's thinking and actions. According to the original Mayer–Salovey–Caruso Emotional Intelligence Test (MSCEIT), EI could be measured in four components: perceiving emotions, facilitating thought, understanding emotions, and managing emotions (Mayer, Salovey, Caruso, and Sitarenios, 2001). In the Polish version (Jaworowska and Matczak, 2005), the PEIQ consists of 94 items with a range of responses from 1 (*I don't agree at all*) to 5 (*I completely agree*), and the results are presented as Total Emotional Intelligence score (TEI) and four branch scores: 15 items – Acceptation (AEI; acceptation, expression, and use of one's own emotion in action), 18 items – Empathy (EEI; reasoning and recognition of other people's emotions), 11 items – Controlling (CEI; behavioural and cognitive controlling of one's own emotions), and 10 items – Reasoning (REI; reasoning and awareness of one's own emotions).[5]

4.1.1 Correlates and predictors of linguistic-colour synaesthesia

Sample A of 79 participants, including 11 linguistic-colour synaesthetes (for more details, see Appendix A), completed a battery of tests and self-report questionnaires to assess creativity (the TCT-DP), absorption (the TAS), general intelligence (Raven's SPM), EI (the PEIQ scales: AEI – Acceptation, EEI – Empathy, CEI – Controlling, REI – Reasoning, TEI – total PEIQ), and TMS scales (preferences and aversions of ST – Sensing-Thinking, NT – Intuition-Thinking, SF – Sensing-Feeling, and NF – Intuition-Feeling). Means, standard deviations, range (min.–max.) and normality (Kolmogorov–Smirnov *D* statistics), and Pearson's correlations analyses were conducted for the variables. All results are shown in Table B4.1 in Appendix B.

To analyse correlations between variables, Pearson's test was conducted, excluding two variables. Since total L-CAT and Raven's SPM did not meet the normality criterion, non-parametric Spearman's correlation analysis was performed to examine relationships between these scales and other variables. Linguistic-colour associations were positively correlated with absorption. Creativity was correlated positively with absorption and aversion to the sensing-thinking (ST) type of mind. General intelligence was

[5] The psychometric characteristics of the questionnaire were satisfactory for TEI ($\alpha = .94$) and for the particular scales AEI, EEI, CEI, and REI (.79, .88, .80, and .78, respectively). In the present study, the scales demonstrated good internal consistency with Cronbach's alphas of .93 for TEI, and .76, .84, .84, and .81, for the other scales respectively.

Table 4.1 *Summary of stepwise regression analysis with forward selection for variables predicting linguistic-colour associations* (n = *75)*

Variables	*B*	*SE B*	β	R^2	ΔR^2	*F*	*df*
				.20	.15	4.28**	4, 68
Absorption	4.14	1.18	0.41***				
Acceptation	−3.40	1.13	−0.37**				
Reasoning	2.02	1.21	0.20				
Creativity	−0.85	0.80	−0.12				

Notes: ** $p < .01$, *** $p < .001$.

positively correlated with acceptation of emotions. Absorption was also positively correlated with acceptation of emotions, preference of intuition-feeling (NF), and aversion to ST type of mind, as well as negatively related to preference of ST and aversion to intuition-thinking (NT). Empathy correlated positively with preference of NF and aversion to ST, and negatively with preference of ST. Controlling of emotions was related positively to the NT type of mind. There were also numerous high correlations among scales in both the PEIQ and the TMS.

A multiple-regression analysis was performed to identify the best predictors of linguistic-colour associations among individual differences in creativity, absorption, general intelligence, EI, and types of mind (Table 4.1). Because many of the explanatory variables represented a strong linear relationship, a stepwise regression method with forward selection was performed to avoid the consequence of multicollinearity. Thus, if the tolerance values of the variable were below .50, the scale was excluded from the regression model. The forward selection procedure was performed on a reduced model containing only those explanatory variables that provided important information about synaesthesia.

The stepwise regression analysis revealed two significant predictors of linguistic-colour associations: absorption and acceptation of emotions. This suggests that stronger linguistic-colour associators represent lower absorption but higher acceptation in comparison with weaker associators. Reasoning of emotions and creativity were the two other variables included in the model of regression, but with an insufficient level of significance. This model accounted for 15% of the variability of synaesthetic associations.

4.1.2 Differences between synaesthetes and non-synaesthetes

Differences between synaesthetes and non-synaesthetes were analysed by Student's *t*-test for most variables, except for Raven's SPM, for which a

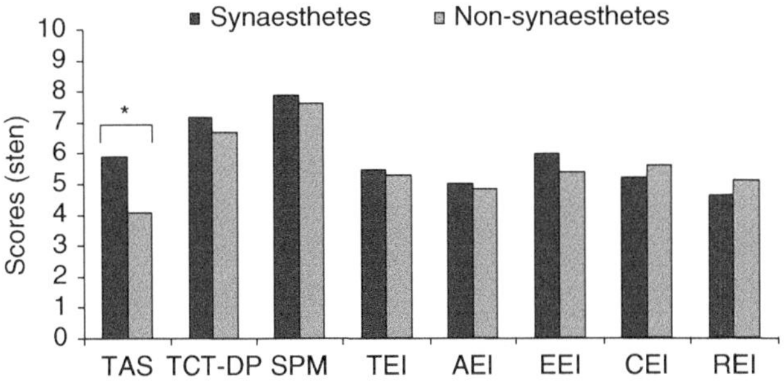

Figure 4.1 Comparison of synaesthetes (n = 11) and non-synaesthetes (n = 68) in absorption, creativity, general intelligence, and emotional intelligence. *Note:* $^{*}p$ < .05. TAS = the Tellegen Absorption Scale; TCT-DP = the Test for Creative Thinking-Drawing Production; SPM = the Raven's Standard Progressive Matrices; TEI = Total Emotional Intelligence; AEI = Acceptation; EEI = Empathy; CEI = Controlling; REI = Reasoning.

non-parametric Mann–Whitney U test was performed. The comparison of synaesthetes with non-synaesthetes in TSM scales is shown in Figure 4.2a for preferences and Figure 4.2b for aversions, while the differences between these groups in the other scales are shown in Figure 4.1. Synaesthetes (M = 5.91, SD = 1.76, n = 11) scored significantly higher than non-synaesthetes (M = 4.07, SD = 1.97, n = 67) in absorption, $t(76)$ = 2.90, p = .005. Non-synaesthetes (M = 13.47, SD = 4.29, n = 64), in comparison to synaesthetes (M = 10.73, SD = 2.49, n = 11), also demonstrated higher aversion to the sensing-feeling type of mind, $t(73)$ = –2.05, p = .044 (see Figure 4.2b). No other significant differences were found.

4.1.3 Exploring the structure of relationships between variables

The initial exploration of relationships between linguistic-colour associations and other variables was conducted by an agglomerative hierarchical clustering method, with Euclidean distance, the unweighted pair-group method with arithmetic mean (UPGMA). Cluster analysis is an iterative process of knowledge discovery, in which a set of variables is grouped into an optimal number of clusters on the basis of similarities between these variables. Connectivity based on clustering algorithms combines variables to form clusters based on their distance (more related variables are nearer).

The results of the hierarchical clustering are shown in Figure 4.3. Linguistic-colour associations were related mostly to the total score of

(a)

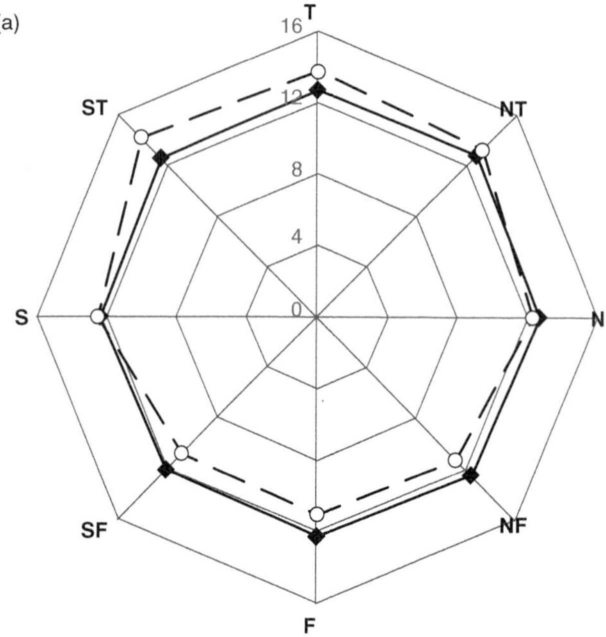

(b)

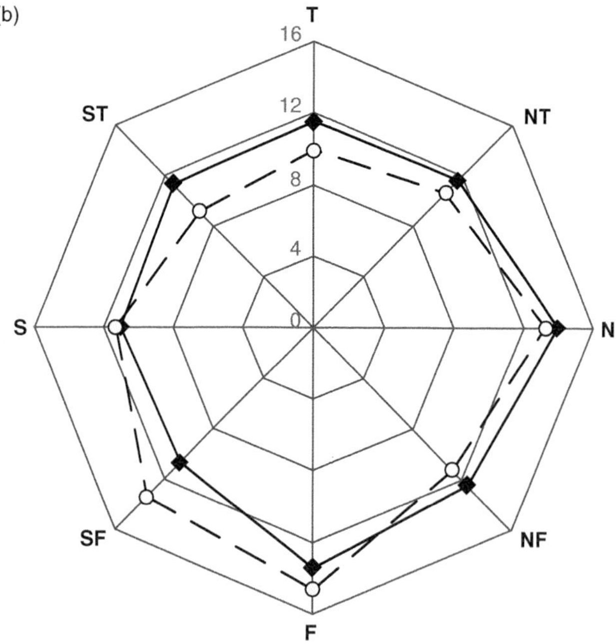

Figure 4.2 Comparison of synaesthetes (continuous line and squares) and non-synaesthetes (dashed line and circles) in TMS scales: (a) preferences, (b) aversions. *Note:* The difference between synaesthetes and non-synaesthetes in aversion of SF is significant ($^{*}p < .05$). S = Sensing; T = Thinking; F = Feeling; N = Intuition; ST = Sensing-Thinking; NT = Intuition-Thinking; SF = Sensing-Feeling; NF = Intuition-Feeling.

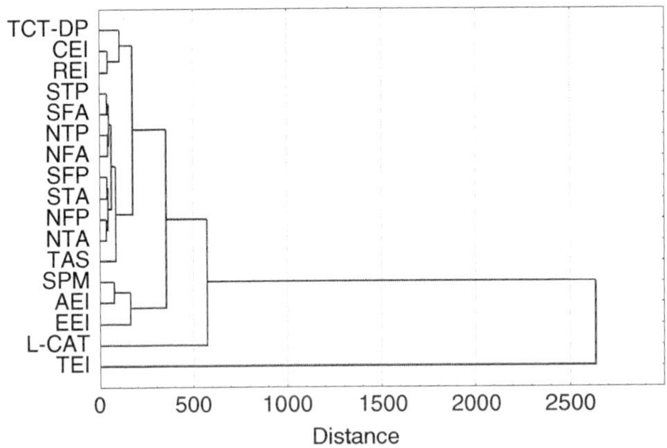

Figure 4.3 Dendrogram of hierarchical cluster analysis with Euclidean distance and average linkage clustering techniques ($n = 79$). *Note:* TCT-DP = the Test for Creative Thinking-Drawing Production; CEI = Controlling; REI = Reasoning; STP = Sensing-Thinking Preference; SFA = Sensing-Feeling Aversion; NTP = Intuition-Thinking Preference; NFA = Intuition-Feeling Aversion; SFP = Sensing-Feeling Preference; STA = Sensing-Thinking Aversion; NFP = Intuition-Feeling Preference; NTA = Intuition-Thinking Aversion; TAS = the Tellegen Absorption Scale; SPM = the Raven's Standard Progressive Matrices; AEI = Acceptation; EEI = Empathy; L-CAT = Linguistic-Colour Association Test; TEI = Total Emotional Intelligence.

EI, and the cluster of empathy, acceptation of emotion, and fluid intelligence. The next close cluster of variables concerned absorption and all dimensions of types of mind: aversion to NT with preference of NF, aversion to ST with preference of SF, aversion to NF with preference of NT, and aversion to SF with preference of ST. The furthest cluster contained reasoning and controlling of emotions together with creativity.

This result shows that emotion may play an important role in the origination of synaesthetic associations, with empathy and acceptation of emotion in the first place. In addition, the general capacity of comprehension as a fluid intelligence may be connected to linguistic-colour associations. However, it is important to note that the distance linking of L-CAT to other variables is relatively long; therefore, the connections are not very strong.

An exploratory factor analysis (EFA) was used to uncover the underlying structure of total variables examined in the present study. There was expectation of detecting a hierarchical structure of associations as a general higher-order capacity responsible for developing cognitive abilities. Fluid intelligence, EI, creativity, absorption, and synaesthesia were based on a hypothetical lower order of primary associative abilities.

The hierarchical factor analysis was performed here in order to find latent constructs underlying a battery of measured variables (Schmid and Leiman, 1957; Wherry, 1959). However, to find the best resolution, two alternative extraction methods were used: principal axis factoring (PAF) and maximum likelihood (ML). Both methods use oblique rotations that permit correlations among factors.

PAF accounts for as much common variance of the first several factors as possible, and can be used when the assumption of normality has been violated. Because two variables did not meet the criteria of normality (i.e., linguistic-colour associations measured by L-CAT and general intelligence assessed by Raven's SPM), PAF seems to be a good method for the present analysis. On the other hand, the maximum likelihood method makes it possible to compute indexes of the goodness-of-fit model and to test the statistical significance of factor loadings.

Factor loadings are shown in Table 4.2, Figures 4.4 and 4.5, and Table B4.2 in Appendix B. The hierarchical analysis by the PAF extraction method yielded a general association as a secondary factor solution that most likely affected all types of cognitive processes. In addition, three primary unique areas of associations, extracted by eigenvalues greater than 1, together accounted for 46% of common variance. These primary factors could be described as Internal, External, and Emotional types of association. The general associations as a secondary latent factor correlated poorly with the Emotional oblique factor ($r = -.16$), and moderately with both Internal ($r = -.66$) and External ($r = -.67$) factors, which seems to refer mostly to the sensing-intuition dimension of type of mind.

Internal association explained 20% of the common variance and included linguistic-colour associations, absorption, general intelligence, and both preference of and aversion to either the intuition-thinking or intuition-feeling type of mind. The internal type of association, referring to Brown's (1827) 'internal affection', may be described as a higher-level (semantic) thinking process that relies only on intrapsychic mental representations. According to Piaget's (1936) formal operations, it is the higher level of abstract thought that makes it possible to use symbols related to abstract concepts, independently of the environmental situation and conditions. The associations may be created between remote abstract concepts, phenomena, or objects. This capability of hypothetical and deductive reasoning is mostly related to imagery, problem-solving, and intelligence.

Table 4.2 *Primary factor loadings of higher-order for both PAF and ML models of EFA*

	PAF model of Association			ML model of Thinking		
Variables	Factor 1 Internal	Factor 2 Emotional	Factor 3 External	Factor 1 Intelligence	Factor 2 Mentality	Factor 3 Openness
TCT-DP	.07	−0.50	**.30**	−.11	.01	**.30**
Raven's SPM	**.16**	0.14	.08	**.16**	.03	.12
TAS	**.35**	0.12	.21	.17	−.04	**.51**
L-CAT	**.13**	0.01	−.03	−.01	.18	**.25**
AEI	.07	**0.58**	.18	**.68**	.01	.05
EEI	.19	**0.43**	.27	**.58**	.10	.23
CEI	−.16	**0.72**	−.19	**.71**	.15	−.26
REI	−.03	**0.81**	−.12	**.77**	.08	−.08
TEI	.00	**1.03**	.06	**.98**	.11	−.02
STP	.32	0.14	**.62**	.06	**.85**	.09
NTP	**.49**	−0.13	.19	.08	**.86**	.00
SFP	−.09	0.05	**.66**	−.04	**.87**	−.12
NFP	**.89**	0.02	.15	.08	**.94**	−.27
STA	.48	0.04	**.65**	.17	**.91**	.18
NTA	**.58**	0.00	.13	.14	**.88**	.23
SFA	.00	0.12	**.75**	.24	**.84**	.36
NFA	**.91**	−0.05	−.07	.15	**.73**	.51

Notes: TCT-DP = Test for Creative Thinking-Drawing Production; Raven's SPM = Raven's Standard Progressive Matrices; TAS = Tellegen Absorption Scale; L-CAT = the Linguistic-Colour Association Test; AEI = Acceptation; EEI = Empathy; CEI = Controlling; REI = Reasoning; TEI = Total Emotional Intelligence; STP = Sensing-Thinking Preference; NTP = Intuition-Thinking Preference; SFP = Sensing-Feeling Preference; NFP = Intuition-Feeling Preference; STA = Sensing-Thinking Aversion; NTA = Intuition-Thinking Aversion; SFA = Sensing-Feeling Aversion; NFA = Intuition-Feeling Aversion. Boldface values indicate the strongest loadings of the variable on the factor.

The external type of association accounts for 17% of the common variance, and it concerns creativity and both preference of and aversion to both sensing-thinking and sensing-feeling types of mind. External associations, referring to Brown's (1827) 'external affection', are connected with sensory experiences and perception of concrete objects in the external world. This kind of cognitive process is concrete and specific and pertains to currently perceived phenomena, objects, or people. Associations are created in interaction with the environment, and they may be described simply as perceptual processes or concrete operations, following Piaget's (1936) theory.

The emotional type of association explains 9% of the common variance and contains all scales of EI, including total EI, empathy, reasoning,

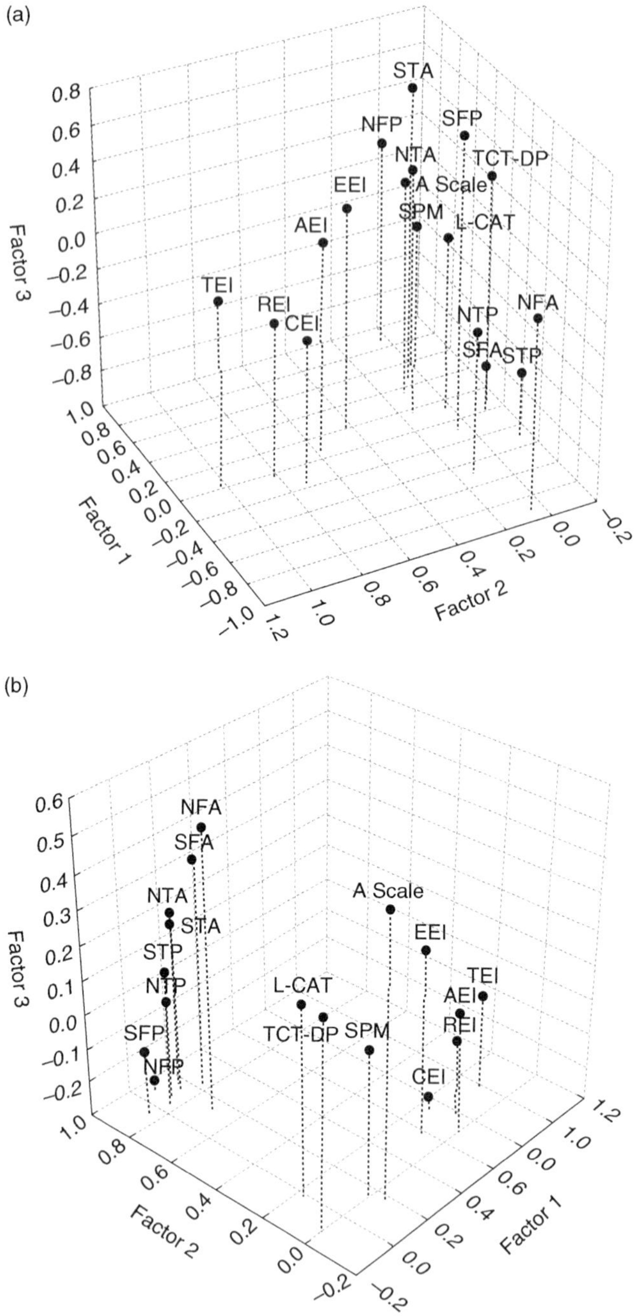

Figure 4.4 Factor loadings of EFA with (a) PAF extracting method, and (b) ML extracting method. *Note:* L-CAT = Linguistic-Colour Association Test; TCT-DP = Test for Creative Thinking-Drawing Production; TAS = Tellegen Absorption Scale; SPM = Raven's

acceptance, and controlling of emotions. The emotional type of association refers to the cognitive level of emotional processes with regard to emotions experienced by oneself and also by others. Usually feeling is placed in opposition to thinking; however, developing emotional intelligence may lead to the controlling and managing of emotions. This type of association may arise on interaction with the environment, as well as independently of current conditions – that is, they may be induced either externally or internally.

The second hierarchical model of EFA, using the ML extraction method and oblique rotations, revealed three primary factors with eigenvalues greater than 1 and one secondary factor that together accounted for 60% of the common variance. However, in comparison with the PAF method, different measured variables were loaded onto particular latent variables, which may be described as Intelligence, Mentality, and Openness (see Table 4.2, Figures 4.4 and 4.5, and Table B4.2 in Appendix B for more details). These three primary factors may be described as distinct dimensions of individual differences in thinking and comprehension.

Intelligence explains 20% of common variance and consists of fluid intelligence (measured with Raven's SPM), and all scales of EI, including total EI, acceptance, empathy, reasoning, and controlling of emotions. Mentality accounts for 34% of the common variance and comprises all types of mind scale, including preferences as well as aversions. Openness to unusual experiences explains 6% of common variance and consists of creativity, absorption, and linguistic-colour associations. This concept seems close to open-mindedness or openness for experience in a Big Five conception.

The hierarchical structure of both models extracted by EFA is shown in Figure 4.5. Both models derived from EFA were validated with the use of confirmatory factor analysis (CFA). In the present study, the EFA results were examined and replicated by CFA on the same set of observations (van Prooijen and van der Kloot, 2001). The aim of the analysis was to

---

Figure 4.4 (cont.)

Standard Progressive Matrices; TEI = Total Emotional Intelligence; EEI = Empathy; AEI = Acceptation; CEI = Controlling; REI = Reasoning; STP = Sensing-Thinking Preference; SFP = Sensing-Feeling Preference; NTP = Intuition-Thinking Preference; NFP = Intuition-Feeling Preference; STA = Sensing-Thinking Aversion; SFA = Sensing-Feeling Aversion; NTA = Intuition-Thinking Aversion; NFA = Intuition-Feeling Aversion.

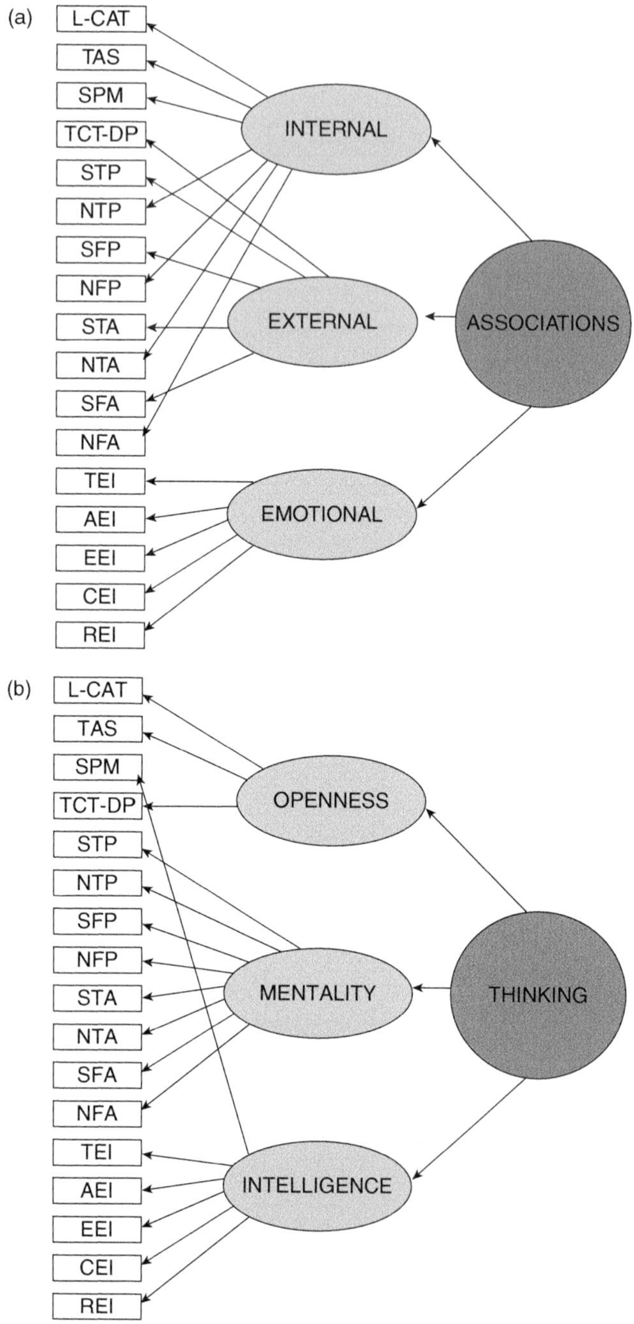

Figure 4.5 Comparison of two models of hierarchical factor structure from EFA: (a) with PAF extracting method, and (b) with ML extracting method. *Note:* L-CAT = Linguistic-Colour Association Test; TAS = Tellegen Absorption Scale; SPM = Raven's Standard Progressive Matrices; TCT-DP = Test for Creative Thinking-Drawing Production; STP = the Sensing-Thinking Preference; SFP = Sensing-Feeling Preference; NTP = Intuition-Thinking Preference; NFP =

assess the extent to which the original exploratory model would be suitable for confirmation.

Absolute fit indices, such as the chi-square test, RMSEA, GFI, AGFI, and SRMR, determine how well a model fits the sample data (McDonald and Ho, 2002) and demonstrate which has the most superior fit (Hooper, Coughlan, and Mullen, 2008). The results of the first EFA hierarchical model with the PAF extracting method were $\chi^2(98) = 191.45$, $\chi^2/df = 1.96$, $p < .001$; SRMR = .307; GFI = .687; AGFI = .512; and RMSEA = .115. The fit indices suggest that the model fit the data poorly. The results of the overall fit of the second EFA hierarchical model with the ML extracting method were more acceptable to the CFA indices: $\chi^2(99) = 141.11$, $\chi^2/df = 1.43$, $p = .004$; SRMR = .136; GFI = .766; AGFI = .639; and RMSEA = .077.

Generally, the bad fit of the first model of associations may suggest that the EFA did not produce the optimal number of factors or the most appropriate factor pattern coefficients. In addition, the obtained results depended on a poor sample size ($n = 75$). The final confirmation of both hierarchical models of EFA requires further research on a more random and much larger sample size. Moreover, the model of association could include, in the future, many other types of association such as explicit-implicit, close-remote, coherent-divergent, and operant-instrumental conditioning related or affected by distinct principles of association: resemblance (e.g., analogy, affinity), contrast, coadjacency (e.g., contiguity, cause and effect), repetition, attention, pleasure-pain, immediacy, homogeneity, or facility. Similarly, the second model of thinking also seems incomplete and could include many other variables in future research. Nevertheless, the current investigation indicates that a structural analysis may be useful in explaining the nature of synaesthetic associations in a wide context of other variables.

4.2 Absorption

According to Tellegen and Atkinson (1974), absorption is openness to absorbing and self-altering experiences, and it is understood as a

---

Figure 4.5 (cont.)

Intuition-Feeling Preference; STA = Sensing-Thinking Aversion; SFA = Sensing-Feeling Aversion; NTA = Intuition-Thinking Aversion; NFA = Intuition-Feeling Aversion; TEI = Total Emotional Intelligence; AEI = Acceptation; EEI = Empathy; CEI = Controlling; REI = Reasoning.

disposition to situations in which a person's total attention fully engages his or her representational resources: perceptual, enactive, imaginative, and ideational. As a state, absorption occurs when a limited number of typically coordinated or related stimuli are focused on the attentional exclusion of other stimuli (external or internal), due to the unifying or aggregative manifestation of cognitive awareness.

Rader and Tellegen (1981, 1987) assumed that synaesthesia is a part of absorption. As such, Synaesthesia is included as one of nine content subscales of the TAS (based on factor analysis), and comprises several items with reference to cross-modal experiences. Rader and Tellegen (1981, 1987) revealed a positive correlation between absorption of the TAS and several measures of synaesthesia. However, when Glicksohn and colleagues (Glicksohn *et al.*, 1992, 1999) tried to replicate these results by similar methods, they did not find any significant relationships.

There is evidence that high absorption is correlated with heightened visual imagery, greater positive affect, increased ability to concentrate and focus, and greater alterations in self-awareness (O'Grady, 1980; Pekala *et al.*, 1985). Absorption correlates positively with fantasy-proneness (Wilson and Barber, 1983b), dream recall, altered states of consciousness such as spontaneous trance, and hypnotizability (Tellegen and Atkinson, 1974; Roche and McConkey, 1990). Moreover, both absorption and synaesthesia-like experiences were shown to be related to aura vision (Zingrone *et al.*, 2009; Milán *et al.*, 2012).

Hypnotic susceptibility that displayed a moderate correlation with absorption was also found to be related to congenital synaesthesia. Recent findings have indicated that congenital synaesthesia can be inhibited by post-hypnotic suggestion (Terhune *et al.*, 2010). Moreover, post-hypnotic suggestion may induce experiences and behaviours in non-synaesthetes similar to those of synaesthetes (Cohen Kadosh, Henik, Catena, *et al.*, 2009). Thus, the present study presumes that synaesthesia is related to absorption.

In the present study, absorption was more related to linguistic-colour associations than any other variable (see Table B4.1 in Appendix B and Figure 4.1). Although synaesthetes scored higher in absorption than non-synaesthetes, the positive result of correlation and regression analysis suggests that stronger linguistic-colour synaesthetes demonstrated lower absorption (Table 4.1). Trait absorption reflects individual differences in cognitive capacity for involvement in sensory and imaginative experiences, in ways that alter an individual's perception, memory, and mood (Roche and McConkey, 1990). As such, weaker linguistic-colour synaesthetes, who scored higher on the TAS in the present study, may be described as emotionally responsive to engagement with sights and sounds, being readily captured by entrancing stimuli, and thinking in images (in contrast to stronger synaesthetes, who scored lower on the TAS).

Synaesthesia can result from disinhibition between brain areas due to the hyperconnectivity hypothesis (Grossenbacher and Lovelace, 2001). This can explain the low level of absorption among stronger synaesthetes. Since the heightened absorption could holistically involve attention, memory, and imagery on a high level of cognition and under conscious control, synaesthesia in disinhibited individuals should be rather connected with the reverse state of mind that joins together selective perceptual features of objects (e.g., timbre of voice, colour, shape) on low and early levels of the perceptual system and without conscious engagement. Thus, spontaneous synaesthesia, not forced by hypnosis or training, may occur due to relatively lower absorption.

On the other hand, absorption is positively correlated with dissociation, depersonalization, hallucination, and schizophrenia (e.g., Glicksohn *et al.*, 2001; Glicksohn and Barrett, 2003; Perona-Garcelán *et al.*, 2011). Thus, the level of absorption may differ between subjects with hallucinations and individuals with synaesthesia. If this hypothesis is appropriate, both absorption and synaesthesia could play an important role in the explanation of schizophrenia.

Furthermore, Ott *et al.* (2005) suggested that individual differences in both absorption and responsiveness to hallucinogenic drugs may be related to the binding potential of the 5-HT2A serotonergic receptor. Brang and Ramachandran (2008) also suggested that serotonin S2a receptors, which can be modulated by various drugs, are responsible for the occurrence of synaesthesia. These 'synaesthesia receptors' in the brain would also predict a higher incidence of synaesthesia in schizophrenics and implicate the *HTR2A* gene on chromosome 13q as the underlying cause of synaesthesia. However, these key questions are still under investigation. In addition, research on possible roles of absorption in synaesthesia should be continued with reference to distinct types of synaesthesia and in different stages of life, especially comparing child and adult populations.

Generally, absorption is associated with overall consciousness alteration, including meditation, biofeedback, mystical-type experiences, marijuana use, and the use of hallucinogenic drugs. Currently, Studerus *et al.* (2012) found that psilocybin-induced pleasant and mystical-type experiences were more likely in individuals having a high level of the personality trait of absorption, remaining in an emotionally excitable and active state immediately before drug intake, and having experienced few psychological problems in past weeks. Moreover, absorption in the TAS most strongly predicted audio-visual synaesthesia after psilocybin ingestion in non-synaesthetes. In these studies the audio-visual synaesthesia scale was significantly related not only to psilocybin response but also to sociability, emotional excitability, activity, alcohol consumption, and drug use.

In the present study on relationships between linguistic-colour synaesthesia and individual differences in personality and temperament (see Chapter 5), linguistic-colour synaesthetes demonstrated a tendency to higher extraversion, excitability, and activity. Therefore, another explanation of the present results is that synaesthesia may be related to the optimal level of arousal. Arousal could influence information processing, perception, attention, memory, the learning process, and emotion (e.g., Easterbrook, 1959). On the behavioural level, arousal is related to temperament and personality (e.g., Eysenck, 1975; Zuckerman, 1979). According to Gray (1981), extraverts experience high energetic arousal, which is characterized by vigour and energy, because of their greater response to reward signals than to punishment, in comparison to introverts.

According to the Yerkes–Dodson law (e.g., Anderson, 1990), the inverted-U relationship between arousal and performance may also be useful in explaining synaesthesia occurrence. For highly excitable extraverts, synaesthesia may be facilitated on a relatively higher optimal level of arousal than in more inhibitable introverts. The other study in this volume of the relation of synaesthesia to traits of temperament and personality (see Chapter 5) revealed that stronger synaesthetes display a higher inhibition of the nervous processes. Because arousal may affect the absorption level, stronger synaesthetes may demonstrate relatively lower absorption than weaker synaesthetes; however, both may show generally higher absorption than non-synaesthetes.

In the second model of EFA with the ML extracting method in the present study, absorption was loaded together with creativity and synaesthesia into one factor (see Table 4.2, Figures 4.4 and 4.5, and Table B4.2 in Appendix B). This seems reasonable, since the results of many studies (e.g., Roche and McConkey, 1990; Glisky, Tataryn, Tobias, and Kihlstrom, 1991) have indicated that absorption is related to openness to experience (especially to fantasy, aesthetics, and feelings), hypnosis and hypnotizability, imagery, daydreaming, consciousness, attentional processing, and psychophysiological responding. Roche and McConkey (1990) suggested that absorption is central to the understanding of the nature of subjective experience, as well as to aspects of cognition and behaviour.

4.3 Creativity

The relationship between art and synaesthesia does not seem to be a simple coincidence (e.g., Berman, 1999; Hertz, 1999; van Campen, 2008). In literature, poetry, and the fine arts, synaesthesia has frequently been applied as a way of styling to transpose sensations – especially in symbolism – following the idea of synthesis and the unity of the arts (e.g., Galeyev, 1993; Nelson and Hitchon, 1999; van Campen and Froger, 1999). Perhaps because synaesthesia is closely related to mental imagery, metaphor, analogy, and remote associations, synaesthetes often become artists (e.g., Rizzo and Eslinger, 1989; Martino and Marks, 2001; Ramachandran and Hubbard, 2001b; Cazeaux, 2002; Seitz, 2005; Barnett and Newell, 2008; Spiller and Jansari, 2008; Brang and Ramachandran, 2010).

Indeed, some authors (e.g., Rich *et al.*, 2005; Ward *et al.*, 2008; Cawley, 2010) have suggested that synaesthetes are more involved in artistic activities. For example, Rich *et al.* (2005) found that 24% of synaesthetes were involved in artistic professions in comparison with the population average of 2%. Synaesthetes were also more likely to be actively engaged in art (e.g., painting, drawing) as a hobby. Ward *et al.* (2008) revealed that synaesthetes spent more time being engaged in creative arts, and this was dependent, at least in part, upon the type of synaesthesia experienced (e.g., musical synaesthetes were more likely to play an instrument). In those studies, synaesthetes scored higher in the Remote Associates Test than controls, but there were no differences in the Alternate Uses Test (both measuring creative thinking). Scientists have concluded that synaesthetes have better bottom-up access to certain associations, but are not necessarily able to use them more flexibly (in divergent thinking).

Nevertheless, synaesthesia seems to be part and parcel of creative individuals. Dailey *et al.* (1997) investigated the relationship between creativity, synaesthetic tendencies, and physiognomic perception with associations between auditory stimuli (pure tones and pure vowel sounds) and colours being measurements of synaesthesia; colours were rated by adjectives with emotional or evaluative connotations for measuring physiognomic perception, and the Remote Associates Test was used to measure creative potential. More creative participants exhibited stronger associations between colours and pure tones, vowels, and emotional terms.

The prevalence of synaesthesia among artists is higher than among the general population (Mulvenna and Walsh, 2005). Rothen and Meier (2010b) revealed a prevalence of grapheme-colour synaesthesia of about 7% in a sample of art students by using the test–retest measure, whereas prevalence in the control sample was only about 2%. Their findings suggested that synaesthesia is more common among art students.

Domino (1989) investigated the relationships between synaesthesia, creativity, and intelligence in a survey of 358 fine art students, using the Synaesthesia Questionnaire, the Quick Word and Vocabulary Tests for measuring verbal intelligence, and four measurements of creativity: the Creativity Scale derived from the Adjective Check List (ACL), the Barron–Welsh Art Scale – Revised (BWAS), the Obscure Figures Test (OFT), and the Similes Test (ST). The prevalence of synaesthesia was about 23% among art students, as indicated during the self-report measurement. Synaesthetes scored significantly higher than controls on all four creativity measurements; however, the frequency and vividness of synaesthesia showed marginal significance when correlated with the measurements of creativity. The intelligence tests did not distinguish between synaesthetes and controls. Domino (1989) argued that synaesthesia can be seen as a metaphorical problem-solving style, which may be particularly effective at generating creative solutions that depend on the perceptions of similarity between elements that are conceptually separate. Synaesthesia may be basically an associative process, a way of thinking analogically, and therefore not a special ability, but potentially available to everyone (Domino, 1999).

The results of the present study rather poorly confirm the previous findings and the assumption that synaesthesia is related to creativity. There was no significant correlation between linguistic-colour associations and creativity as assessed by the TCT-DP, and the creativity score did not reveal differences between synaesthetes and non-synaesthetes (see Table B4.1 in Appendix B and Figure 4.1). This result may be connected with the fact that creativity is a very difficult variable to measure. A variety of measures and protocols have been developed to assess aspects of creativity. The most frequent indices of creativity were the fluency, originality, and flexibility of responses (Torrance, 1966; Guilford, 1967). Moreover, the TCT-DP drawing test serves to assess the level of creative thinking on the basis of divergent thinking, general competences, specific knowledge and abilities, task-oriented engagement, motives, and tolerance of ambiguity. However, in the sample in the present study, Cronbach's alpha was not very high ($\alpha = .63$), suggesting an acceptable but rather poor reliability.

Nevertheless, the TCT-DP was included together with synaesthesia and absorption in one factor variable (Openness to unusual experiences) in the second model of thinking that was the effect of EFA with ML (see Table 4.2, Figures 4.4 and 4.5, and Table B4.2 in Appendix B). The negative correlation indicated that stronger linguistic-colour associators demonstrated a poor (non-significant) relationship with heightened creativity. This seems to be supported by the results of other studies (Wild *et al.*, 1995), in which absorption was positively correlated with openness to experience and with participation in arts, with effects of art on mood, and with ratings of the importance of art to daily life. In this study, absorption was also negatively correlated with speed, positively correlated with productivity of visual figure-ground differentiation, and positively correlated with cross-modal elaborative processing. Therefore, the results of both earlier and the present study may be indications for the need for further exploration of the relationships between synaesthesia, openness, and creativity.

According to the Big Five model of personality, openness refers to a receptive orientation towards varied feelings, trials, and ideas (Costa and McCrae, 1992). Openness to new experience is manifested by an active and vivid imagination, aesthetic sensitivity, attentiveness to inner emotional states and feelings, preference for variety and novelty, and intellectual curiosity (Costa and McCrae, 1992). On the other hand, people closed to experience tend to be conventional in their outlook and behaviour and have a narrow range of interests. Openness characterizes people with a high level of creativity (e.g., McCrae, 1987; King, McKee Walker, and Broyles, 1996; Feist, 1998; Griffin and McDermott, 1998; Dollinger, Urban, and James, 2004).

Openness as a trait is also associated with high intelligence, wide knowledge, and a fluid style of consciousness that allows the making of novel associations between remotely connected ideas (e.g., Chamorro-Premuzic, Furnham, and Ackerman, 2006; Moutafi, Furnham, and Crump, 2006; Mussell, 2010). Thus, instead of a direct relation between synaesthesia and creativity, more appropriate is the kind of connection in which synaesthesia, absorption, and creativity are three types of latent and higher-order variables – that is, openness to unusual experiences. Openness also correlated positively with strength of excitation (Strelau and Zawadzki, 1998; Michielsen, de Vries, and van Heck, 2003) and sensory sensitivity (Strelau and Zawadzki, 1995; Strelau, 1996; Zawadzki and Strelau, 1997), which was found to be related to linguistic-colour synaesthesia in the other study in this volume of the relation of synaesthesia to temperament and personality (see Chapter 5). Further research using a battery of creativity assessments and various types of synaesthesia is necessary to describe precisely the nature of these relationships.

Synaesthesia as a trait seems to be a kind of giftedness. Kalbfleisch (2009) describes giftedness as a particular biological adaptation based on the brain's implicit sense of when to organize according to each rule. Giftedness, based on neural plasticity, is related to fluid cognition, including non-verbal reasoning, mental rotation, and creativity. The perceptual capabilities of synaesthetes are similar to the extraordinary calculation abilities in mathematics or facility for instrumental music shown in the savant syndrome (Heaton and Wallace, 2004), which are also specific examples of giftedness. According to the compensatory hypothesis

(Rogowska, 2011), spatial configurations of ordinal sequences in the mind's eye or peripersonal space of a savant, as well as of a synaesthete (e.g., in grapheme-colour, time-space synaesthesia), could represent the conversion of abstract concepts into concrete shape or colour (Simner, Mayo, and Spiller, 2009; Murray, 2010). Compensatory synaesthesia would arise as an answer to individual needs, and thus it may indicate cognitive problems at a given stage of development.

On the other hand, hypercompensation may provide synaesthetes with the extraordinary skills displayed by famous musicians (e.g., L. Bernstein, D. Ellington), composers (e.g., F. Liszt, J. Sibelius, O. Messiaen, G. Ligeti), artists (e.g., W. Kandinsky, D. Hockney, M. Smilack, C. Steen), novelists (e.g., V. Nabokov), and scientists (e.g., R. Feynman, E. Bleuler). Thus, the education of gifted children with synaesthesia should be based on their preferred learning style with the use of synaesthetic associations to release their unique potential, as suggested by Cawley (2010).

4.4 Type of mind

According to Jung (1921/1971), people differ in the way in which they perceive information about things, people, or events in the environment and the way in which they make judgements about their perceptions. *Sensing* refers to an immediate experience of the objective world, realistically and concretely, without any kind of evaluation of the experience. It fails to consider contexts, implications, meanings, or alternative interpretations, but instead attempts to represent the process of information factually and fragmentarily. Contrary to sensing, *intuition* ignores details and globally focuses on the general context instead of the atmosphere. *Thinking* is an objective mode of evaluation concerned with the truth or falsity of experience; it is based upon the intellectual comprehension of things, particularly their conceptual interrelationships. It is a rational systematic process that seeks to understand reality through analysis and logical inference, whereas *feeling* is an affective and sentimental function involving judgement of the value of things on the basis of likes and dislikes.

The ST type of mind displays a tendency to a local, analytical, concrete, and objective style of perception, and may join together three phenomena: savantism, synaesthesia, and autism. According to Baron-Cohen *et al.* (2007), the combination of autism spectrum conditions (ASC) and synaesthesia may increase the likelihood of savantism. According to Witkin's concept of perceptual styles, field-dependence (global perceptual style) and field-independence (local perceptual style) differ from each other in the contextual influence of the visual scene, when estimating features in object recognition processing (Witkin, Dyk, Faterson, Goodenough, and Karp, 1962). A field-independent individual tends to perceive an element independently of its context.

Although evidence suggests a universal tendency to perceive the global prior to the local (Milne and Szczerbinski, 2009), individuals with autism seem to ignore the global aspects of the visual scene. Instead, they show the tendency to focus on smaller details and indicate a reduced ability to integrate material objects into appropriate contexts (Frith, 2003). This indicates the weak central coherence in autism.

Bor, Billington, and Baron-Cohen (2007) examined a male savant with abilities of numerical memory and mathematical calculations that co-occurred with grapheme-colour synaesthesia and Asperger syndrome, who preferentially attended to local features of stimuli. The research demonstrated that relative to controls, an autistic synaesthete was faster at finding a target at the local level, and was less distracted by interference from the global level. The researchers (Bor *et al.*, 2007) concluded that the propensity to focus on local detail, in concert with a form of synaesthesia that provides structure to all digits, may account for exceptional numerical memory and calculation ability. Following earlier findings (Rogowska, 2007), in the present study a relationship between linguistic-colour synaesthesia and the sensing-thinking type of mind was expected.

Contrary to expectations (Rogowska, 2007), the present analysis did not reveal a direct correlation between synaesthesia and type of mind (see Table B4.1 in Appendix B). Synaesthetes differed from non-synaesthetes in lower aversion to the SF type of mind (see Figure 4.2). No other relationships were found; in particular, there was no assumed relation to the preference of the ST type of mind. However, the mediation role may be played by an association as a higher-order factor extracted by the PAF method in EFA (see Table 4.2, Figures 4.4 and 4.5, and Table B4.2 in Appendix B). The results of this analysis showed that linguistic-colour associations were loaded, together with fluid intelligence, absorption, and intuitive types of mind in both preferences and aversions, into one factor, described as the internal type of association.

Linguistic-colour associations are triggered by words and arbitrary systems of signs (graphemes) such as letters of the alphabet and numbers. In relation to intelligence, the thinking process and comprehension are based on a semantic, higher level of mind system that operates on abstract concepts and internal mental representations of objects rather than sensations processed on a lower sensory level. Therefore, linguistic-colour associations may be more related to the intuition-sensing dimension of type of mind, with the dominant preference of intuition, than to the thinking-feeling dimension. The relationships found in the previous study (Rogowska, 2007) concerned auditory-colour synaesthesia triggered by the sounds of speech and music. Those types of synaesthesia could be more related to the sensory dimension of the type of mind, in contrast to the linguistic-colour synaesthesia examined in the present study.

Moreover, in the other study in this volume of the relation of synaesthesia to temperament and personality (Chapter 5), synaesthetes demonstrated rather low sensory sensitivity as a temperamental trait and also a poor self-reported sensory perception, especially touch perception. Contrary to the suggestions of Banissy, Walsh, and Ward (2009) that a hypersensitive concurrent perceptual system is a general property of synaesthesia, the synaesthetes in the present study did not reveal a higher colour sensitivity than non-synaesthetes. The dominance of ST represents local and more primary features of mind that may be shared by children and autistic individuals (e.g., Baron-Cohen *et al.*, 2007; Bor *et al.*, 2007). The intuition-feeling type of mind seems to characterize the global, deeper, and more advanced cognitive process of information. However, it is also possible that, due to maturation or older age, more people develop the intuition-feeling style and use this type of processing and evaluation of information more frequently; thus, the preference of and aversion to local *vs.* global cognitive styles can change over time.

As Förster (2012) suggested, the global versus local processing model includes predictions about cognitive mechanisms (the how) and functionalities (the why) of two processing systems: one that processes information holistically and one that processes the parts that carry over other perceptual and conceptual tasks. Furthermore, global processing is functional for understanding the general meaning of novel events, whereas local processing supports the encoding of details in familiar situations and when novel events are threatening. Although distinct types of synaesthesia may rely more on either global (intuition--feeling) or local (ST) cognitive processes, further research is necessary to resolve these issues.

4.5 Intelligence

The relationship between synaesthesia and intelligence seems controversial. The study by Domino (1989) using a questionnaire to measure synaesthesia did not show significant correlations with intelligence, as measured with the Quick Word Test by Borgatta and Corsini.

Participants consisted of 385 undergraduates enrolled in the introductory psychology course. Rader and Tellegen (1981) did not find correlations between intelligence assessed with the Brief Intelligence Test (an adaptation of the Mill Hill Vocabulary Scale) and synaesthesia measured by three scales: the Synaesthesia Questionnaire, the Auditory Synaesthesia Performance Test, and the Paper-and-Pencil Synaesthesia Performance Test. Synaesthetes have demonstrated higher scores on the absorption scale and positive self-view in the Tellegen Multidimensional Personality Questionnaire (MPQ). The vividness of synaesthetic imagery was not found to be associated with personality dysfunction or with intelligence. The same procedure was repeated (Rader and Tellegen, 1987) among 374 university students, and again the results were similar. However, when synaesthesia was measured by the computer test–retest procedure for colour-word associations (Rogowska, 2007), the results indicated a marginal ($r = .19, p < .05$) but significant and positive correlation between synaesthesia and fluid intelligence assessed with Raven's SPM. The divergence may be the result of the different methods used to assess synaesthesia and intelligence in various studies.

The relationship between linguistic-colour associations and general intelligence may shed some light on neurocognitive mechanisms as well as on the genetics of synaesthesia (Bargary and Mitchel, 2008; Brang and Ramachandran, 2011). According to the two-stage model of grapheme-colour synaesthesia (Hubbard and Ramachandran, 2005; Hubbard, 2007), synaesthetic experience may arise from abnormal cross-activation between the grapheme area and the colour area in the fusiform gyrus (FG) due to altered local connections. Indeed, functional imaging studies seem to provide support for this idea (e.g., Sperling, Prvulovic, Linden, Singer, and Stirn, 2006). Moreover, Rouw and Scholte (2007) found increased structural connectivity for the white matter underlying the FG and the parietal cortex in grapheme-colour synaesthetes. In addition, Weiss and Fink's (2009) study on the neuroanatomical basis of grapheme-colour synaesthetic perceptions revealed increased grey-matter volumes in the fusiform and intraparietal cortices, a finding that also suggested cross-activation at the level of the FG and 'hyperbinding' at the level of the parietal cortex. Furthermore, Jäncke Beeli, Eulig, and Hänggi (2009) indicated increased cortical thickness, volume, and surface area in the right and left FG, and in the lingual gyrus and the calcarine cortex in grapheme-colour synaesthetes. They suggested that the detected effects may be a consequence of the lifelong experience of grapheme-colour synaesthesia.

Neuroimaging research related to the activation of brain areas during reasoning by highly intelligent individuals has revealed some similarities to synaesthetic perception. For example, Lee *et al.* (2006) demonstrated that the prefrontal cortex is a key brain region for reasoning and novel problem-solving. Individuals with higher Gf (fluid intelligence) scores, as assessed with Raven's SPM, showed greater neural activity in the lateral prefrontal and parietal cortices during the most demanding tasks. Moreover, Colom, Jung, and Haier (2006) found that the general factor of intelligence correlates with the grey- and white-matter volumes in the frontal lobe, particularly in the frontal Brodmann area, FG, lingual gyrus, and sublobar insula. The results of an fMRI study (Masunaga, Kawashima, Horn, Sassa, and Sekiguchi, 2008) designed to investigate neural substrates of fluid reasoning indicated that higher-order cognition is supported by neural networks in both the parietal cortex (involved in activating possible responses based on learned stimulus–response associations) and the prefrontal cortex (recruited when there is a need to generate and evaluate hypotheses and select between competing responses). Those results were consistent with previous neuroimaging studies of reasoning with Raven's SPM that revealed activations of the prefrontal and parietal cortices during Gf reasoning tasks (e.g., Prabhakaran, Smith, Desmond, Glover, and Gabrieli, 1997; Houde and Tzourio-Mazoyer, 2003).

Van Leeuwen *et al.*'s (2009) study on a population-based sample of 112 nine-year-old twin pairs of children examined the association among total brain volume, grey-matter and white-matter volume, and intelligence assessed by Raven's SPM and the Wechsler Intelligence Scale for Children (WISC-III). The phenotypic correlations between brain volumes and intelligence traits ranged between .20 and .33, a finding that may be explained by both genetic and environmental factors. The authors concluded that at 9 years of age, variation in brain structure is associated with individual differences in intelligence measures and the genes that influence brain volume and probably influence intelligence via a causal pathway or via pleiotropy. Some analogies between synaesthesia and intelligence genes may exist; however, in the light of current research into the genetics underlying synaesthesia, this question remains unresolved (Brang and Ramachandran, 2011).

Contrary to expectations (Rogowska, 2007), the fluid intelligence of Raven's SPM did not show here any significant relationships with linguistic-colour associations (see Figure 4.1. and Table B4.1 in Appendix B). This result may be supported by other studies (Rader and Tellegen, 1981; Domino, 1989) in which synaesthesia was not correlated with intelligence assessed with distinct tests. However, hierarchical factor analysis demonstrated here that linguistic-colour synaesthesia is related to intelligence on a higher level by the common association factor (see Table 4.2, Figures 4.4 and 4.5, and Table B4.2 in Appendix B).

Raven's SPM is a non-verbal, multiple-choice measurement of two main components of reasoning: educative and reproductive abilities. The common theme of relationship, which has to be deduced from the figures by means of analogical reasoning, could be described as a form of continuation, supplementation, or concatenation (van der Ven and Ellis, 2000). Detection of associations between abstract shapes and forms is the basis of correct problem-solving in Raven's SPM. Perhaps, this kind of general intellectual ability is close to linguistic-colour associations.

Schwenzer and Mathiak (2012) have recently investigated the relationship between inductive reasoning and perception. They revealed that Raven's Advanced Progressive Matrices (APM), as a measure of inductive reasoning, correlated with the simultaneous perception of locus and pitch, and with the perception of four distinct colours (red, yellow, green, and blue). They suggested that inductive reasoning and the correlating perception skills may share a multidimensional mental representation, because all of them require the processing of unrelated categories.

According to the compensatory hypothesis (Rogowska, 2011), colour may be an excellent concrete cue for searching memory storage, and thus may be very helpful for individuals with some difficulty in operating abstract concepts. For example, a person with mathematical difficulty may develop number-colour synaesthesia, and an individual with face-recognition problems may use forename-colour synaesthesia. Perhaps, for a child at early school age, synaesthesia facilitates memorization and later finding a single linguistic item in a sequence of numbers (number-colour synaesthetes), days of the week (day-colour synaesthetes), letters of the alphabet (grapheme-colour synaesthetes), or names in a register (forename-colour synaesthetes). Synaesthesia may arise when a child is at a preoperational stage of intelligence, and categorization is still impossible, before the concrete operational stage has completely developed. At this time, a helpful synaesthetic strategy could occasionally provide hypercompensation and (in consequence) lead to better memory and intelligence. Further research should examine these possibilities as well as general connections between synaesthesia and the development of abstract thinking in children.

4.6 Emotional intelligence

One of the most interesting aspects of intelligence is emotionality. Emotional intelligence (EI) is defined as a cognitive ability to understand and reason about emotions. It comprises perception, appraisal, and integration of emotions, as well as reasoning by using and managing emotions (Mayer, Caruso, and Salovey, 1999). Mayer *et al.* (1999) revealed that emotional synaesthesia, which is a measure of people's ability to describe emotional sensations and their parallels to other sensory modalities, is involved in assimilation and understanding emotion, as a factor of EI. Moreover, emotional synaesthesia is one of the EI scales that distinguishes adolescents from adult participants and shows that EI grows from early adolescence to young adulthood.

Understanding emotion is defined as the ability to comprehend emotional information about relationships, transitions from one emotion to another, and linguistic information about emotions. The conception of emotion contains a central locus of abstract processing and reasoning about emotions and emotional information in relation to intelligence and personality (Mayer *et al.*, 2001). According to the EI conception, abstract processing of emotion refers to the ability to analyse an emotion and identify its parts and their combination. From this point of view, abstract linguistic-colour associations should correlate with the understanding scale of EI in the present study.

Recent research has shown that empathy is related to some other types of synaesthesia. For example, in mirror-touch synaesthetes, observing touch to another person induces a subjective tactile sensation for the synaesthete (Banissy, Cohen Kadosh, *et al.*, 2009). A fMRI experiment revealed that synaesthesia for touch exhibited higher levels of activity in the mirror system for touch (Blakemore *et al.*, 2005). Moreover, Banissy and Ward (2007) provided evidence that these systems may be crucial for empathy. They suggested that, in particular, experiencing aspects of affective empathy may depend on shared interpersonal representations. In their research, mirror-touch synaesthesia was correlated with heightened empathic ability, particularly with the emotional reactivity subscale, Empathy Quotient (EQ). This subscale measures automatic emotional reactions directed towards other people (e.g., sharing their sadness) rather than the more cognitive aspects of empathy. Moreover, mirror-touch synaesthesia in amputees was predicted by the emotional reactivity of the EQ (Goller, Richards, Novak, and Ward, 2013).

Similarly to mirror-touch, mirror-pain synaesthesia occurs when the observation of noxious stimulation to another induces an actual experience of pain (Giummarra and Bradshaw, 2009). Mirror-pain synaesthesia in amputees may be the result of the painful and traumatic experiences causing disinhibition in the mirror system that underlies empathy for pain (Fitzgibbon *et al.*, 2010). Fitzgibbon, Enticott, Rich, *et al.* (2012) suggested that atypical connectivity or altered function may produce

hyperactivity of the somatosensory mirror systems that may result in both developmental and acquired forms of mirror-sensory synaesthesia.

Nevertheless, Fitzgibbon, Enticott, Bradshaw, *et al.* (2012) found in another study that amputees who report synaesthetic pain have not scored higher than controls in self-reported measures of empathy (the EQ). In addition, when the EQ was used in relation to grapheme-personification synaesthesia (Amin *et al.*, 2011), a group of 10 personifying synaesthetes did not exhibit heightened empathy. It was concluded that heightened empathy is not necessary to personify graphemes.

However, this form of synaesthesia may provide a unique point of view on understanding others' state of mind. According to Corricelli (2005), there are two levels of understanding of another person's mind. The first level refers to automatic-preconceptual phenomena, which are based on early imitation, action, and emotion recognition. The second level of mindreading is conceptual and voluntary, based on intentionality, empathy, and higher depths of reasoning. On the other hand, de Vignemont and Singer (2006) suggested that empathic brain responses are modulated by appraisal processes which take into account information about the emotional stimuli, their situative context, characteristics of the empathizers, and their relationship with the target. Thus, self-reported scores might not be the best measure of empathy.

There is other evidence that synaesthesia is linked to affect. Strong emotional responses to colours and photisms in synaesthetes were reported in numerous studies (e.g., Cytowic, 1993, 2002; Ramachandran and Hubbard, 2001b; Ward, 2004). Ramachandran and Brang (2008) investigated tactile-emotion synaesthesia, in which specific textures (e.g., denim, wax, sandpaper, silk) evoked equally distinct emotions (e.g., depression, embarrassment, relief, and contentment, respectively). Scientists suggested that those types of synaesthesia may represent an enhancement of pre-existing, evolutionarily primitive interactions between touch and emotions.

Emotionally mediated synaesthesia was reported by Ward (2004), in particular, as a reaction to the affective valence of words (e.g., 'love') and to faces of known persons. Hochel *et al.* (2009) described emotional synaesthesia as a type in which coloured photisms were subjectively categorized in line with emotional valence. A common connotation seems to exist in normal human modes of aesthetic expression between colours, emotions, musical sounds, and abstract shapes that may be shared in synaesthesia (e.g., Collier, 1996; Dailey *et al.*, 1997; Hupka, Zaleski, Otto, Reidl, and Tarabrina, 1997; Pozella and Hassen, 1997).

Regardless of synaesthesia type, synaesthetes often report negative affective reactions related to synaesthetic perceptions, by means of an evaluation task, when stimulation is incongruent with their own experiences. For grapheme-colour synaesthetes, the perception of an incorrectly coloured word (e.g., the letter *A* printed in blue while their synaesthetic association is red) affects the judgement of emotional valence (Callejas, Acosta, and Lupiáñez, 2007). This affective reaction was automatic and difficult to ignore. Therefore, it was concluded that emotion is a part of the set of subjective experiences of synaesthesia. In a recent review study, Dael, Sierro, and Mohr (2013) hypothesized that the synaesthetic experience is determined by, or even altered through, cognitive appraisal processes, and it changes temporarily on a quantitative level according to either the affective appraisal of the inducing stimulus or the current affective state of the individual.

Although earlier studies investigated emotionally mediated synaesthesia, EI has never been examined in the context of linguistic-colour synaesthesia. If emotionality is a universal characteristic of synaesthesia, it should be reflected in some way in each type of this phenomenon. Because of the exploratory character of this study, it was only hypothesized generally that at least some of the EI scales are related to linguistic-colour synaesthesia.

The result of the present study revealed that linguistic-colour associations were not correlated with any of the PEIQ scales (see Table B4.1 in Appendix B). Moreover, EI was not a distinguishing factor between synaesthetes and non-synaesthetes (see Figure 4.1). However, when an explorative stepwise analysis of regression with forward selection was performed for linguistic-colour association as an explained variable, acceptation and reasoning of emotions of the PEIQ were included in the regression model along with absorption and creativity, although only two predictor variables – absorption and acceptation of emotion – demonstrated sufficient levels of significance (Table 4.1). Nevertheless, the general assumption for the emotional component in synaesthesia seems to be currently supported.

According to Mayer *et al.* (1999), EI is a cognitive ability to understand and reason about emotions. This ability comprises perception, appraisal, and integration of emotions as well as reasoning by exploiting and managing emotions. Emotional synaesthesia is, rather, related to cognitive factors such as assimilation and understanding emotions. In the present study, the acceptation of emotions scale of the PEIQ seems to respond to this description. Banissy *et al.* (2011) showed mirror-touch synaesthesia to be associated with superior ability in facial expression recognition, which is also one of the indicators of EI, especially with the Perceive

Emotion scale (Mayer *et al*, 1999; Edgar, McRorie, and Sneddon, 2012) – the ability to perceive and identify the emotional content of a variety of stimuli.

Perhaps, the cognitive capacity of EI to perceive emotions, assimilate emotion-related feelings, and understand the information of those emotions (Mayer *et al.*, 1999) has an influence on forming concrete colour-word connotations, because heightened emotional ability enhances memory. Research by Kensinger and Corkin (2003) supported the well-known relation that emotional words are more vividly remembered than neutral words. The recent study of Toyota (2011) showed that the level of EI determined the effectiveness of recalling the neutral episodes of targets as retrieval cues. In that research, participants who demonstrated high EI recalled targets with pleasant, neutral, and unpleasant episodes equally, whereas participants with low EI indicated targets with neutral episodes less frequently than those with pleasant or unpleasant ones.

Another study (Mikolaczak, Roy, Verstrynge, and Luminet, 2009) indicated that the Self-Control (SC) scale of EI moderates the impact of stress on memory and attention. Contrary to stressful conditions, in neutral conditions, high SC was characterized by an intentional focus on neutral material and a facilitated memory for positive events, whereas low SC was characterized by an intentional focus on emotional material (regardless of valence) and a facilitated memory for negative events.

Some relationships between empathy and linguistic-colour associations were revealed here using cluster analysis. Empathy together with acceptation of emotions and fluid intelligence were grouped together into one nearest cluster of the linguistic-colour associations scale. According to research on EI, all of the empathy subscales (Empathic Suffering, Positive Sharing, Responsive Crying, Avoidance, and Feeling for Others) correlated significantly with Assimilation and Understanding Emotion, the factor of EI that contained Emotional Synaesthesia scores (Mayer *et al.*, 1999). Freedberg and Gallese (2007) proved that mirroring mechanisms and embodied simulation for empathetic responses to images are universal and essential to the understanding of the effectiveness of both everyday images and works of art. Automatic empathetic responses constitute the basic level that enables direct experiential understanding of the intentional and emotional contents of images. Thus, the weak connection between empathy and linguistic-colour associations found in the present study could imply that the mirror system may play a universal role in all visual forms of synaesthesia.

It seems probable that different types of synaesthesia are related to distinct dimensions of individual differences, including various dimensions of EI. Future research on the relationships between EI and synaesthesia should include different types and kinds of synaesthesia by using neuroimaging, and behavioural and self-reported measures for particular dimensions of emotional abilities (Schlegel, Grandjean, and Scherer, 2012; Thingujam, Laukka, and Elfenbein, 2012).

4.7 Conclusions

The results of the present study show that linguistic-colour synaesthesia is directly and strongly correlated with absorption, and poorly correlated with acceptation of emotions. Indirectly it could also be connected with either creativity or fluid intelligence together with the global type of mind, depending on higher-order factor solutions. Synaesthesia may be considered one of the dimensions included in either general association or the general thinking process. As such, research on synaesthesia could embrace a cognitive view in a wide context of emotion, perception, attention, memory, imagination, and intelligence. Exploration of these relationships may be useful in explaining not only the development and evolution of language and human thinking, but also mental disorders such as autism, schizophrenia, depression, and mania (e.g., Glicksohn *et al.*, 2001; Ramachandran and Hubbard, 2001b; Ott *et al.*, 2005).

The present study had some limitations. One major concern is that the university sample was not large and fully representative of the general population, and thus the findings may not be generalizable. Because of the great individual differences among synaesthetes (Day, 2005), the findings cannot be generalized with reference to other types and categories of synaesthesia. Thus, the future exploration of relationships between various types of synaesthesia and different dimensions of individual differences assessed by various measures and methods is necessary. This kind of research may shed some light on the neurocognitive mechanisms of synaesthesia and their evolutionary nature.

5 Exploring the relationships between linguistic-colour associations and self-reported traits of personality and temperament

5.1 Personality

Personality is a psychological construct that characterizes the enduring psychological qualities that contribute to the coherence and uniqueness of an individual and to differences among individuals. Among numerous personality theories and methods of personality assessment, trait taxonomy and factor-analytic programmes have gained prominence in recent decades. Personality traits are relatively stable over time, differing among individuals and influencing behaviour. A nearly unlimited number of potential traits could be used to describe personality. The majority of standardized personality questionnaires consist of self-reports (Smith, 1999).

Currently, the Big Five model (neuroticism/emotional stability, extraversion, openness, agreeableness, and conscientiousness) seems to be one of the most notable nomothetic procedures that describe all individuals in terms of a common set of personality variables (Just, 2011). Extraversion reflects the disposition to sociability, cheerfulness, and high activity. According to Costa and McCrae (1992), the dimension of neuroticism-emotional stability stands for the tendency to experience distressing emotions such as frustration, guilt, and fear. Openness indicates a receptive orientation towards varied feelings, trials, and ideas. Agreeableness summarizes the inclination to consideration of others and interpersonal trust. Conscientiousness represents the tendency to persistence, organizing, planning, industriousness, sense of duty, and self-discipline.

By factor analysis, Eysenck (1967) suggested that personality is reducible to three major traits: extraversion, neuroticism, and psychoticism. According to Eysenck's theory (1967, 1992), extraversion and neuroticism are very similar to their counterparts in the Big Five model, whereas psychoticism corresponds to two traits in the Big Five model: conscientiousness and agreeableness. Persons with high psychoticism are inclined to be cruel, inhumane, socially indifferent, hostile, aggressive, inconsiderate in the face of danger, insular, glacial, and intolerant. They show a propensity to make trouble for others, to belittle others, to act disruptively, and to lack empathy, thus displaying tendencies to develop psychotic disorders. Eysenck's personality system does not address openness to experience. Although Eysenck's three-dimensional conception of personality is similar to the Big Five, the theories differ in their understanding of and the number of basic personality traits, demonstrating that they are more complementary than alternative methods of assessing personality.

In the present chapter, the synaesthetic trait is seen as inheriting a strong tendency to create abstract intra- or cross-modal associations, which arise in some key period of life and remain relatively constant in response to a need for integrative or compensatory cognitive processes, influenced by the external environment, unique stimulations, and experiences acquired by enculturation and socialization. This idiosyncratic character, as well as the resource of various forms, types, and kinds of synaesthesia, seems to be confirmed by this assumption. Exploration of the relationship between synaesthetic and cognitive/behavioural traits could shed new light on the phenomenon of synaesthesia from a psychological point of view.

Although research on synaesthesia has developed greatly over the last decade, studies of the relationships of synaesthesia with individual differences in personality have been very scarce. Rader and Tellegen (1981, 1987) examined the interrelationships of synaesthesia (assessed by the Synaesthesia Questionnaire, the Auditory Synaesthesia Performance Test, and the Paper-and-Pencil Synaesthesia Performance Test) with intelligence (Brief Intelligence Test) and personality (Differential Personality Questionnaire and Multidimensional Personality Questionnaire). With respect to personality traits, synaesthetes demonstrated higher scores for absorption and positive self-view than non-synaesthetes. The vividness of synaesthetic imagery was not found to be associated with personality dysfunction or with intelligence.

It is likely that over the past 30 years there have not been any other systematically conducted studies on personality or temperament with reference to synaesthesia. However, a description of the synaesthete's personality profile could be helpful in predicting synaesthesia among children and adults, and also in identifying synaesthetes on the basis of the configuration of individual differences in personality and temperament. The purpose of the present study was to explore interrelations between synaesthesia and traits of personality and temperament by self-report methods. Because personality and temperament are present in early childhood, and are determined by inborn mechanisms, it was assumed that personality and temperament could be primary psychobiosocial factors that play a role in the emergence of synaesthesia.

In the present study, a total Sample B of 79 students (see Appendix A) completed a self-reported measure of the following traits of personality following the Big Five model: Neuroticism (N), Extraversion (E), Openness (O), Agreeableness (A), and Conscientiousness (C). The Neuroticism-Extraversion-Openness Five-Factor Inventory (NEO-FFI) consists of 60 items, 12 for each of the five dimensions of adult personality (Costa and McCrae, 1992) answered on a 5-point Likert scale from 1 (*strongly disagree*) to 5 (*strongly agree*).[1]

Pearson's correlation analysis was used to examine the relationships between linguistic-colour associations and traits of personality and temperament. In addition, synaesthetes' personality and temperament trait scores were compared with the scores of non-synaesthetes, using the *t*-test. Means, standard deviations, and normality (Kolmogorov–Smirnov *D* statistics) analyses were conducted for the NEO-FFI scales and total L-CAT. There were no gender differences in the NEO-FFI scales; thus, further analysis was conducted without dividing the sample into two sex groups. Descriptive statistics for the total sample ($N = 79$), as well as for synaesthetes ($n = 8$) and non-synaesthetes ($n = 71$), are shown in Table B5.1 in Appendix B.

The sample scored low on openness to experience and moderately on other personality traits. Linguistic-colour synaesthetes demonstrated significantly higher scores than non-synaesthetes in conscientiousness. There were no other differences between synaesthetes and non-synaesthetes in neuroticism, extraversion, openness, or agreeableness (Figure 5.1).

Synaesthetes revealed a positive correlation between the total range of linguistic-colour associations of the L-CAT and two personality traits: extraversion and agreeableness. No other relationships were found either in non-synaesthetes or in the total sample. Stronger synaesthetes tended to be introvert and disagreeable, meaning that stronger synaesthetes preferred to be with their own thoughts instead of being with other people (they avoided social situations). Because introverts are more concerned with the inner world of the mind, and enjoy thinking, and exploring their thoughts and feelings, it is not surprising that they experience conscious linguistic-colour synaesthesias on a daily basis. Introversion as a trait may

[1] The reliabilities indicated an acceptable internal consistency (Cronbach's alpha) for the Polish version of NEO-FFI (Zawadzki, Strelau, Szczepaniak, and Śliwińska, 1998) for the following scales: Neuroticism (α = .80), Extraversion (α = .77), Openness (α = .68), Agreeableness (α = .68), and Conscientiousness (α = .82). In the present study, the Cronbach's alphas were .87, .70, .56, .64, and .85, respectively.

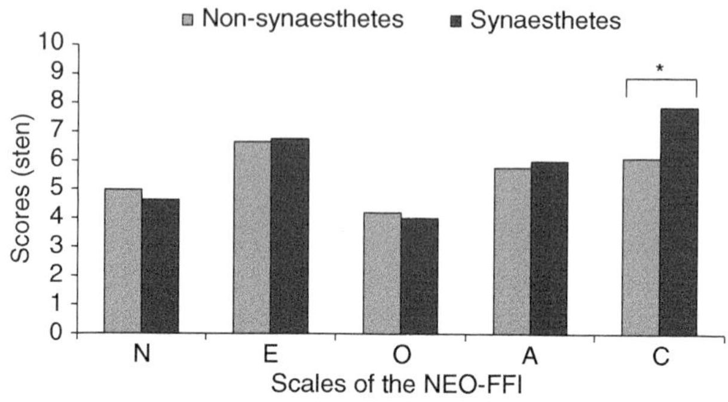

Figure 5.1 Mean sten scores in the NEO-FFI for non-synaesthetes B (n = 71) and synaesthetes B (n = 8). *Note:* $^*p < .05$. N = Neuroticism, E = Extraversion, O = Openness, A = Agreeableness, C = Conscientiousness.

favour reinforcement of synaesthetic associations. However, it is important to note that synaesthetes as a group represent generally a high level of extraversion (a mean sten score of almost 7).

Moreover, the introversion tendency of stronger synaesthetes seems to correspond with their tendency to score low on agreeableness. Agreeableness is the tendency to be pleasant, empathetic, considerate, friendly, generous, helpful, and accommodating in social situations. In contrast, stronger linguistic-colour synaesthetes may be less concerned with others' well-being, and they may be more sceptical about other people's motives, resulting in suspicion and unfriendliness. People scoring low on agreeableness are also more likely to compete than to co-operate. Because linguistic-colour synaesthetes in Sample B were athletes, who also often participated in sports competitions as physical education students, low agreeableness seems to be understandable.

On the other hand, individuals with synaesthesia perceive the world in a different way from non-synaesthetes. Synaesthetes may distrust other people because others do not believe in their vision and experiences. Nonconformity and high self-control, which seem to characterize both disagreeable and creative individuals (Guencer and Oral, 1993; Runco, 2007), could also be a link connecting synaesthetes with low agreeableness. Nevertheless, further research is necessary to examine this speculation.

Furthermore, the sample of linguistic-colour synaesthetes revealed higher conscientiousness than that of non-synaesthetes. This may mean that linguistic-colour synaesthetes demonstrate a stronger tendency to being efficient, organized, neat, and systematic, with a high level of deliberation, carefulness, thoroughness, self-discipline, and need for achievement. This characteristic of synaesthetes may provide them with success, and that seems to explain why so many famous people have been synaesthetes.[2]

The Big Five model of personality was compared with Eysenck's three-dimensional model (Eysenck and Eysenck, 1975; Eysenck, Eysenck, and Barrett, 1985) in the present study. The Eysenck Personality Questionnaire – Revised (EPQ-R) was administered to Sample A consisting of 79 students (see Appendix A). The EPQ-R in its Polish adaptation (Brzozowski and Drwal, 2008) consisted of 100 items, including 24 items for Neuroticism (N), 23 items for Extraversion (E), 32 items for Psychoticism (P), and 21 items for the Lie (L) Scale.[3]

Descriptive statistics such as means and standard deviations, were calculated for the EPQ-R scales and total L-CAT range (Table B5.2 in Appendix B). The Kolmogorov–Smirnov *D* statistic showed that Extraversion and total L-CAT deviated from normality in the total Sample A ($n = 79$) and in non-synaesthetes A ($n = 68$): thus, non-parametric statistics were used for these scales. No gender differences were found in using *t*-tests and the *U* test (alternatively) on the EPQ-R scales.

Synaesthetes demonstrated significantly higher extraversion than non-synaesthetes (see Table B5.2 in Appendix B and Figure 5.2). According to the EPQ-R assumptions (Eysenck and Eysenck, 1975), individuals who score high in extraversion tend to be outgoing, impulsive, and uninhibited; have many social contacts; and often take part in group activities. Extraverts, according to Eysenck's (1967) arousal theory, are chronically under-aroused and bored, and are therefore in need of external stimulation to bring them up to an optimal level of performance. Typically, extraverts are highly social, like gatherings, and have many friends. The heightened extraversion of linguistic-colour synaesthetes seems to be consistent with the results of a recent study by Amin *et al.* (2011) on grapheme personification as a variant of the linguistic type of synaesthesia. The study found that grapheme personification provides a very interesting aid to our understanding of certain key social skills – that is, how people encode and represent their own and other people's intentions, beliefs, and feelings.

[2] See the list of famous synaesthetes, http://en.wikipedia.org/wiki/List_of_people_with_synesthesia#

[3] The internal consistency (Cronbach's alpha) for scales N, E, P, and L of the EPQ-R in the Polish adaptation (Brzozowski and Drwal, 2008) was .84, .83, .67, and .75, respectively. In the present study, reliability was acceptable, with Cronbach's alphas of .84, .89, .65, and .75, respectively.

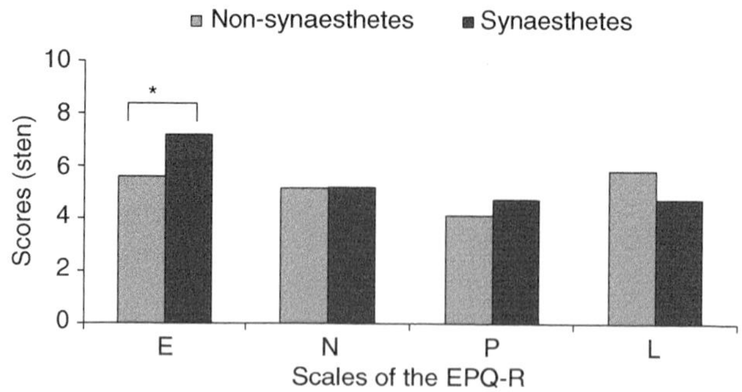

Figure 5.2 Mean sten scores in the EPQ-R for non-synaesthetes (n = 68) and synaesthetes (n = 11). *Note:* $^*p < .05$. E = Extraversion, N = Neuroticism, P = Psychoticism, L = Lie Scale.

On the other hand, the heightened extraversion in the synaesthetes from Sample A seems to be inconsistent with the lower extraversion tendency in stronger synaesthetes from Sample B. However, the present results of linguistic-colour synaesthetes as a group (a sten score of 7 on the extraversion scale for Sample A) did not differ significantly from those of the previous study (a sten score of almost 7 for Sample B). Moreover, although the correlation between total L-CAT and Extraversion of the NEO-FFI was not significant, the coefficient was quite high in synaesthetes from Sample A ($r_s = .56, p = .08$), especially in comparison to relationships with other variables and other groups – that is, non-synaesthetes and the total sample.

Synaesthetes revealed a positive correlation between the Lie Scale of the EPQ-R and total L-CAT. Thus, stronger linguistic-colour synaesthetes scored lower on the Lie Scale. No correlation between these variables was found in non-synaesthetes or in the total samples. This result may be seen as a confirmation of the authenticity of synaesthetes and the accuracy of synaesthesia assessment with the use of L-CAT. According to Eysenck and Eysenck (1976), lying is diagnosed when a set of rarely performed acts is endorsed by the respondent as being habitually done and when frequently performed non-desirable acts are denied by the respondent.

Lie scales were originally introduced into personality measures in order to detect the 'faked good' scores on other scales or falsification tests (O'Donovan, 1969). Moreover, when the motivation to fake good is high, a negative correlation between lie scores and neuroticism scores occurs, but when motivation to fake good is low, there is no correlation between the two variables (Jackson and Francis, 1999). Because, in the present study, there was no correlation between lie and neuroticism ($r = -.12$; $p = .73$), it may be concluded that synaesthetes were not highly motivated to fake good. However, a significantly negative correlation between the Lie Scale and neuroticism was found in non-synaesthetes ($r = -.39$; $p = .001$). This may imply that non-synaesthetes were highly motivated to fake good. Furthermore, it can be proposed that non-synaesthetic individuals with a strong tendency to fake good tried to perform the L-CAT even though they did not have daily word-colour associations. Because they used accidental linguistic-colour connotations, the test–retest colours were less consistent (positive mean scores) in total L-CAT than in the sample of synaesthetes. When we consider all of these results, the Lie Scale of the EPQ-R seems to confirm the good validity of the L-CAT for strong–weak synaesthesia measurement.

5.2 Temperament

Temperament is usually defined as a set of biologically based individual differences in emotional and physiological reactivity and self-regulation of behaviour influenced over time by heredity and experience (Putnam, Ellis, and Rothbart, 2001). Reactivity refers to motor, emotional, and attentive responses to internal and external stimuli, whereas self-regulation refers to processes serving to modulate reactivity, including approach/withdrawal, inhibitory control, and effortful control of attention. Temperament is particularly related to perception (Barclay, 1993).

Temperament differs from personality and consists of the following characteristics: occurrence in people and animals, strong constitutional basis (is genetically influenced by neuro-biochemical mechanisms), earlier childhood manifestations, broader effects on behaviour, and more formal characteristics (e.g., tempo, endurance) instead of specific content of behaviour (Thomas and Chess, 1985; Strelau, 1987; Angleitner and Riemann, 1991; Kagan and Snidman, 1991; Strelau and Zawadzki, 1993; Michielsen *et al.*, 2003). Although temperament pertains to relatively stable dispositions, its elicitors and expressions often change during the course of human development.

Temperament and personality become increasingly fixed from childhood to adulthood. Nevertheless, both generic and environmental mechanisms can be used to account for changes in temperament and personality. Stable temperament or personality characteristics are produced by the cumulative effects of experiences or environmental pressures such as the internalization of emotion-display rules, the acquisition of new coping strategies, or becoming embedded within a stable social environment (Ganiban, Saudino, Ulbricht, Neiderhiser, and Reiss, 2008).

Despite the fact that the concept of temperament measurement has been established for many years, there is still debate regarding the validity and categorization of the temperament concept, as pointed out by Mathiesen and Tambs (1999). Although some differences are concerned with conceptualizing temperament traits, there is general agreement that some features of emotionality, activity, and sociability refer to the basic characteristics of individual differences between people.

In Buss and Plomin's (1984) conception of temperament, emotionality is defined as primordial distress, which is assumed to differentiate into fear and anger during the first 6 months of life; activity is described as the sheer expenditure of physical energy; and sociability is defined as a preference for being with others rather than being alone. The Emotionality-Activity-Sociability Temperament Survey (EAS-TS) was developed by Buss and Plomin (1984). The survey for adults (EAS-TS) measures three components of emotionality: anger, distress, and fearfulness, beside the activity and sociability scales (Buss and Plomin, 1984). The EAS-TS for adults in its Polish version (Oniszczenko, 1997) is composed of five scales: Sociability (So, $\alpha = .57$), Activity (Ac, $\alpha = .66$), Fear (Fe, $\alpha = .70$), Distress (Di, $\alpha = .74$), and Anger (An, $\alpha = .59$).[4] The results of a study conducted by Naerde, Røysamb, and Tambs (2004), which investigated the psychometric properties of the EST-TS for adults, confirmed the structure and stability of this instrument.

The descriptive statistics used here in Sample B of 77 participants (see Appendix A) for the EAS-TS scales are shown in Table B5.3 in Appendix B and Figure 5.3. Means, standard deviations, and normality analyses (Kolmogorov–Smirnov D statistics) were calculated for the EAS-TS scales and the L-CAT total range. No gender differences were found in the EAS-TS scales. Synaesthetes B, like non-synaesthetes B, demonstrated a typical and average level of temperament traits on the EAS-TS, except for a tendency to a slightly (but not significantly) higher activity. However, heightened activity may be related to sports activity, which characterizes athletes within the physical education students of Sample B.

There were no differences between synaesthetes and non-synaesthetes in any of the temperament scales of the EAS-TS. Synaesthetes demonstrated significantly lower scores than non-synaesthetes in the L-CAT range. They also revealed a negative correlation between anger and the

[4] In the present study, Cronbach's alphas for scales So, Ac, Fe, Di, and An were .65, .68, .60, .77, and .54, respectively.

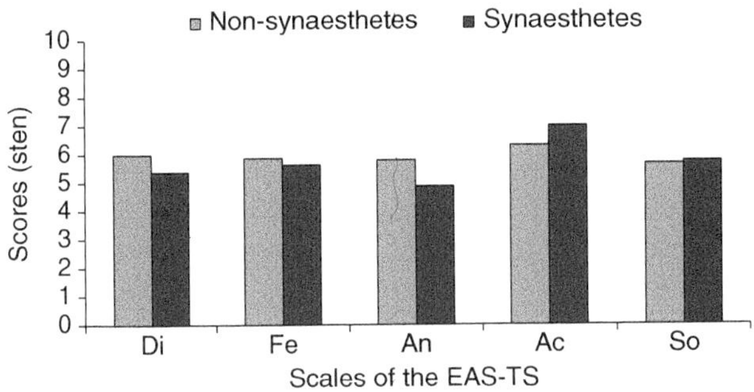

Figure 5.3 Mean sten scores in the EAS-TS for non-synaesthetes (n = 69) and synaesthetes (n = 8). *Note:* Di = Distress, Fe = Fear, An = Anger, Ac = Activity, So = Sociability.

range of linguistic-colour associations. This is an indication that stronger synaesthetes more frequently, easily, and intensely experienced negative emotions, especially anger.

In Buss and Plomin's (1975) conception of temperament, emotionality encompasses autonomic nervous system functions including arousal, tempers, fearful responses, and mood swings. A highly emotional person has a lower threshold for experiencing distress, fear, and anger, and therefore may experience these more often and with greater intensity than an unemotional person. Synaesthetes frequently experience discomfort and strong aversive emotional reactions when the inducer is presented in a colour different from their photism (Ramachandran and Hubbard, 2001b; Cytowic, 2002; Callejas *et al.*, 2007). Hence, grapheme-colour synaesthetes could often experience a negative emotional response and anger if they read a text with the 'wrong colours' on billboards, on television, or in books.

On the other hand, for emotion-colour synaesthetes, only words that have emotional connotations (e.g., 'anger') can elicit a synaesthetic response, and the valence of the emotion (positive vs. negative) may play some role in determining the synaesthetic colour of concurrent sensation (Ward, 2004). Because there have been no studies on the prevalence of emotion-colour synaesthesia, the presence of emotion-colour synaesthetes among linguistic synaesthetes remains unknown. Nevertheless, the emotional component of synaesthesia seems to explain the current results.

Moreover, the present results seem to be consistent with earlier research that revealed a positive correlation between agreeableness of the NEO-FFI and the L-CAT range of linguistic-colour associations. In their research using a structural quotation modelling approach, Finch and Graziano (2001) found a relationship between low agreeableness and high anger. Moreover, the negative correlation between these two variables may affect depression by the meditational role of highly negative social exchange and low level of support satisfaction. Because a significantly negative correlation was found between agreeableness of the NEO-FFI and anger of the EAS-TS in synaesthetes B ($r = -.73$, $p = .04$), stronger linguistic-colour synaesthetes may apparently be more prone to depression.

One of the most influential temperament models, that constructed by Pavlov (1941), is based on the assumption that nervous system traits can explain individual differences in responses to conditioning situations (Strelau, 1983). According to the Pavlovian conception of temperament (Strelau, Angleitner, and Newberry, 1999), the strength of excitation refers to the nervous system's capacity to work, particularly under prolonged or intense stimulation, whereas strength of inhibition is the system's ability to develop and maintain a conditioned inhibition, as seen in such phenomena as extinction, delay, and stimulus discrimination. The mobility of nervous processes refers to the ability to respond adequately to changes in stimulus conditions, including environmental demands. The Pavlovian Temperament Survey (PTS) was created by Strelau *et al.* (1999). The Polish version (Strelau and Zawadzki, 1998) consists of three scales: Strength of Excitation (SE, $\alpha = .80$), Strength of Inhibition (SI, $\alpha = .72$), and Mobility of the Nervous Processes (MO, $\alpha = .82$).[5] Studies using the Polish version (Strelau, Zawadzki, and Angleitner, 1995) and an American English version (Newberry *et al.*, 1997; Strelau *et al.*, 1999) of the PTS have appeared to demonstrate an adequate level of psychometric properties of the inventory.

The PTS scales and total L-CAT were examined here in a Sample B of 78 participants (see Appendix A) with the use of descriptive statistics: means and standard deviations (Table B5.4 in Appendix B). All variables met the normality criteria with the use of Kolmogorov–Smirnov *D* statistics. The parametric *t*-test and Pearson's correlation were conducted next. Women were shown not to differ from men in temperament scales. Generally, synaesthetes demonstrated higher scores (sten scores of above 6) in SI, and non-synaesthetes in SE. However, there were no significant differences between synaesthetes and non-synaesthetes in SE, SI, or MO, as shown in Figure 5.4.

[5] In the present study, all scales demonstrated acceptable reliability coefficients, with Cronbach's alphas of .82, .56, and .82 for scales SE, SI, and MO, respectively.

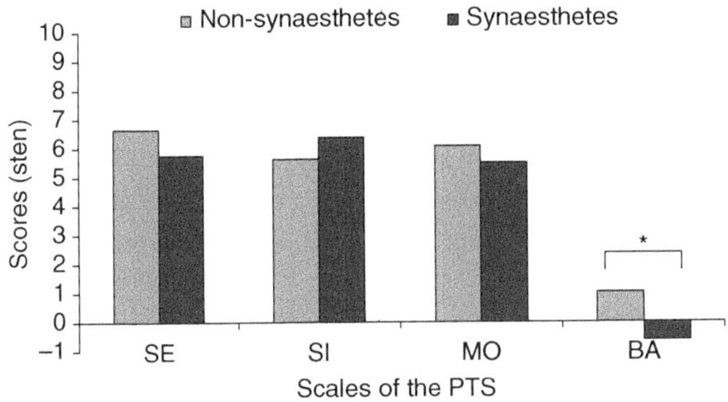

Figure 5.4 Mean sten scores in the PTS for non-synaesthetes (n = 70) and synaesthetes (n = 8). *Note:* $^{*}p < .05$. SE = Strength of excitation, SI = Strength of inhibition, MO = Mobility of nervous processes, BA = Balance of Nervous System Processes.

The only difference between synaesthetes and non-synaesthetes was found in the Balance of Nervous System Processes (BA) scale. In the Pavlovian conception of temperament (see Corulla, Strelau, Angleitner, and Ruch, 1993), the BA is described and estimated with the SE/SI ratio. Strength of excitation is defined as the capacity of the nervous system to endure long-lasting or short-lived but intense stimulation. Contrary to SE, SI is described as the system's capacity for conditioned inhibition, and is manifested in the capacity to refrain from action, delay action, or interrupt action.

Excitation and inhibition may be balanced or unbalanced, depending on the correlation of their force. That is, both processes may be equally strong, or one of them may predominate. In the present study, SI predominated slightly over SE in linguistic-colour synaesthetes, whereas in non-synaesthetes, SE predominated slightly over SI. The difference between these two samples in the BA was significant (see Figure 5.4). The obtained results may be explained in the context of the interrelationships of linguistic-colour synaesthesia with personality and temperament scales.

According to the regulative theory of temperament (RTT), developed by Strelau (1996, 1998), temperament refers mainly to the formal aspects of behaviour such as energetic and temporal characteristics. On the basis of broad psychometric studies, the Formal Characteristics of Behaviour – Temperament Inventory (FCB-TI) (Strelau and Zawadzki, 1993; Strelau, 1996) distinguishes six temperamental traits: briskness and perseveration as dimensions referring to the temporal characteristics of behaviour; and sensory sensitivity, endurance, emotional reactivity, and activity as traits representing the energetic aspect of behaviour.[6] Each scale comprises 20 items. Briskness (BR) is described as the tendency to react quickly, to keep a high tempo of performing activities, and to shift easily in response to changes in the surroundings from one type of behaviour (reaction) to another. Perseveration (PE) refers to the tendency to continue and repeat behaviour after the cessation of stimuli (situations) evoking this behaviour. Sensory Sensitivity (SS) is the ability to react to sensory stimuli of low stimulative value. Emotional Reactivity (ER) means the tendency to react intensively to emotion-generating stimuli, expressed in high emotional sensitivity and in low emotional endurance. Endurance (EN) describes the ability to react adequately in situations demanding long-lasting or high stimulative activity and under intensive external stimulation. Finally, Activity (AC) is the tendency to undertake behaviour of high stimulative value or to supply by means of behaviour strong stimulation from the surroundings. Because of their strong biological bases, the universal temperamental traits derived from FCB-TI should be common to humans and independent of their specific cultural environment (Strelau and Angleitner, 1994). Indeed, a study on an Italian sample (de Pascalis, Zawadzki, and Strelau, 2000) revealed similar psychometric properties to the original Polish sample (Strelau and Zawadzki, 1993).

Descriptive statistics were used in Sample B (n = 73, see Appendix A) to analyse the means, standard deviations, and Kolmogorov–Smirnov D statistics in the FCB-TI scales and in total L-CAT (Table B5.5 in Appendix B and Figure 5.5). The t-test did not reveal significant gender differences in any of the variables. Synaesthetes differed significantly from non-synaesthetes in the total range of linguistic-colour associations of the L-CAT. No other differences were found.

In addition, Pearson's correlation analysis did not show any relationships between synaesthetic associations and the temperament scales of the FCB-TI in synaesthetes B and total Sample B. However, non-synaesthetes B demonstrated a negative correlation between linguistic-colour associations and SS. This suggests that stronger linguistic-colour associators are highly sensitive. People with high SS possess the ability to react to sensory stimuli of low stimulative value, and therefore detect more input than others, whereas the strength of excitation refers to the

[6] The FCB-TI in its Polish version developed by Zawadzki and Strelau (1997) revealed good reliability for the following scales: Briskness (α = .77), Perseveration (α = .79), Sensory Sensitivity (α = .73), Emotional Reactivity (α = .83), Endurance (α = .85), and Activity (α = .83). In the present study, the reliability coefficients (Cronbach's alpha) were .69, .81, .75, .85, .87, and .84, respectively.

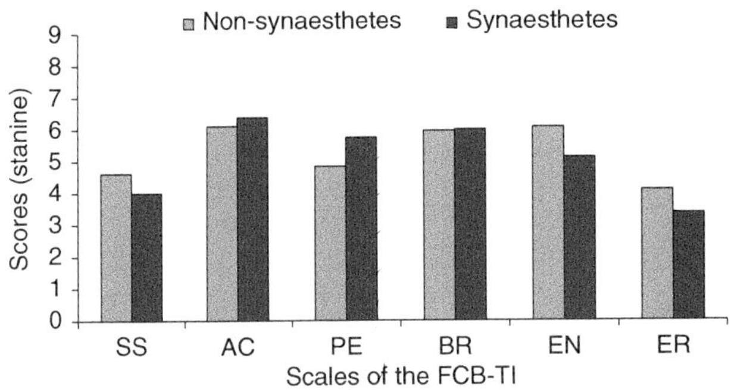

Figure 5.5 Mean stanine scores in the FCB-TI for non-synaesthetes ($n = 65$) and synaesthetes ($n = 8$). *Note:* SS = Sensory Sensitivity, AC = Activity, PE = Perseveration, BR = Briskness, EN = Endurance, ER = Emotional Reactivity.

nervous system's capacity to work under prolonged or intense stimulation. It is noteworthy that research on the behavioural genetics of temperament among 546 adolescent and adult twin pairs indicated additive genetic variance in SS temperamental traits (Strelau, 1996, 1998). The results of the present study seem to correspond with some recent findings (Yaro and Ward, 2007; Banissy, Walsh, *et al.*, 2009; Brang *et al.*, 2012), according to which linguistic synaesthesia characterizes people with a hypersensitive colour perceptual system.

Nevertheless, it is not clear why synaesthetes did not show any relationship between these two variables. Moreover, synaesthetes demonstrated a positive (although non-significant) correlation with SS, a finding that suggests rather a tendency to the lower level of SS in stronger linguistic-colour synaesthetes. Generally, synaesthetes B demonstrated low levels of SS (sten score of 4) as well as low ER (sten score of 3). According to the conception of Strelau and Zawadzki (1993), highly ER individuals demonstrate the tendency to react intensively to emotion-inducing stimuli. Low ER is usually connected with high extraversion. The fact that synaesthetes B revealed high extraversion in the previous study may partially explain the present results.

However, low SS may be explained by the compensatory hypothesis of synaesthesia (Rogowska, 2011), according to which individuals who demonstrate deficiency in one sensory modality may develop an extraordinary ability in another sensory modality, because of the compensation mechanism and plasticity of the brain. This can take place if an individual has some predispositions, such as weak control of nervous processes connected with disinhibition.

5.3 Interrelationships between personality, temperament, and synaesthesia

Structural analyses such as clustering and partial least squares regression (PLS) were performed to investigate relationships between all variables, and also for synthesis of a large number of data and detection of latent variables that may be important for explaining the phenomenon of synaesthesia. First, a cluster analysis was used on Sample B for an initial exploration of the structure and configuration of interrelated variables. Clustering is the task of grouping a set of similar variables into particular clusters.

The two-way joining method was used to cluster similar individuals among synaesthetes B (n = 8) and simultaneously to cluster similar variables among traits of personality and temperament. This method is particularly useful when both cases and variables may simultaneously contribute to the uncovering of meaningful patterns of clusters. The resulting structure (clusters) does not appear to be homogeneous: thus, further analysis is necessary to explore the structure of the variables. However, the two-way joining of tree clustering provided a comprehensive insight into the total dimensions of personality and temperament separately for each synaesthete, an insight that may be helpful in the interpretation of further exploratory data analysis (see Plate 7).

Hierarchical clustering is a connectivity-based clustering incorporating the core idea of objects being more related to objects nearby than to objects farther away. Hierarchical clustering provides an extensive hierarchy of clusters that merge with each other at certain distances, as demonstrated in a dendrogram. In the complete linkage method, the distances between clusters are determined by the greatest distance between any two objects in different clusters (i.e., by the 'furthest neighbours'). The hierarchical cluster analysis with a Euclidean distance and complete linkage clustering method (the maximum of object distances) was used for all variables assessed in the present study (Figure 5.6). The aim of this analysis was to examine the cluster structure and specific relationships between linguistic-colour synaesthesia (total L-CAT) and the total of 20 self-reported traits of both personality (NEO-FFI) and temperament (EAS-TS, FCB-TI, and PTS).

In the sample of synaesthetes (Figure 5.6a), the most related variables included BA, SS linked with Openness to experience, and some of the temperamental traits related to the nervous system – that is, SI, Mobility of the Nervous Processes, SE, and endurance. The next clusters included mostly traits responsible for contact with other people, such as Sociability, Agreeableness, Conscientiousness, Activity, Briskness, and Extraversion. The most distant cluster

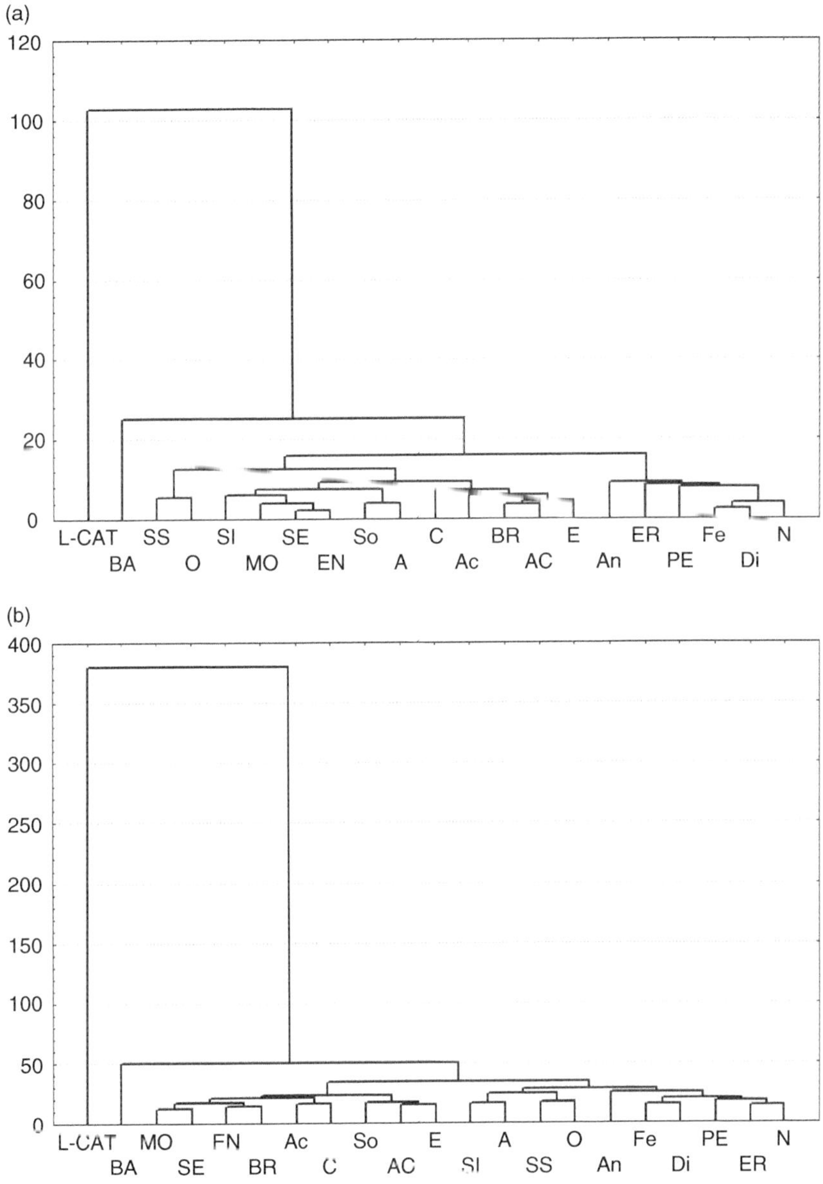

Figure 5.6 The vertical hierarchical tree plot as a result of hierarchical cluster analysis with Euclidean distance and complete linkage clustering method for all scales of the NEO-FFI, the EAS-TS, the FCB-TI, the PTS, and total L-CAT, in samples B: (a) synaesthetes (n = 8); (b) non-synaesthetes (n = 71). *Note:* NEO-FFI = the Neuroticism Extraversion Openness Five-Factor Inventory; N = Neuroticism; E = Extraversion; O = Openness; A = Agreeableness; C = Conscientiousness; EAS-TS = the Emotionality-Activity-Sociability Temperament Survey; Di = Distress; Fe = Fear; An = Anger; Ac = Activity; So = Sociability; FCB-TI = the Formal Characteristics of Behaviour – Temperament Inventory;

concerned the following traits of Emotionality: Anger, ER, Perseveration, Fear, Distress, and Neuroticism.

Although the first trait (balance – the closer to total L-CAT) and the last trait (neuroticism – the furthest from total L-CAT) within the cluster analysis were the same in the sample of non-synaesthetes as in synaesthetes, these groups differed from each other in the sequence of the other traits (Figure 5.6b). The closer cluster of synaesthetic associations included traits of temperament, the middle cluster mixed traits of personality and temperament, and, finally, the most distancing cluster concerned dimensions of Emotionality. The total L-CAT was more related (closer distance in the dendrogram) to traits of temperament and personality in synaesthetes than in non-synaesthetes (longer distance); however, in both samples, these connections were relatively poor.

The second step of the analysis was the exploration of a regression model that would explain synaesthesia variability on the basis of individual differences in temperament and personality. The purpose of that study was to find latent higher-order factors that may explain synaesthesia variability better than primary traits.

In parallel to Spearman's general factor of intelligence (G), Musek (2007) found the general factor of personality (GFP) for the first time by using different personality measures of the Big Five in three samples. A major effort was made to extract the GFP from highly diverse measures of personality in order to provide strong evidence for its merit as a universal personality construct rather than a statistical artefact (Just, 2011). A review study by Rushton and Irwing (2011) on over 24 different personality inventories (including the Big Five and the EAS) revealed that GFP reliably occupies the apex of the hierarchy of personality and its disorders. However, depending on a given criterion, some primary traits (e.g., personality facets existing *below* the Big Five) may sometimes be better predictors than higher-order traits. Nevertheless, this evidence seems to confirm Rushton's (1985, 1990) assumption that much of the field of individual differences can be organized under a hierarchy of broad, heritable dimensions that comprise a fast–slow life history.

Figure 5.6 (cont.)

SS = Sensory Sensitivity; AC = Activity; PE = Perseveration; BR = Briskness; EN = Endurance; ER = Emotional Reactivity; PTS = the Pavlovian Temperament Survey; SE = Strength of Excitation; SI = Strength of Inhibition; MO = Mobility; BA = Balance; L-CAT = the Linguistic-Colour Association Test.

Zawadzki and Strelau (2010) examined the GFP in the structure of six Polish-language inventories (32 scales, including NEO-FFI, EPQ-R, EAS-TS, PTS, and FCB-TI) and found the GFP to be most saturated by temperament traits located within Neuroticism and Extraversion. The results of their study suggested that arousability is the pivotal biological mechanism for these traits (and the GFP), and that above this, the GFP may primarily reflect only a classification of basic dimensions of personality, based on their shared variances, which it is not useful to reduce to one general factor.

PLS (also called projection on latent structures) regression analysis was also used in the present study to predict linguistic-colour synaesthetic associations from a set of independent variables assessed with the use of personality and temperament inventories such as NEO-FFI, EAS-TS, FCB-TI, and PTS. PLS is a recent technique that combines features from, and generalizes, principal-components analysis (PCA) and multiple linear regression. It originated in the social sciences with Wold (1966). Diagnostic PLS tools based on score and loadings plots allow better understanding of data structure, observing existing relations among data sets but also detecting outliers in the measured data.

Prediction is achieved by extracting from the predictors a set of orthogonal factors called *latent* variables which have the best predictive power (Abdi, 2003). Moreover, PLS balances the two objectives of explaining both response and predictor variation. PLS, by using a cross-validation procedure, could fit the model to part of the data and minimize the prediction error for the unfitted part. This is a useful multivariate technique in the social sciences for non-experimental data. Moreover, PLS is a particularly useful alternative to the linear multiple regression model when the number of predictors is relatively high as compared with the number of observations, and the X-variables are correlated (Abdi, 2010). Because these problems concern the present data, the PLS seems to be the best alternative for examining the regression model here, instead of a common linear regression model, which is in this case inappropriate.

The initial intercorrelation analysis was performed separately for the samples of synaesthetes ($n = 8$) and non-synaesthetes ($n = 71$). As Tables B5.6 and B5.7 in Appendix B show, numerous scales of personality and temperament were correlated with each other. Because the present study was of an explorative character, there was no assumption concerning the number of latent variables that may be the most useful to explain synaesthesia. Thus, a non-linear iterative partial least squares (NIPALS) algorithm was performed, which is the most commonly used to compute the first few components in a PLS analysis.

Table 5.1 *Variance of* X *and* Y *explained by the latent vectors and* Q^2 *in synaesthetes* (n = *8)*

Latent vector	R^2X	Total R^2X	Eigen-value	R^2Y	Total R^2Y	Q^2	Boun-dary	Total Q^2	Signif-icance	Iteracy
1	.52	.52	9.03	.63	.63	0.11	.00	0.11	Yes	1
2	.19	.71	3.28	.26	.89	0.33	.01	0.40	Yes	1
3	.07	.78	1.32	.10	.89	−0.43	.02	0.15	Yes	1
4	.09	.87	1.31	.01	.99	−0.36	.03	−0.16	Yes	1

This analysis revealed that four latent variables accounted together for 87% of the variance of linguistic-colour synaesthetic associations. They also accounted for 99% of the variance of individual differences in both personality and temperament traits (see Table 5.1). The most important variables for the model included extraversion, agreeableness, anger, conscientiousness, and briskness, whereas the less important variables were SS, strength of inhibition, activity, endurance, and openness to experiences (see Figure 5.7).

The results of the PLS regression analysis are shown in Tables 5.1 and 5.2, Figure 5.8, and Plate 8. The most important latent variables for linguistic-colour synaesthesia (explaining 52% of variance), as well as for individual differences in personality and temperament (explaining 63%), was the first component (sociability), which included extraversion, agreeableness, sociability, and activity as primary factors. The second latent variable (arousability or sensation seeking) comprised strength of excitation, endurance, perseveration, and activity. This latent variable is more predictive of dimensions of temperament (accounting for 26% of variance) than for synaesthesia (19%). The third unobserved latent variable (emotionality) was related to neuroticism, ER, distress, sensory sensitivity, briskness, and conscientiousness (explaining 7% of synaesthesia and 10% of individual differences). The last latent variable (disinhibition) pertained mostly to the PTS scales, such as strength of inhibition, balance, and mobility of the nervous system processes, and also anger, fear, and openness to experiences (together accounting for 9% of synaesthesia variability and 1% of both temperament and personality).

However, when PLS regression analysis was conducted on the non-synaesthete sample ($n = 71$), only one latent factor was extracted. Thus, the hierarchical model of individual differences in personality and temperament does not seem to be appropriate for explaining the variability of total L-CAT in non-synaesthetes.

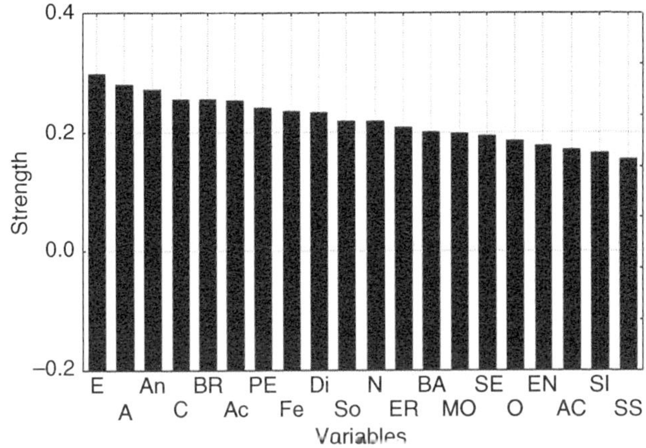

Figure 5.7 Variable importance for the PLS regression model. *Note:* NEO-FFI = the Neuroticism Extraversion Openness Five-Factor Inventory; N = Neuroticism; E = Extraversion; O = Openness; A = Agreeableness; C = Conscientiousness; EAS-TS = the Emotionality-Activity-Sociability Temperament Survey; Di = Distress; Fe = Fear; An = Anger; Ac = Activity; So = Sociability; FCB-TI = Formal Characteristics of Behaviour – Temperament Inventory; SS = Sensory Sensitivity; AC = Activity; PE = Perseveration; BR = Briskness; EN = Endurance; ER = Emotional Reactivity; PTS = the Pavlovian Temperament Survey; SE = Strength of Excitation; SI = Strength of Inhibition; MO = Mobility; BA = Balance.

As the correlation analysis implied, stronger synaesthetes tended to display heightened negative emotionality, as demonstrated in frequent and intense experiencing of anger, and also in a higher but non-significant degree of both fear and distress. According to some research (Royce and Diamond, 1980), high excitability may be negatively related to emotional stability. Negative emotionality involves individual differences in arousability of fear and frustration, and is related to both internalizing and externalizing problems (Rothbart and Bates, 1998). Self-regulation processes modulate emotionality, facilitating or inhibiting affective responses, and include attention, inhibitory control, and impulsivity (Goldsmith and Rothbart, 1991). However, inhibitory control seems to be particularly relevant to the regulation of emotion-related physiological processes, internal emotional states, and emotion-related behaviours (Lengua, Long, Smith, and Meltzoff, 2005).

In the present study, the sample of linguistic-colour synaesthetes also demonstrated heightened extraversion and activity (mean sten scores of 7) and low SS (mean sten scores of 4) and ER (mean sten scores of 3), due

Table 5.2 *Loadings and weights of four upper-level latent variables extracted from the lower-level response variables by PLS regression procedure*

	Loadings				Weights			
Variables	1	2	3	4	1	2	3	4
NEO-FFI								
Neuroticism	**−.29**	.08	**.29**	−.19	−.22	.19	.27	−.07
Extraversion	**.29**	.05	.23	.00	.34	.15	.2	.12
Openness	.10	−.38	.33	**−.45**	−.03	−.33	.14	−.54
Agreeableness	**.27**	.21	−.10	.01	.33	.16	−.14	−.11
Conscientiousness	.27	−.05	**.29**	.07	.29	.07	.31	.06
EAS-TS								
Distress	−.30	−.02	**.33**	−.15	−.26	.11	.31	−.05
Fear	−.28	−.07	.19	**−.36**	−.29	−.02	.13	−.18
Anger	−.30	−.07	−.14	**.33**	−.33	−.09	−.05	.24
Activity	−.09	**−.45**	.42	.10	−.20	.28	.45	.08
Sociability	**.28**	.03	−.19	.02	.27	−.02	−.13	.16
FCB-TI								
Sensory Sensitivity	.21	−.20	**.24**	−.01	.16	−.13	.17	−.21
Activity	**.23**	−.30	.06	.04	.12	−.28	.05	−.01
Perseveration	−.14	**.38**	.12	.21	.04	.45	.18	.18
Briskness	.24	−.14	**.49**	.10	.26	.04	.47	−.06
Endurance	.24	**−.32**	.06	−.16	.13	−.29	.08	.06
Emotional Reactivity	**−.27**	.21	**.27**	−.12	−.15	.30	.24	−.10
PTS								
Strength of Excitation	.23	**−.37**	.05	−.06	.10	−.34	.07	.06
Strength of Inhibition	.23	−.09	.08	**−.49**	.19	−.10	−.03	−.29
Mobility	.27	−.18	.00	**.29**	.22	−.14	.13	.36
Balance	−.04	−.34	−.05	**.62**	−.15	−.29	.12	.49

Notes: NEO-FFI: Neuroticism Extraversion Openness Five-Factor Inventory; EAS-TS = Emotionality-Activity-Sociability Temperament Survey; FCB-TI = Formal Characteristics of Behaviour – Temperament Inventory; PTS = Pavlovian Temperament Survey. Boldface values indicate the strongest loadings of the variable on the factor.

to the average level (sten scores of 5–6) of SE, SI, and mobility. In Gray's (1964) arousability postulate, the strong type of nervous system and low arousability are features of the extravert, while the weak type of nervous system and high arousability characterize the introvert. Moreover, the strength of the nervous system has a negative correlation with sensitivity, according to Tieplov's conception of temperament (Kustubayeva, 2010). Eysenck's (1967) theory postulates that extraverted patterns of behaviour develop according to slow and relatively weak excitatory processes, whereas introverted patterns of behaviour develop due to strong excitatory processes (Eysenck and Eysenck, 1964). Generally, extraverts tend to be under-aroused, and

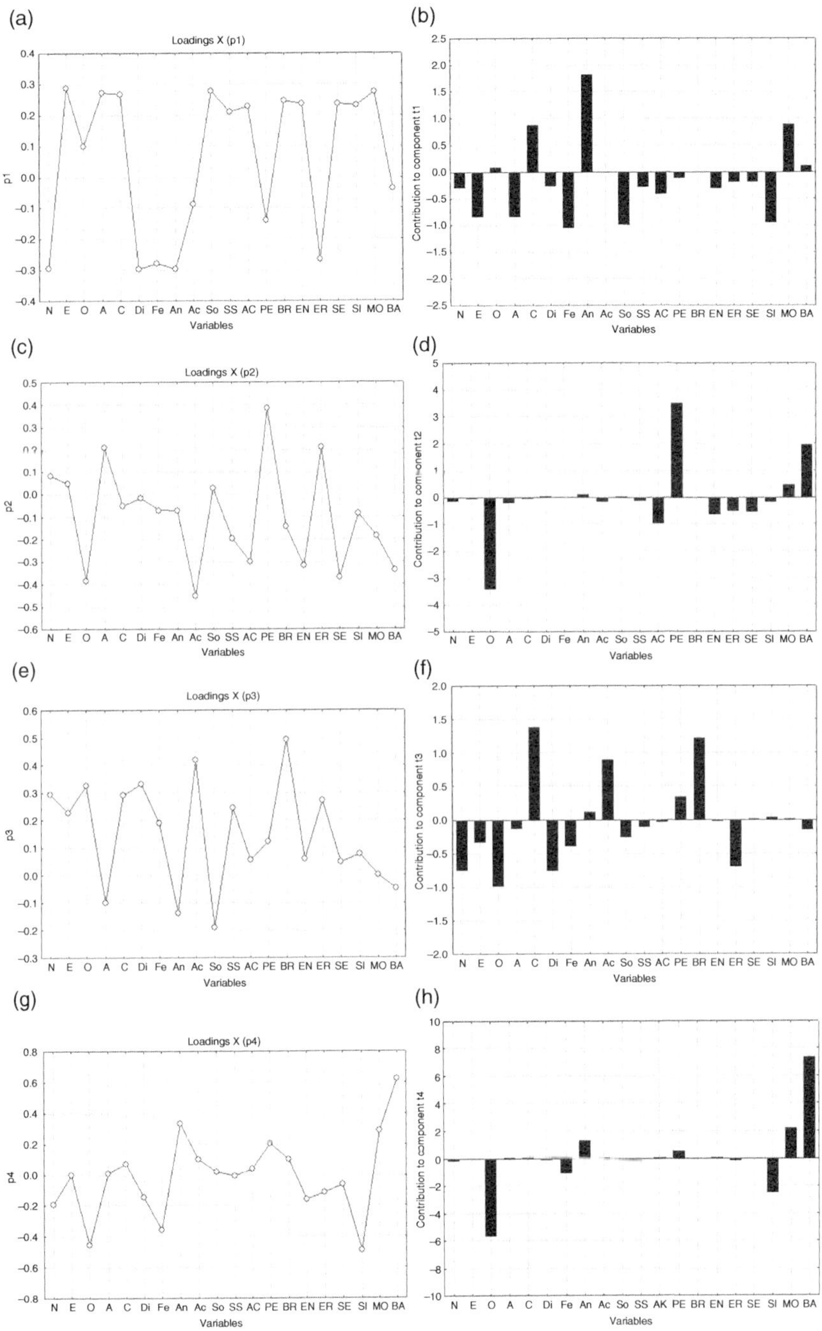

Figure 5.8 Factor loadings of *X*: (a) p1, (c) p2, (e) p3, and (g) p4; and contributions to components: (b) t1, (d) t2, (f) t3, and (h) t4. *Note*: t1, t2, t3, and t4 are the score vectors; p1, p2, p3, and p4 are the loading vectors. NEO-FFI = the Neuroticism Extraversion Openness Five-Factor Inventory; N = Neuroticism; E = Extraversion; O = Openness; A = Agreeableness; C = Conscientiousness; EAS-TS =

thus seek maximum stimulation from the environment. They are very excitable, but an excess of excitation is quickly altered into protective inhibition. On the other hand, introverts are already over-aroused and seek to minimize external stimulation.

Buss and Plomin (1975) suggested that the initial parameters of temperament characteristics are modified by the individual's interactions with environmental stimulation and learning. According to the regulative theory of temperament (Strelau, 1996, 1998), people regulate arousal in order to attain or maintain its optimal level. High-reactive individuals (high sensitivity and low endurance) demonstrate low levels of activity, while low-reactive individuals (low sensitivity and high endurance) show high levels of activity. In general, low reactives prefer situations of high stimulative value and may be characterized as sensation-seekers, sociable, fast decision-makers, and impulsive as compared with high reactives. On the other hand, high reactives prefer situations of low stimulative value and appear to be sensation-controllers or reducers, slow decision-makers, and inhibited as compared to low reactives.

In the present study, synaesthetes demonstrated high levels of extraversion, but also quite high levels of both excitation and negative emotionality. Because extraversion is connected with a high need of acceptance in highly social individuals, it is most likely that synaesthetes developed protective inhibition that even predominated over the excitation level. Protective inhibition usually develops in response to very strong stimulation. However, it may be difficult to maintain the height level of inhibition in this way in their configuration of both personality and temperament traits; thus, synaesthetes may be more prone to disinhibition.

Disinhibition is the opposite of inhibition, which is conscious or unconscious restraint of a behavioural process, desire, or impulse. Disinhibition refers to a temporary state of reduced control over one's behaviours, impulses, attention, and emotions, usually caused by an outside stimulus such as substance use (alcohol or a drug), traumatic brain injury, or psychiatric disorders. Individuals who show disinhibited behaviour

---

Figure 5.8 cont.

Emotionality-Activity-Sociability Temperament Survey; Di = Distress; Fe = Fear; An = Anger; Ac = Activity; So = Sociability; FCB-TI = Formal Characteristics of Behaviour – Temperament Inventory; SS = Sensory Sensitivity; AC = Activity; PE = Perseveration; BR = Briskness; EN = Endurance; ER = Emotional Reactivity; PTS = Pavlovian Temperament Survey; SE = Strength of Excitation; SI = Strength of Inhibition; MO = Mobility; BA = Balance.

display a tendency to show verbal aggression, physical aggression, socially inappropriate behaviour, sexual disinhibition, wandering, and repetitive behaviour. Disinhibition may be manifested in several ways on the behavioural level, including disregard for social conventions, violent tendencies, impulsivity, and poor risk assessment.

According to Pavlovian classical conditioning, disinhibition describes the fundamental process of associative learning. Disinhibition is a temporary increase in the strength of an extinguished response due to an unrelated stimulus effect. Pavlov suggested specific types of higher nervous systems based on the development of the first and second signal systems: (1) artists with prevalence of the first signal system; (2) thinkers with the prevalence of the second signal system; (3) the middle, or mixed type with equal proportions and activity of both signals (Kustubayeva, 2010). The first signal system is a system of response to immediate objects. The second signal system depends on the mediation of signals of the second order – namely, the primary signals in the form of words (spoken, heard, seen), thoughts, abstractions, and generalizations. Conditioned reflexes play a significant role in both signal systems.

According to Pavlov's concept (1941), the second signalling system is the highest regulator of human behaviour. However, weakness of the second signalling system and of the emotional background may occur in artistic types in the form of fantasies with unrestrained motivation and disturbance of the general nervous system, such as hysteria or neurosis. On the other hand, a general weakness in the first signal in the thinking type, on the basis of emotions, may result in a lack of grasp of reality, complete incapability and uselessness, ideas of compulsion, phobias, and constant, distorted melancholy. Generally, constitutional neurasthenia is the effect of a weakness in the middle type, hysteria is the result of general weakness in the artistic type, and psychasthenia is a product of weakness in the thinking type. The excitable type corresponds to the manic-depressive psychoses, whereas generally the weak type is connected with schizophrenia.

In this view, linguistic-colour synaesthesia may be seen as an effect of a poor process of differentiating a second-order signal during language acquisition in a person representing a strong artistic type of nervous system processes as well as either an unbalanced person with a predominance of excitatory process or labile inhibitory process. In a strongly unbalanced person, in whom excitation distinctly prevails over inhibition, positive conditioned reflexes develop with relative ease, but inhibitory conditioned reflexes develop with great difficulty and require long conditioning (Pavlov, 1941). The differentiating reflex is not always complete and is easily disinhibited. Higher nervous activity caused by pronounced inhibition is difficult and often impossible, since a conflict arises between the weakened process of inhibition and the greatly intensified process of excitation.

Linguistic-colour synaesthetes demonstrated a relatively high level of excitation in the present study. This is confirmed by the findings of previous research (Terhune *et al.*, 2011) using transcranial magnetic stimulation. It indicates that grapheme-colour synaesthesia is characterized by enhanced cortical excitability in the primary visual cortex. These results indicate that hyperexcitability acts as a source of noise in the visual cortex that influences the availability of neuronal signals underlying the awareness of synaesthetic photisms.

Hyperexcitability also seems to explain numerous cases of acquired and drug-induced synaesthesia (Afra *et al.*, 2009). For example, acute visual deprivation (by blindfolding) causes cortical enhanced excitability in specific brain regions of visual modality, which in some individuals may induce synaesthetic experiences. When synaesthesia occurs as a result of neuropathological insult to the anterior optic pathways, the imbalance between the excitation and inhibition could result in increased excitability in the surrounding deafferented area. The reorganization of the brain and change in weight of synaptic neurons can produce synaesthetic experience in some cases.

In addition, the mechanism of hallucinogenic (e.g., LSD) drug-induced synaesthesia has been attributed to chemical deafferentation through serotonin mediation, which causes deprivation of the occipital cortex of visual stimuli (Brang and Ramachandran, 2008). Similarly to the disinhibited feedback theory (DFT) (Grossenbacher and Lovelace, 2001) of synaesthesia, when the activity of an inhibitory neurotransmitter is decreased, the next neuron in the chain is freed from inhibition and becomes more active (Sinke *et al.*, 2012). The explanation of the actions of LSD and other hallucinogens by their disinhibition of serotonergic systems may also be useful in the control of sensation, sleep, attention, and mood. The cases of acquired and drug-induced synaesthesia seem necessary for the complete explanation of congenital synaesthesia, since both types of synaesthesia may share the compensatory mechanism of arousal (Rogowska, 2011).

On the other hand, taking into consideration the low SS of the examined synaesthetes, an alternative explanation for the results obtained is that linguistic-colour synaesthesia may be the result of the dominant process of a second-order signal in a person, representing a strong thinking type of nervous system processes and an unbalanced nervous system with a predominance of either inhibitory processes or labile excitatory processes. Pavlov (1941) suggested that the predominance of inhibition may lead to involuntary sleep and many phases of hypnosis. The paradoxical and ultra-paradoxical phases in the latter state may involve many pathological symptoms, including narcolepsy, cataplexy, catalepsy, and catatonia. The weakness of the excitatory process is produced either by its strain or by its collision with the inhibitory process.

Zingrone *et al.* (2009) reported that individuals who claimed to be 'aura viewers' reported a higher frequency of synaesthesia-like experiences as well as other seemingly psychic, mystical, and lucid dream experiences. In the explanation of the synaesthetic process (Zingrone *et al.*, 2009), acquisition of information about another person may be transformed into a hallucination of light or an 'energy' field. Moreover, other findings (Terhune *et al.*, 2010) demonstrate that the conscious experience of synaesthesia can be temporarily abolished by cognitive control – namely, by post-hypnotic suggestion in highly suggestible face-colour synaesthetes.

Furthermore, Cohen Kadosh, Henik, Catena, *et al.* (2009) showed that post-hypnotic suggestion induces abnormal cross-modal experiences similar to those observed in congenital grapheme-colour synaesthesia. They concluded that synaesthetic experience may be induced by disinhibition of signals within or between brain areas (the disinhibition-unmasking hypothesis; Cohen Kadosh and Henik, 2007; Cohen Kadosh and Walsh, 2008). Because hypnosis affects the level of inhibition, decreased inhibitory effects via the modulation of top-down processes might be the mechanism behind synaesthesia (Cohen Kadosh and Henik, 2007).

The DFT was proposed for the first time by Grossenbacher and Lovelace (2001). According to this theory, synaesthesia is entirely mediated by neural connections that exist in normal adult human brains; it emphasizes limbic mediation and cortical depression instead of cortical mediation. This functional concept of synaesthesia mechanisms presumes that the feed-forward origins of synaesthetic induction lead to feedback activation of the concurrent representation. The synaesthetic induction can originate in feed-forward signals from the inducer representation, and it may culminate in an activation of the concurrent representation through feedback signals by virtue of convergence between the inducer and concurrent pathways (Grossenbacher and Lovelace, 2001). Synaesthesia may use the same (or an analogous) mechanism of exogenous cross-modal orientation as normal perception (Ward, Huckstep, and Tsakanikos, 2006). Bargary and Mitchell (2008) reviewed the evidence that developmental synaesthesia is most likely mediated by direct, feed-forward connections between adjacent areas.

The correlation analysis on the sample of synaesthetes in the present sample indicated that the strength of inhibition increases alongside decreasing scores of linguistic-colour synaesthesia; however, on an insufficient level of significance ($r = .42, p > .05$). The results of the correlation may suggest that stronger linguistic-colour synaesthetes demonstrate a tendency to a weaker inhibition of the nervous process. However, the PLS regression model, which involved an interaction between all variables, indicated that stronger synaesthetes represented rather a lower tendency to display predominating excitation over inhibition. Nevertheless, this unbalanced dominancy of excitatory processes seems to be linked with heightened anger (lower fear). In general, synaesthetes may experience hyperexcitability, which must be strongly inhibited in order to preserve the balance of nervous system processes. Because the strength of excitation is positively correlated with the mobility of nervous processes in the sample of synaesthetes ($r = .82, p < .05$), highly excitable synaesthetes also showed heightened mobility. This continuous conversion of excitation into inhibition could provide the nervous system of synaesthetes with frequent states of disinhibition.

The unstable inhibition of the nervous processes in childhood may facilitate synaesthesia arising in critical periods of life (e.g., during acquisition of reading and writing in the case of linguistic synaesthesia), and can help to support synaesthesia in later life. Although synaesthesia seems to be relatively consistent over time, many synaesthetes report that synaesthetic associations increase or decrease during adolescence and adulthood (see Section 2.1.2, for more details).

Meier and Rothen (2007) found that a group of 13 grapheme-colour synaesthetes, but not a control group, showed a startle in their response to a colour-inducing grapheme after a startle response was conditioned to the specific corresponding colour. When the startle response was associated with the real colour, an association between shock and the grapheme was also established. The conditioned response to the real colour was generalized to the synaesthetic colour on the basis of an implicit cross-activation mechanism. This evidence suggests that bidirectional cross-activation occurred in digit-colour synaesthetes at an implicit level. These results were consistent with previous studies that found implicit activations in number-colour synaesthesia (e.g., Cohen Kadosh *et al.*, 2005; Cohen Kadosh and Henik, 2006; Simner and Hubbard, 2006).

However, conditioning seems insufficient to induce synaesthetic associations in non-synaesthetes. In a more recent study (Meier and Rothen, 2009), 20 non-synaesthetes were trained for 10 minutes on 7 consecutive days to associate four different letters with four specific colours. After

1 week of training, the synaesthetic Stroop test and the synaesthetic conditioning test were administered, and there was no evidence of a conditioned synaesthetic response as measured by a skin conductance response in the synaesthetic conditioning test, whereas the synaesthetic Stroop effect was elicited. Because the synaesthetic Stroop effect is not unique to true synaesthetes, it could not be used as a single test for diagnosing synaesthesia. Nevertheless, these results suggest that, although conditioning seems to be the most likely mechanism for the arising of synaesthesia, some special predispositions (e.g., traits of nervous system processes that may be measured by using the neuroscience method as well as by application of psychological questionnaires and tests) or some (as yet unknown) circumstances are necessary in order for a person to become a synaesthete.

This report is the first investigation of the interrelationships between linguistic-colour synaesthetic associations and traits of personality and temperament. The study has indicated that the synaesthetic trait may be (at least in some way) connected with personality and temperament. However, the small study sample size was a limitation to the interpretation and confidence levels of the results obtained. The preliminary character of the current analysis may encourage other researchers to undertake their own studies on relationships between various types of synaesthesia and other dimensions of individual differences. This kind of research seems necessary in order to better understand the phenotype of individual differences in synaesthesia and to explain its neurocognitive mechanisms.

General conclusions

The present study seems to indicate that consistency of linguistic-colour synaesthesia is a continuous variable, with weaker and stronger abstract forms of associations. Individual differences between linguistic-colour synaesthetes refer to the strength of synaesthesia (measured by consistency of linguistic-colour associations), as well as to various categories of linguistic inducers (e.g., numbers, letters of the alphabet, forenames, days). Thus, a range of consistent linguistic-colour associations seems to be the best measure of strength of linguistic-colour associations.

However, the L-CAT reveals that a range of consistent concrete word-colour associations, such as fruit-colour (e.g., lemon-yellow), did not differ between synaesthetes and non-synaesthetes. Thus, the analysis of differences between synaesthetic and non-synaesthetic word-colour associations by neuroimaging methods could help to resolve problems with describing features that can distinguish between synaesthetic and non-synaesthetic associations. This problem seems to have a key meaning for the definition and understanding of the nature of synaesthesia. Similar to cross-modal perception, synaesthesia seems to be a kind of tacit knowledge. Thus, future research on synaesthetic mechanisms should take into consideration environmental factors as well as biological factors. Memory and learning processes seem to play an important role in the origination of synaesthesia.

Identification of synaesthetes within the general population seems to be one of the most difficult problems in the current view. If consistency of synaesthetic associations is a continuous variable, with normal distribution, the question arises as to how far from the mean we can identify synaesthesia. Is the answer the first, the second, or only the third standard deviation from the mean? Usually, 80–100% of test–retest consistency was sufficient to identify synaesthesia. However, every arbitrary decision seems inappropriate. The other open question is, if a subject uses memory strategies to remember these associations, how can we identify it and distinguish a synaesthete from an excellent mnemonist? To minimize type 1 and type 2 errors, the present study proposed to use both kinds of assessment of synaesthesia: a self-report subjective view and objective experimental testing (e.g., test–retest consistency of associations or a modified Stroop test).

The present study suggests that linguistic-colour synaesthesia may be associated with a specific cerebral organization or processing. There seems to be a greater likelihood of linguistic-colour synaesthesia occurring in lateralized men and one-sided women. Moreover, linguistic-colour synaesthetes more frequently experienced headaches or migraine than non-synaesthetes. As the regression analysis indicated, linguistic-colour synaesthesia may be related to weaker functioning of the sensorimotor cortex (in touch and movement perception). Future research should rely on neuroimaging methods for the confirmation and verification of the present findings and hypothesis.

Linguistic-colour synaesthetes also have some other contrasting characteristics when compared to non-synaesthetes. Linguistic-colour synaesthetes outperformed non-synaesthetes in attention, absorption, imagination, and memory. They also revealed heightened excitation, negative emotionality (especially in anger), heightened extraversion and activity, and low SS and ER, as compared to non-synaesthetes. Stronger linguistic-colour synaesthetes seemed to demonstrate a tendency to a weaker inhibition of the nervous process, which may be consistent with disinhibited feedback theory.

Linguistic-colour synaesthesia seems not to be directly connected with either creativity or intelligence as measured by non-verbal tests. Moreover, the present study did not find strong evidence that linguistic-colour synaesthesia is related to emotional intelligence or specific types of mentality. However, as latent higher-level variables, intelligence, openness, and mentality may be connected with linguistic-colour associations.

In the present study, linguistic-colour synaesthesia was considered as a trait in the wide context of individual differences. As the current result suggests, probably people are more or less prone to synaesthesia in general, and they revealed particular types and categories of synaesthesia with distinct strength. Like many other traits, synaesthesia may depend on many factors, such as genes, personality, absorption, type of nervous system (temperament), and serotonin distribution. Environmental factors and learning processes may determine the final form of synaesthetic associations. As suggested here, some problems with the mental organization of cognitive processes in the early stage of development may provide congenital (developmental) synaesthesia, whereas some other problems with the reorganization of cognitive systems may affect other types of synaesthesia in adulthood (e.g., acquired, narcotic, virtual, temporary).

The present result did not provide strong evidence for most of the questions. Instead, new possibilities for explaining the phenomenon of synaesthesia were explored here. Further research about relationships between individual differences and synaesthesia is necessary, using a larger sample of participants, which should also be more representative of the general population. For a complete understanding of linguistic-colour synaesthesia, future research should also include other types, kinds, categories, and forms of synaesthesia. One of the most important objectives for an explanation of the nature of synaesthesia is to find what is common to all types (e.g., neonatal, congenital, acquired, temporary) and forms (e.g., linguistic-colour, mirror-touch, time-space) of synaesthesia, and the ways in which they differ from each other. This research seems to be helpful in explaining synaesthetic perception, as well as non-synaesthetic cognitive processes, in the areas of genetics, evolutionary psychology, developmental psychology, cognitive neuroscience, and personality and linguistics.

Appendix A Participants

The subjects were 161 students of the Opole University of Technology, a large public university in southern Poland. Of the students, 82 were women (51%) and 79 were men (49%); the average age was 23 years (ranged between 20 and 44 years, $M = 22.67$; $SD = 2.40$). Participants represented second-year undergraduate students of two faculties: Physiotherapy (51%) and Physical Education (49%).

The total sample of 161 participants consisted of two groups with regard to both the faculty and test–retest procedure for linguistic-colour associations (the L-CAT):

- Sample A consisted of 82 students of physiotherapy, including 58 women (71%), aged between 21 and 29 years ($M = 22.52$, $SD = 1.18$); the L-CAT retest was conducted during the same session, immediately after the test. Among the participants, 11 were considered linguistic-colour synaesthetes as determined with the L-CAT and the SAQ, including the following single types of synaesthesia: four forename-colour (FC), two day-colour (DC), and two number-colour (NC). There were also three double types: FC with grapheme-colour (GC), FC with DC, and NC with GC.
- Sample B consisted of 79 students of physical education, including 24 women (30%) aged between 20 and 44 years ($M = 22.82$, $SD = 3.22$); the L-CAT retest was performed during the other session, 1 month after the test. Sample B included eight linguistic-colour synaesthetes, including three FC and three DC single types, one double type DC with GC, and one multiple type who combined FC, DC, NC, and GC.

The L-CAT was conducted in a computer laboratory in groups of up to 10 participants in one session. The other tests and self-administered questionnaires were distributed in the second session, during class hours, in groups of up to 30 participants in one classroom, with the agreement of their professors to participate.

However, not all subjects completed all of the tests and questionnaires (some data were missing), and some of the students were absent during the second session. Thus, in the study described in Chapter 2 of the present book, only 141 students of the total sample (including 73 students from Sample A, 52%; and 74 women, 52%) completed both the L-CAT and the SAQ. In Chapter 3, the participants were 74 students of Sample A, including 54 women (73%), who completed all tests and questionnaires (including the L-CAT, the d2 Test of Attention, the TAS, the II, the BVRT, and the WLRT). In the study described in Chapter 4, 79 students from Sample A (including 57 women, 72%) participated. Finally, in Chapter 5, 79 subjects from Sample A participated; participation also ranged from 73 to 79 subjects of the total of Sample B, depending on the test.

All of the students were white Polish and native speakers of Polish. Participation in the study was voluntary, anonymous, and confidential. The study was approved by the Bioethics Committee of the Opole Medical Chamber.

Appendix B Tables

Table B1.1 *Differences in the colour consistency of linguistic associations between two samples representing distinct test–retest intervals*

	Procedure						
	Retest 1 month later Sample B (n = 79)			Retest immediately Sample A (n = 82)			
Scales of the L-CAT	*M (SD)*	*MS*	K–S *D*	*M (SD)*	*MS*	K–S *D*	*t (df)*
Test–retest consistency of linguistic-colour associations							
Colours	14.42 (6.86)	46.71	.07	10.01 (5.12)	26.19	.08	4.65 (159)***
Fruits	20.47 (8.11)	65.72	.14	13.71 (5.95)	35.39	.10	6.04 (159)***
Verbs	54.88 (27.41)	751.15	.08	32.61 (21.69)	470.51	.10	5.71 (158)***
Adjectives	39.96 (24.57)	603.83	.06	19.51 (14.45)	208.92	.12	6.37 (154)***
Days	67.31 (33.30)	1,109.10	.11	42.58 (28.29)	800.52	.13	4.64 (132)***
Months and Seasons	37.52 (20.13)	405.34	.12	26.01 (11.81)	139.39	.10	4.44 (158)***
Forenames	54.24 (32.11)	1,030.91	.13	28.15 (22.44)	503.65	.15	5.64 (140)***
Pseudowords	72.69 (41.67)	1,736.62	.13	35.51 (27.93)	779.93	.11	5.43 (106)***
Numbers	67.33 (31.52)	993.37	.13	37.92 (26.73)	714.32	.14	5.86 (133)***
Alphabet	67.66 (35.19)	1,238.31	.10	36.28 (28.41)	807.17	.10	5.66 (130)***
Total	46.23 (20.15)	406.19	.11	27.49 (14.53)	211.27	.16*	6.79 (159)***
VCD	10.47 (18.56)	344.51	.32**	8.58 (16.00)	255.88	.34**	

Table B1.1 *(cont.)*

	Procedure						
	Retest 1 month later Sample B ($n = 79$)			Retest immediately Sample A ($n = 82$)			
Scales of the L-CAT	*M (SD)*	*MS*	K–S *D*	*M (SD)*	*MS*	K–S *D*	*t (df)*
Mean RT(s) of linguistic-colour associations							
Colours	66.58 (41.03)	1,683.68	.11	83.61 (35.69)	1,273.60	.06	−2.81 (159)**
Fruits	68.27 (39.70)	1,575.74	.09	85.24 (36.30)	1,317.96	.07	−2.83 (159)**
Verbs	53.72 (31.57)	996.92	.12	64.55 (27.42)	751.63	.07	−2.33 (159)*
Adjectives	47.03 (26.00)	676.02	.11	56.84 (23.11)	534.16	.07	−2.53 (159)*
Days	40.85 (23.40)	547.72	.11	49.35 (20.80)	432.65	.07	−2.44 (159)*
Months and Seasons	40.48 (21.61)	466.79	.08	52.24 (22.78)	519.03	.17*	
Forenames	38.92 (23.08)	532.87	.09	44.55 (17.54)	307.66	.06	−1.85 (159)
Pseudowords	34.75 (20.93)	438.04	.10	40.85 (19.07)	363.56	.12	−1.94 (159)
Numbers	40.19 (22.73)	516.67	.10	49.63 (23.12)	534.61	.09	−2.61 (159)*
Alphabet	9.71 (6.25)	39.06	.23**	9.77 (3.74)	13.98	.12	
Total	37.82 (18.38)	337.76	.09	45.74 (15.02)	225.67	.09	−3.00 (159)**
VCD	20.95 (6.45)	41.66	.12	22.45 (7.74)	59.83	.10	−1.34 (159)

Notes: $^{*}p < .05$, $^{**}p < .01$, $^{***}p < .001$. L-CAT = Linguistic-Colour Association Test; VCD = Visual Colour Discrimination training subtest.

Table B1.2 *Descriptive statistics for the colour consistency of linguistic associations*

Scales of the L-CAT	1	2	3	4	5	6	7	8	9	10	11
Items within scale	10	10	10	10	10	16	10	10	14	35	135
n	161	161	160	156	134	160	142	108	135	132	161
K–S *D*	.05	.08	.06	.08	.06	.08	.05	.09	.07	.06	.04
Cronbach's α	.31	.49	.53	.66	.59	.73	.64	.56	.68	.90	.89
1. Colours		−.01	.07	−.06	.19	−.14	.11	.15	.23*	.21*	.30**
2. Fruits			.11	.20	.14	.07	.20	.12	.23*	.19	.31**
3. Verbs				.47***	.53***	.34**	.42***	.34**	.36**	.42***	.61***
4. Adjectives					.43***	.44***	.44***	.40***	.38***	.45***	.66***
5. Days						.39***	.58***	.29**	.49***	.49***	.71***
6. Months and Seasons							.33**	.30**	.27*	.30**	.59***
7. Forenames								.18	.47***	.51***	.68***
8. Pseudowords									.29**	.41***	.54***
9. Numbers										.72***	.73***
10. Alphabet											.82***
11. Total											

Notes: The table includes the names of scales, number of items on the scales, number of participants who selected colours for items within the linguistic category (*n*), Kolmogorov–Smirnov *D* statistic (K–S *D*), Cronbach's alpha and intercorrelation between scales with *r* (Pearson's coefficient) ($N = 161$, including 82 women); $^{*}p < .05$, $^{**}p < .01$, $^{***}p < .001$. A lower mean result denotes a strong and constant association over time (the same test–retest colours for the item), whereas a higher result indicates a connotation or a weak association. L-CAT = Linguistic-Colour Association Test.

Table B1.3 *Descriptive statistics for two clusters extracted with the EM algorithm*

	Complete Associators $n = 65$					Selective Associators $n = 96$					
Scales of the L-CAT	Min.	Max.	*M*	*SD*	K–S *D*	Min.	Max.	*M*	*SD*	K–S *D*	*F(df)*
Colours	−21.10	23.02	0.92	10.22	.07	−18.07	19.87	−0.72	9.53	.08	1.08(159)
Fruits	−13.29	30.71	0.83	9.33	.14	−18.11	34.80	−0.55	10.08	.07	0.07(159)
Verbs	−10.63	27.75	5.21	8.32	.06	−10.18	8.54	−1.33	3.43	.12	47.58(159)***
Adjectives	−11.15	42.85	5.75	9.90	.07	−12.74	8.28	−2.08	3.83	.06	49.18(159)***
Days	−14.07	21.60	4.00	7.74	.06	−10.18	10.98	−0.69	4.06	.22**	25.17(159)***
Months	−18.16	53.85	8.21	16.10	.08	−23.65	26.23	−3.99	9.71	.08	35.92(159)***
Forenames	−11.15	27.32	4.40	7.79	.10	−10.96	7.75	−1.17	3.11	.16*	39.77(159)***
Pseudowords	−13.67	30.36	2.66	7.32	.15	−6.07	5.53	−0.57	1.82	.25**	17.11(159)***
Numbers	−17.44	38.05	6.86	10.39	.08	−13.14	10.05	−1.21	4.28	.16*	46.42(159)***
Alphabet	−47.44	83.11	17.32	27.30	.07	−19.03	9.97	−1.75	4.37	.17**	45.25(159)***

Notes: L-CAT = Linguistic-Colour Association Test. $^{*}p < .05$, $^{**}p < .01$, $^{***}p < .001$.

Table B2.1 *Descriptive statistics for total sample of participants and for synaesthetes and non-synaesthetes in several scales of the SAQ and total L-CAT*

	Total sample $N = 141$					Synaesthetes $n = 19$		Non-synaesthetes $n = 122$		
Variables	*Min.*	*Max.*	*M*	*SD*	r_s	*M*	*SD*	*M*	*SD*	*z*
Sidedness	−9	9	5.74	3.70	−.23**	6.84	3.27	5.57	3.75	1.53
Vision defect	0	6	1.06	1.38	.06	1.16	1.50	1.05	1.37	0.25
Vision	19	45	34.58	5.18	−.05	35.95	5.52	34.37	5.12	1.33
Hearing	20	44	32.99	5.30	.05	34.63	4.89	32.73	5.33	1.39
Taste	5	18	12.55	2.84	.12	10.89	3.20	12.80	2.71	−2.31*
Smell	6	18	12.11	3.11	.00	11.47	3.63	12.20	3.03	−1.15
Touch	8	21	15.96	3.02	.23**	15.58	3.34	16.02	2.98	−0.37
Movement	2	6	4.32	1.08	.15	4.00	1.15	4.37	1.07	−1.27
Total sensing	73	151	112.50	15.24	.08	112.53	16.98	112.49	15.03	−0.02
Language	0	3	1.66	.71	−.04	1.58	.84	1.67	.69	−0.43
Face	0	9	6.99	2.00	−.02	6.95	2.46	7.00	1.93	0.43
Colour	3	9	7.15	1.63	−.07	7.95	1.31	7.02	1.64	2.26*
Inscription	2	9	6.49	1.36	−.13	6.79	1.87	6.44	1.27	0.77
Shape	3	9	6.87	1.60	.13	6.95	1.75	6.86	1.58	0.55
Total L-CAT	−80.60	241.00	16.88	55.25		−23.59	24.51	12.19	56.08	−3.76***

Notes: The table includes range (*Min.* and *Max.*), mean (*M*), standard deviation (*SD*), Spearman's correlation coefficient (r_s), and Mann–Whitney *U* test coefficient (*z*). *$p < .05$, **$p < .01$, ***$p < .001$. L-CAT = Linguistic-Colour Association Test; SAQ = Synaesthetic Association Questionnaire.

Table B3.1 *Descriptive statistics for total sample and differences between synaesthetes and non-synaesthetes in cognitive traits*

Scales	Total sample $N = 74$				Synaesthetes A $n = 11$		Non-synaesthetes A $n = 63$		
	M	*SD*	K-S *D*	r_s	*M*	*SD*	*M*	*SD*	*t* or *z*
Total L-CAT	15.71	64.10	.21**		−28.81	20.83	23.48	65.99	*−3.03***
Total VCD	8.96	16.79	.33**	.02	4.47	1.83	9.74	18.09	*−0.74*
RT (s)									
L-CAT	45.31	14.92	.10	−.09	45.27	11.01	45.32	15.57	−0.01
VCD	22.39	7.89	.11	.09	17.64	4.95	23.22	8.04	−2.22*
Total II	19.22	5.25	.09	.22	25.18	5.40	18.17	4.51	4.61***
VSI	6.65	2.88	.10	.08	9.00	3.00	6.24	2.67	3.11**
CI	2 80	1.12	.22**	.01	3.55	.93	2.67	1.11	*2.54**
EE	9.77	3.17	.12	.31**	12.64	3.78	9.27	2.80	3.49***
d2 Test									
TN	532.69	71.20	.08	.20	563.64	66.16	527.29	71.16	1.58
E	34.32	25.69	.17*	.21	27.64	25.16	35.49	25.80	*−1.48*
E %	6.38	4.47	.15	.16	5.06	4.83	6.61	4.41	−1.06
TN-E	498.36	69.02	.08	.15	536.00	75.39	491.79	66.30	2.00*
CP	197.38	40.00	.09	.10	222.09	49.58	193.06	36.88	2.28*
BVRT									
NES	1.26	2.20	.31**	−.05	1.09	1.38	1.29	2.32	*0.17*
NCS	9.45	0.85	.34**	.04	9.36	.92	9.46	0.84	*−0.31*
WLRT	52.82	28.55	.09	−.15	72.82	22.23	49.27	28.21	2.62*
AW	14.59	3.43	.08	−.10	16.45	3.14	14.26	3.39	2.00*
CW	12.41	4.16	.10	−.17	15.55	3.53	11.85	4.04	2.84**

Notes: $^{*}p < .05$, $^{**}p < .01$, $^{***}p < .001$; a non-parametric *z* test in italics. L-CAT = the Linguistic-Colour Association Test; VCD = the Visual Colour Discrimination training subtest; RT = reaction time (seconds); II = the Imagination Inventory; VSI = Vividness of Sensory Imaginings; CI = Childhood Imagination; EE = Engagement in Experiences; d2 Test = the d2 Test of Attention; TN = Total Number of Items Processed; E = Raw Score of Errors; E% = Percentage of Errors; TN-E = Total Number of Items Minus Error Scores; CP = Concentration Performance; BVRT = the Benton Visual Retention Test; NCS = Number Correct Score; NES = Number Error Score; WLRT = the Word List Recall Test; CW = Concrete Words; AW = Abstract Words.

Table B4.1 *Descriptive statistics and intercorrelations between linguistic-colour associations, creativity, intelligence, absorption, emotional intelligence, and types of mind*

Variables	*N*	*M*	*SD*	*Range*	K–S D	1	2	3	4	5	6	7	8	9	10	11	12	13	14	15	16
1. L-CAT	79	13.74	63.01	−63–241	.21**																
2. TCT-DP	75	33.09	9.16	18–57	.14	_−.01_															
3. SPM	79	51.76	7.44	0–60	.19**	_−.09_	_−.10_														
4. TAS	78	18.72	6.55	1–34	.10	_.25*_	.23*	_−.02_													
PEIQ																					
5. AEI	79	53.53	7.09	36–71	.09	_−.10_	−.10	_.24*_	.23*												
6. EEI	79	69.52	6.41	57–89	.11	_.01_	.09	_.06_	.17	.39**											
7. CEI	79	31.14	7.58	16–51	.10	_.06_	−.21	_.08_	−.01	.23	.09										
8. REI	79	30.76	6.41	17–45	.11	_.05_	−.14	_.18_	−.02	.41***	.21	.76***									
9. TEI	79	330.97	30.72	270–438	.09	_−.03_	−.12	_.17_	.14	.68***	.58***	.73***	.78***								
TMS																					
10. STP	75	13.92	4.60	0–23	.09	_−.11_	−.22	_−.10_	−.25*	−.08	−.39**	.00	−.01	−.17							
11. NTP	75	13.21	4.60	0–25	.13	_−.06_	−.06	_−.01_	−.23	−.15	.01	.24*	.13	.13	.01						
12. SFP	75	11.00	3.86	0–20	.09	_.03_	.08	_.10_	.05	.18	.05	−.03	.00	.05	−.49***	−.30*					
13. NFP	75	11.41	4.92	0–24	.09	_.05_	.11	_.00_	.37**	.07	.31**	−.14	−.06	.03	−.49***	−.55***	−.09				
14. STA	75	9.44	3.85	0–21	.09	_.02_	.30*	_.14_	.31**	.09	.28*	−.16	−.02	.08	−.63***	−.26*	.33**	.49***			
15. NTA	75	10.79	3.50	0–19	.10	_.01_	−.05	_−.11_	.12	.10	.03	−.09	.04	−.01	−.16	−.50***	.07	.52***	.26*		
16. SFA	75	13.07	4.18	0–23	.10	_.12_	−.19	_.02_	−.13	−.21	−.20	.03	−.05	−.16	.40**	.17	−.53***	−.08	−.55***	−.36**	
17. NFA	75	15.89	4.83	0–25	.07	_−.19_	−.03	_−.06_	−.23*	.03	−.07	.15	.01	.06	.29*	.39**	.13	−.71***	−.52***	−.62***	−.14

Notes: Spearman's correlation coefficient in italics; *p < .05, **p < .01, ***p < .001. L-CAT = the Linguistic-Colour Association Test; TCT-DP = Test for Creative Thinking-Drawing Production; SPM = Raven's Standard Progressive Matrices; TAS = Tellegen Absorption Scale; PEIQ = Popular Emotional Intelligence Questionnaire; AEI = Acceptation; EEI = Empathy; CEI = Controlling; REI = Reasoning; TEI = Total Emotional Intelligence; TMS = Types of Mind Scale; STP = Sensing-Thinking Preference; NTP = Intuition-Thinking Preference; SFP = Sensing-Feeling Preference; NFP = Intuition-Feeling Preference; STA = Sensing-Thinking Aversion; NTA = Intuition-Thinking Aversion; SFA = Sensing-Feeling Aversion; NFA = Intuition-Feeling Aversion.

Table B4.2 *Comparison of secondary and primary factor loadings for two models of hierarchical factor analysis with either the PAF or ML extracting method*

	PAF				ML			
Variables	g	f1	f2	f3	g	f1	f2	f3
TCT-DP	.19	.00	−.16	.23	.09	−.12	−.01	.28
Raven's SPM	.14	.11	.13	.03	.11	.14	.00	.09
TAS	.32	.24	.09	.10	.23	.13	−.10	.45
L-CAT	.06	.12	.01	−.05	.18	−.04	.13	.21
AEI	.20	.01	.56	.12	.24	.64	−.05	.00
EEI	.29	.09	.41	.17	.32	.53	.01	.16
CEI	−.12	−.12	.73	−.15	.20	.68	.10	−.30
REI	.00	−.02	.81	−.12	.25	**.73**	.01	−.13
TEI	.14	−.04	1.02	.02	.35	**.92**	.02	−.10
STP	−.53	−.14	−.11	−.44	.47	−.03	**.72**	−.02
NTP	−.36	−.37	.15	−.07	.44	.00	**.73**	−.11
SFP	.32	−.20	.02	.54	.37	−.11	**.76**	−.20
NFP	.57	.69	−.02	−.04	.38	.00	**.83**	−.36
STA	.63	.27	.00	.44	.57	.06	**.75**	.05
NTA	.39	.45	−.03	.00	.56	.03	**.72**	.10
SFA	−.43	.15	−.09	−.60	.63	.12	.67	.21
NFA	−.45	−.76	.08	.23	.60	.04	.56	.37

Notes: TCT-DP = Test for Creative Thinking-Drawing Production; SPM = Raven's Standard Progressive Matrices; TAS = Tellegen Absorption Scale; L-CAT = Linguistic-Colour Association Test; AEI = Acceptation; EEI = Empathy; CEI = Controlling; REI = Reasoning; TEI = Total Emotional Intelligence; STP = Sensing-Thinking Preference; NTP = Intuition-Thinking Preference; SFP = Sensing-Feeling Preference; NFP = Intuition-Feeling Preference; STA = Sensing-Thinking Aversion; NTA = Intuition-Thinking Aversion; SFA = Sensing-Feeling Aversion; NFA = Intuition-Feeling Aversion. Boldface values indicate the strongest loadings on the factor.

Table B5.1 *Mean (M), standard deviation (SD), and* t*-test results for the NEO-FFI scales, and Pearson's correlation* (r) *between personality and the L-CAT range of linguistic-colour associations*

	Total Sample B N = 79			Synaesthetes B n = 8			Non-synaesthetes B n = 71			
Scales	*M*	*SD*	*r*	*M*	*SD*	*r*	*M*	*SD*	*r*	*t*(77)
NEO-FFI										
Neuroticism	4.94	2.35	−.02	4.63	2.88	−.53	4.97	2.31	.01	−0.39
Extraversion	6.66	2.14	.01	6.75	1.75	.82*	6.65	2.19	−.03	0.13
Openness	4.16	1.70	−.13	4.00	2.14	−.07	4.18	1.66	−.15	−0.29
Agreeableness	5.78	1.99	−.10	6.00	2.14	.79*	5.76	1.99	−.16	0.32
Conscientiousness	6.28	2.34	−.10	7.88	2.03	.70	6.10	2.32	−.09	2.08*
Total L-CAT	13.49	46.77		−16.40	28.69		16.75	47.35		−1.93

Notes: $^{*}p < .05$. NEO-FFI = Neuroticism Extraversion Openness Five-Factor Inventory; L-CAT = Linguistic-Colour Association Test.

Table B5.2 *Mean (M), standard deviation (SD), and t-test for the EPQ-R scales, and Spearman's correlation (r_s) between personality and range of linguistic-colour associations of the L-CAT*

	Total Sample A $n = 79$			Synaesthetes A $n = 11$			Non-synaesthetes A $n = 68$			
Scales	*M*	*SD*	r_s	*M*	*SD*	r_s	*M*	*SD*	r_s	*t*(77)
EPQ-R										
Extraversion	5.81	1.91	*−.11*	7.18	1.89	*.58*	5.59	1.83	*−.07*	*2.41**
Neuroticism	5.15	2.06	*.04*	5.18	1.99	*.07*	5.15	2.08	*.03*	0.05
Psychoticism	4.19	2.03	*.00*	4.73	2.20	*.13*	4.10	2.01	*.04*	0.94
Lie Scale	5.67	2.01	*.19*	4.73	1.49	*.62**	5.32	2.05	*.11*	−1.70
Total L-CAT	13.74	63.01		−28.81	20.83		20.62	64.90		*−2.89***

Notes: Instead of the *t* test, a non-parametric Mann-Whitney *U* test was used in Extraversion and total L-CAT scales (in italics).
**p* < .05, ***p* < .01. EPQ-R = Revised Eysenck Personality Questionnaire; L-CAT = Linguistic-Colour Association Test.

Table B5.3 *Means (M), standard deviation (SD), and t-test for the EAS-TS scales, and Pearson's correlation (r) between temperament and range of linguistic-colour associations of the L-CAT*

	Total sample B $N = 77$			Synaesthetes B $n = 8$			Non-synaesthetes B $n = 69$			
Scales	*M*	*SD*	*r*	*M*	*SD*	*r*	*M*	*SD*	*r*	$t(75)$
EAS-TS										
Distress	5.92	1.97	−.05	5.38	2.20	−.61	5.99	1.95	−.04	−0.83
Fear	5.84	2.25	.05	5.63	2.50	−.69	5.87	2.24	.10	−0.29
Anger	5.70	2.41	−.15	4.88	3.40	−.79*	5.80	2.28	−.14	−1.03
Activity	6.38	2.21	−.21	7.00	1.20	−.47	6.30	2.29	−.19	0.84
Sociability	5.66	2.36	.02	5.75	2.60	.64	5.65	2.35	−.02	0.11
Total L-CAT	15.15	45.82		−16.40	28.69		18.81	46.16		−2.10*

Notes: $^{*}p < .05$. EAS-TS = Emotionality-Activity-Sociability Temperament Survey; L-CAT = Linguistic-Colour Association Test.

Table B5.4 *Means (M), standard deviation (SD), and t-test for the PTS scales, and Pearson's correlation (r) between temperament and range of linguistic-colour associations of the L-CAT*

	Total sample $n = 78$			Synaesthetes B $n = 8$			Non-synaesthetes B $n = 70$			
Scales	*M*	*SD*	*r*	*M*	*SD*	*r*	*M*	*SD*	*r*	*t*(76)
PTS										
Strength of Excitation	6.56	1.88	.08	5.75	1.98	.24	6.66	1.86	.04	−1.30
Strength of Inhibition	5.71	1.56	.06	6.38	2.26	.46	5.53	1.47	.06	1.28
Mobility	6.03	1.92	.09	5.50	2.07	.53	6.09	1.91	.04	−0.82
Balance	0.86	2.21	.03	−0.63	1.60	−.35	1.03	2.21	−.01	−2.05*
Total L-CAT	13.89	46.86		−16.40	28.69		17.35	47.42		

Notes: $^{*}p < .05$. PTS = Pavlovian Temperament Survey; L-CAT = Linguistic-Colour Association Test.

Table B5.5 *Means (M), standard deviation (SD), and t-test for the FCB-TI scales, and Pearson's correlation (r) between temperament and the L-CAT range of linguistic-colour associations*

	Total sample B $N = 73$			Synaesthetes B $n = 8$			Non-synaesthetes B $n = 65$			
Scales	*M*	*SD*	*r*	*M*	*SD*	*r*	*M*	*SD*	*r*	$t(71)$
FCB-TI										
Sensory Sensitivity	4.55	2.08	−.19	4.00	2.51	.38	4.62	2.04	−.28*	−0.79
Activity	6.14	1.97	.00	6.38	1.85	.29	6.11	1.99	−.01	0.36
Perseveration	4.95	1.79	.05	5.75	2.05	.08	4.85	1.75	.09	1.35
Briskness	5.96	1.90	−.04	6.00	1.51	.62	5.95	1.96	−.07	0.06
Endurance	5.97	1.84	−.02	5.13	2.17	.30	6.08	1.79	−.10	−1.39
Emotional Reactivity	4.03	1.85	.02	3.38	1.69	−.36	4.11	1.86	.01	−1.06
Total L-CAT	15.41	44.69		−16.40	28.69		19.33	44.89		−2.19*

Notes: $^*p < .05$. FCB-TI = Formal Characteristics of Behaviour – Temperament Inventory; L-CAT = Linguistic-Colour Association Test.

Table B5.6 *Intercorrelation among scales representing traits of personality, temperament, and synaesthesia in the sample of synaesthetes* (n = 8)

Scales	1	2	3	4	5	6	7	8	9	10	11	12	13	14	15	16	17	18	19	20
NEO-FFI																				
1. N																				
2. E	−.62																			
3. O	−.14	.27																		
4. A	−.70	.72*	−.03																	
5. C	−.67	.67	.36	.39																
EAS-TS																				
6. Di	.97***	−.60	−.03	−.79*	−.63															
7. Fe	.93***	−.64	.11	−.80*	−.63	.94***														
8. An	.61	−.85**	−.41	−.73*	−.73*	.66	.55													
9. Ac	.25	−.14	.61	−.56	.00	.43	.38	.32												
10. So	−.74*	.86**	.10	.82*	.40	−.75*	−.72*	−.73*	−.32											
FCB-TI																				
11. SS	−.54	.42	.61	.53	.51	−.52	−.48	−.52	.24	.37										
12. AC	−.64	.61	.62	.54	.40	−.57	−.52	−.51	.32	.68	.83*									
13. PE	.47	−.46	−.65	−.07	−.32	.31	.20	.36	−.41	−.49	−.22	−.61								
14. BR	−.56	.75*	.57	.49	.79*	−.47	−.57	−.64	.32	.47	.75*	.72*	−.41							

Table B5.6 (*cont.*)

Scales	1	2	3	4	5	6	7	8	9	10	11	12	13	14	15	16	17	18	19	20
15. EN	−.61	.61	.68	.22	.72*	−.52	−.36	−.68	.28	.54	.50	.66	−.76*	.61						
16. ER	.92***	−.45	−.32	−.48	−.69	.88**	.75*	.56	.07	−.56	−.61	−.65	.49	−.50	−.76*					
PTS																				
17. SE	−.67	.56	.71*	.24	.70	−.57	−.42	−.60	.36	.51	.63	.77*	−.75*	.67	.97***	−.82*				
18. SI	−.46	.60	.59	.32	.70	−.46	−.25	−.87**	−.11	.48	.35	.37	−.53	.46	.83*	−.57	.72*			
19. MO	−.85**	.59	.29	.45	.83*	−.80*	−.76*	−.58	.06	.56	.63	.65	−.40	.68	.78*	−.92***	.84*	.53		
20. BA	−.18	−.17	.04	−.17	−.12	−.05	−.17	.48	.60	−.04	.29	.43	−.19	.18	.03	−.22	.21	−.52	.28	
L-CAT	−.53	.82*	−.07	.79*	.70	−.61	−.69	−.79*	−.47	.64	.38	.29	.08	.62	.30	−.36	.24	.46	.53	−.35

Notes: *$p < .05$, **$p < .01$, ***$p < .001$. NEO-FFI = Neuroticism Extraversion Openness Five-Factor Inventory; N = Neuroticism; E = Extraversion; O = Openness; A = Agreeableness; C = Conscientiousness; EAS-TS = Emotionality-Activity-Sociability Temperament Survey; Di = Distress; Fe = Fear; An = Anger; Ac = Activity; So = Sociability; FCB-TI = Formal Characteristics of Behaviour – Temperament Inventory; SS = Sensory Sensitivity; AC = Activity; PE = Perseveration; BR = Briskness; EN = Endurance; ER = Emotional Reactivity; PTS = Pavlovian Temperament Survey; SE = Strength of Excitation; SI = Strength of Inhibition; MO = Mobility; BA = Balance; L-CAT = Linguistic-Colour Association Test.

Table B5.7 *Intercorrelation among scales representing traits of personality, temperament, and synaesthesia in the sample of non-synaesthetes (n = 71)*

Scales	1	2	3	4	5	6	7	8	9	10	11	12	13	14	15	16	17	18	19	20.
NEO-FFI																				
1. N																				
2. E	−.50***																			
3. O	.11	.02																		
4. A	−.30*	.27*	−.01																	
5. C	−.48***	.33**	.00	.20																
EAS-TS																				
6. Di	.74***	−.23	.04	−.27*	−.36**															
7. Fe	.56***	−.36**	−.14	−.15	−.47***	.60***														
8. An	.16	.14	−.05	−.26*	−.02	.45***	.12													
9. Ac	−.35**	.50***	−.17	.09	.58***	−.20	−.34**	.12												
10. So	−.48***	.65***	−.09	.10	.27*	−.18	−.28*	.08	.42**											
FCB-TI																				
11. SS	−.16	.05	.38**	.09	.08	−.06	−.14	.14	−.08	.06										
12. AC	−.47***	.65***	.05	.14	.29*	−.29*	−.18	.05	.40**	.53***	.20									
13. PE	.43***	−.15	.22	−.03	−.12	.39**	.28*	.32	−.14	−.09	.18	−.21								
14. BR	−.69***	.38**	.09	.23	.41***	−.55***	−.54***	−.20	.32*	.26*	.38**	.47***	−.25*							
15. EN	−.44***	.03	.07	.05	.28*	−.45***	−.48***	−.12	.16	.04	.26*	.09	−.28*	.55***						
16. ER	.73***	−.39**	.04	−.11	−.38**	.63***	.57***	.14	−.35**	−.40**	−.23	−.49***	.48***	−.63***	−.60***					
PTS																				
17. SE	−.46***	.27*	−.15	−.22	.22	−.29*	−.49***	.15	.29*	.31*	.04	.27*	−.49***	.47***	.49***	−.60***				
18. SI	−.19	.05	.05	.30*	.05	−.25*	−.15	−.34**	.12	−.02	.02	.03	−.20	.17	.29*	−.24	.07			
19. MO	−.65***	.52***	−.09	.18	.36**	−.45***	−.47***	−.08	.39**	.42***	.07	.44***	−.59***	.55***	.32*	−.58***	.69***	.12		
20. BA	−.27*	.26*	−.16	−.37**	.16	−.08	−.32*	.33**	.17	.27*	.02	.20	−.29*	.28*	.23	−.36**	.79***	−.56***	.50***	
L-CAT	.12	−.14	−.17	−.16	−.21	.05	.14	−.06	−.17	−.01	−.29*	−.05	.11	−.13	−.13	.06	.01	.18	−.04	−.10

Notes: *$p < .05$, **$p < .01$, ***$p < .001$. NEO-FFI = Neuroticism Extraversion Openness Five-Factor Inventory; N = Neuroticism; E = Extraversion; O = Openness; A = Agreeableness; C = Conscientiousness; EAS-TS = Emotionality-Activity-Sociability Temperament Survey; Di = Distress; Fe = Fear; An = Anger; Ac = Activity; So = Sociability; FCB-TI = Formal Characteristics of Behaviour – Temperament Inventory; SS = Sensory Sensitivity; AC = Activity; PE = Perseveration; BR = Briskness; EN = Endurance; ER = Emotional Reactivity; PTS = Pavlovian Temperament Survey; SE = Strength of Excitation; SI = Strength of Inhibition; MO = Mobility; BA = Balance; L-CAT = Linguistic-Colour Association Test.

References

Abdi, H. (2003). Partial least squares (PLS-regression). In M. Lewis-Beck, A. Bryman, and T. Futing (Eds.), *Encyclopedia for research methods for the social sciences* (pp. 792–5). Thousand Oaks, CA: Sage.

(2010). Partial least squares regression and projection on latent structure regression (PLS regression). *Wiley Interdisciplinary Reviews: Computational Statistics, 2*, 97–106.

Afra, P., Funke, M., and Matsuo, F. (2009). Acquired auditory-visual synesthesia: a window to early cross-modal sensory interactions. *Psychology Research and Behavior Management, 2*, 31–7.

Ahmadi, J., Keshtkar, M., and Pridmore, S. (2011). Methamphetamine induced synesthesia: a case report. *American Journal on Addictions, 20*(3), 306.

Allbutt, J., Ling, J., Rowley, M., and Shafiullah, M. (2011). Vividness of visual imagery and social desirable responding: correlations of the vividness of visual imagery questionnaire with the balanced inventory of desirable responding and the Marlowe-Crowne Scale. *Behavior Research Methods, 43*, 791–9.

Alstadhaug, K. B., and Benjaminsen, E. (2010). Synesthesia and migraine: case report. *BMC Neurology, 10*, 121.

Amin, M., Olu-Lafe, O., Claessen, L. E., Sobczak-Edmans, M., Ward, J., Williams, A. L., and Sagiv, N. (2011). Understanding grapheme personification: a social synaesthesia? *Journal of Neuropsychology, 5*, 255–82.

Anderson, K. J. (1990). Arousal and the inverted-U hypothesis: a critique of Neiss's 'Reconceptualizing arousal.' *Psychological Bulletin, 107*, 96–100.

Angleitner, A., and Riemann, R. (1991). What can we learn from the discussion of personality questionnaires for the construction of temperament inventories? In J. Strelau and A. Angleitner (Eds.), *Explorations in temperament: international perspectives on theory and measurement* (pp. 191–204). New York: Plenum Press.

Armel, K. C., and Ramachandran, V. S. (1999). Acquired synesthesia in retinitis pigmentosa. *Neurocase, 5*, 293–6.

Arnau, R. C., Green, B. A., Rosen, D. H., Gleaves, D. H., and Melancon, J. G. (2003). Are Jungian preferences really categorical?: an empirical investigation using taxometric analysis. *Personality and Individual Differences, 34*, 233–51.

Arteaga, C., and Poblano, A. (2008). Handedness of children determines preferential facial and eye movements related to hemispheric specialization. *Arquivos de Neuro-Psiquiatria, 66*, 488–93.

Asano, M., and Yokosawa, K. (2012). Synesthetic colors for Japanese late acquired graphemes. *Consciousness and Cognition, 21*, 983–93.

Asher, J. E., Aitken, M. R. F., Farooqi, N., Kurmani, S., and Baron-Cohen, S. (2006). Diagnosing and phenotyping visual synaesthesia: a preliminary evaluation of the Revised Test of Genuineness (TOG-R). *Cortex*, *42*, 137–46.

Asher, J. E., Lamb, J. A., Brocklebank, D., Cazier, J.-B., Maestrini, E., Addis, L., Sen, M., Baron-Cohen, S., and Monaco, A. P. (2009). A whole-genome scan and fine-mapping linkage study of auditory-visual synesthesia reveals evidence of linkage to chromosomes 2q24, 5q33, 6p12, and 12p12. *American Journal of Human Genetics*, *84*, 279–85.

Bailey, M. E. S., and Johnson, K. J. (1997). Synaesthesia: is genetic analysis feasible? In S. Baron-Cohen and J. Harrison (Eds.), *Synaesthesia: classic and contemporary readings* (pp. 182–210). Oxford: Blackwell.

Banissy, M. J., Cohen Kadosh, R., Maus, G. W., Walsh, V., and Ward, J. (2009). Prevalence, characteristics and a neurocognitive model of mirror-touch synaesthesia. *Experimental Brain Research*, *198*, 261–72.

Banissy, M. J., Garrido, L., Kusnir, F., Duchaine, B., Walsh, V., and Ward, J. (2011). Superior facial expression, but not identity recognition, in mirror-touch synesthesia. *Journal of Neuroscience*, *31*, 1820–4.

Banissy, M. J., Walsh, V., and Ward, J. (2009). Enhanced sensory perception in synaesthesia. *Experimental Brain Research*, *196*, 565–71.

Banissy, M. J., and Ward, J. (2007). Mirror-touch synaesthesia is linked with empathy. *Nature Neuroscience*, *10*, 815–16.

Barber, T. X., and Wilson, S. C. (1979). Guided imagining and hypnosis: theoretical and empirical overlap and convergence in a new creative imagination scale. In A. A. Sheikh and J. T. Shaffer (Eds.), *The potential of fantasy and imagination* (pp. 67–88). New York: Random House.

Barclay, J. R. (1993). The regulative theory of temperament: implications for assessment and teaching. *McGill Journal of Education*, *28*, 181–212.

Bargary, G., Barnett, K. J., Mitchell, K. J., and Newell, F. N. (2009). Colored-speech synaesthesia is triggered by multisensory, not unisensory, perception. *Psychological Science*, *20*, 529–33.

Bargary, G., and Mitchell, K. J. (2008). Synaesthesia and cortical connectivity. *Trends in Neurosciences*, *31*, 335–42.

Barnett, K. J., Feeney, J., Gormley, M., and Newell, F. N. (2009). An exploratory study of linguistic–colour associations across languages in multilingual synaesthetes. *Quarterly Journal of Experimental Psychology*, *62*, 1343–55.

Barnett, K. J., Finucane, C., Asher, J. E., Bargary, G., Corvin, A. P., Newell, F. N., and Mitchell, K. J. (2008). Familial patterns and the origins of individual differences in synaesthesia. *Cognition*, *106*, 871–93.

Barnett, K. J., Foxe, J. J., Molholm, S., Kelly, S. P., Shalgi, S., Mitchell, K. J., and Newell F. N. (2008). Differences in early sensory-perceptual processing in synesthesia: a visual evoked potential study. *NeuroImage*, *43*(3), 605–13.

Barnett, K. J., and Newell, F. N. (2008). Synaesthesia is associated with enhanced, self-rated visual imagery. *Consciousness and Cognition*, *17*, 1032–9.

Baron-Cohen, S., Bor, D., Billington, J., Asher, J., Wheelwright, S., and Ashwin, C. (2007). Savant memory in a man with colour form-number synaesthesia and Asperger syndrome. *Journal of Consciousness Studies*, *14*, 237–51.

Baron-Cohen, S., Burt, L., Smith-Laittan, F., Harrison, J., and Bolton, P. (1996). Synaesthesia: prevalence and familiarity. *Perception, 25*, 1073–9.

Baron-Cohen, S., Harrison, J., Goldstein, L. H., and Wyke, M. (1993). Coloured speech perception: is synaesthesia what happens when modularity breaks down? *Perception, 22*, 419–26.

Baron-Cohen, S., Wyke, M. A., and Binnie, C. (1987). Hearing words and seeing colours: an experimental investigation of a case of synaesthesia. *Perception, 16*, 761–7.

Benton, A. L. (1992). *Benton Visual Retention Test* (5th edn.). San Antonio, TX: Psychological Corporation.

Berman, G. (1999). Synesthesia and the arts. *Leonardo, 32*, 15–22.

Berteletti, I., Hubbard, E. M., and Zorzi, M. (2010). Implicit versus explicit interference effects in a number-color synesthete. *Cortex, 46*, 170–7.

Bien, N., ten Oever, S., Goebel, R., and Sack, A. T. (2012). The sound of size crossmodal binding in pitch-size synesthesia: a combined TMS, EEG and psychophysics study. *NeuroImage, 59*, 663–72.

Biocca, F., Kim, J., and Choi, Y. (2001). Visual touch in virtual environments: an exploratory study of presence, multimodal interfaces, and cross-modal sensory illusions. *Presence, 10*, 247–65.

Blakemore, S.-J., Bristow, D., Bird, G., Frith, C., and Ward, J. (2005). Somatosensory activations during the observation of touch and a case of vision–touch synaesthesia. *Brain, 128*, 1571–83.

Bor, D., Billington, J., and Baron-Cohen, S. (2007). Savant memory for digits in a case of synaesthesia and Asperger syndrome is related to hyperactivity in the lateral prefrontal cortex. *Neurocase, 13*, 311–19.

Borst, G., and Kosslyn, S. M. (2008). Visual mental imagery and visual perception: structural equivalence revealed by scanning processes. *Memory and Cognition, 36*, 849–62.

Brang, D., and Ramachandran, V. S. (2008). Psychopharmacology of synaesthesia: the role of serotonin S2a receptor activation. *Medical Hypotheses, 70*, 903–4.

(2010). Visual field heterogeneity, laterality, and eidetic imagery in synesthesia. *Neurocase, 16*, 169–74.

(2011). Survival of the synesthesia gene: why do people hear colors and taste words? *PloS Biology, 9*, e1001205. doi:10.1371/journal.pbio.1001205.

Brang, D., Rouw, R., Ramachandran, V. S., and Coulson, S. (2011). Similarly shaped letters evoke similar colors in grapheme–color synesthesia. *Neuropsychologia, 49*, 1355–8.

Brang, D., Teuscher, U., Miller, L. E., Ramachandran, V. S., and Coulson, S. (2011). Handedness and calendar orientations in time–space synaesthesia. *Journal of Neuropsychology, 5*, 323–32.

Brang, D., Teuscher, U., Ramachandran, V. S., and Coulson, S. (2010). Temporal sequences, synesthetic mappings, and cultural biases: the geography of time. *Consciousness and Cognition, 19*, 311–20.

Brang, D., Williams, L. E., and Ramachandran, V. S. (2012). Grapheme-color synaesthetes show enhanced crossmodal processing between auditory and visual modalities. *Cortex, 48*, 630–7.

Brickenkamp, R. (1962). *Aufmerksamkeits-Belastungs-Test (Test d2)*. [The d2 Test of Attention]. Göttingen: Hogrefe.

(1994). *Test d2 Aufmerksamkeits-Belastungs-Test. Handanweisung* (8th expanded and revised edition). Göttingen: Hogrefe.

(2002). *Test d2. Test badania uwagi. Podręcznik* [The d2 Test of Attention. Manual].Warszawa: ERDA.

Brown, T. (1827). Of the external affections combined with desire. In T. Brown (Ed.), *A treatise on the philosophy of the human mind, being the lectures of the late Thomas Brown* (vol. I, pp. 209–20). Cambridge, MA: Hilliard and Brown. doi:10.1037/11701-016.

Brzozowski, P., and Drwal, R. Ł. (2008). *Kwestionariusz Osobowości Eysencka. Polska adaptacja EPQ-R. Podręcznik* [Eysenck Personality Questionnaire: Polish adaptation of the EPQ-R. Manual]. Warszawa: Pracownia Testów Psychologicznych PTP.

Buss, A., and Plomin, R. (1975). *A temperament theory of personality development*. New York: Wiley-Interscience.

(1984). *Temperament: early developing personality traits*. Hillsdale, NJ: Lawrence Erlbaum.

Callejas, A., Acosta, A., and Lupiáñez, J. (2007). Green love is ugly: emotions elicited by synesthetic grapheme-color perceptions. *Brain Research, 1127*, 99–107.

Carriere, J. S. A., Eaton, D., Reynolds, M. G., Dixon, M. J., and Smilek, D. (2008). Grapheme–color synesthesia influences overt visual attention. *Journal of Cognitive Neuroscience, 21*, 246–58.

Cattell, R. B. (1971). *Abilities: their structure, growth, and action*. New York: Houghton Mifflin.

Cawley, V. (2010). The synaesthete: a new type of 'gifted student' and how to teach them. *Procedia – Social and Behavioral Sciences, 7*(C), 574–9.

Cazeaux, C. (2002). Metaphor and categorization of senses. *Metaphor and Symbol, 17*, 3–26.

Chamorro-Premuzic, T., Furnham, A., and Ackerman, P. L. (2006). Ability and personality correlates of general knowledge. *Personality and Individual Differences, 41*, 419–29.

Chiou, R., Stelter, M., and Rich, A. N. (2013). Beyond colour perception: auditory-visual synaesthesia induces experiences of geometric objects in specific locations. *Cortex, 49*(6), 1750–63.

Clements, A. M., Rimrodt, S. L., Abel, J. R., Blankner, J. G., Mostofsky, S. H., Pekar, J. J., Denckla, M. B., and Cutting, L. E. (2006). Sex differences in cerebral laterality of language and visuospatial processing. *Brain and Language, 98*, 150–8.

Cohen Kadosh, R., Cohen Kadosh, K., and Henik, A. (2007). The neuronal correlate of bidirectional synesthesia: a combined event-related potential and functional magnetic resonance imaging study. *Journal of Cognitive Neuroscience, 19*, 2050–9.

Cohen Kadosh, R., and Henik, A. (2006). Color congruity effect: where do colors and numbers interact in synesthesia? *Cortex, 42*, 259–63.

(2007). Can synaesthesia research inform cognitive science? *Trends in Cognitive Sciences*, *11*, 177–84.

Cohen Kadosh, R., Henik, A., Catena, A., Walsh, V., and Fuentes, L. J. (2009). Induced cross-modal synaesthetic experience without abnormal neuronal connections. *Psychological Science*, *20*, 258–65.

Cohen Kadosh, R., Henik, A., and Walsh, V. (2007). Small is bright and big is dark in synaesthesia. *Current Biology*, *17*, 834–5.

(2009). Synaesthesia: learned or lost? *Developmental Science*, *12*, 484–91.

Cohen Kadosh, R., Sagiv, N., Linden, D. E. J., Robertson, L. C., Elinger, G., and Henik, A. (2005). When blue is larger than red: colors influence numerical cognition in synesthesia. *Journal of Cognitive Neuroscience*, *17*, 1766–73.

Cohen Kadosh, R., and Walsh, V. (2008). Synaesthesia and cortical connections: cause or correlation? *Trends in Neurosciences*, *31*, 549–50.

Collier, G. L. (1996). Affective synesthesia: extracting emotion space from simple perceptual stimuli. *Motivation and Emotion*, *20*, 1–32.

Collins, A. M., and Quillian, M. R. (1969). Retrieval time from semantic memory. *Journal of Verbal Learning and Verbal Behavior*, *8*, 240–7.

Colom, R., Jung, R. E., and Haier, R. J. (2006). Finding the g-factor in brain structure using the method of correlated vectors. *Intelligence*, *34*, 561−70.

Coricelli, G. (2005). Two-levels of mental states attribution: from automaticity to voluntariness. *Neuropsychologia*, *43*, 294–300.

Corulla, W. J., Strelau, J., Angleitner, A., and Ruch, W. (1993). The development of the Revised Pavlovian Temperament Survey in England: continuing research. *Personality and Individual Differences*, *14*, 323–8.

Costa, P. T., and McCrae, R. R. (1992). *NEO personality inventory professional manual*. Odessa, FL: Psychological Assessment Resources.

Cudeck, R., and O'Dell, L. L. (1994). Applications of standard error estimates in unrestricted factor analysis: significance tests for factor loadings and correlations. *Psychological Bulletin*, *115*, 475–87.

Cui, X., Jeter, C. B., Yang, D., Montague, P. R., and Eagleman, D. M. (2007). Vividness of mental imagery: individual variability can be measured objectively. *Vision Research*, *47*, 474–8.

Cytowic, R. E. (1993). *The man who tasted shapes* (4th edn.). London: Abacus.

(1997). Synaesthesia: phenomenology and neuropsychology – a review of current knowledge. In S. Baron-Cohen and J. Harrison (Eds.), *Synaesthesia: classic and contemporary readings* (pp. 17–39). Oxford: Blackwell.

(2002). *Synaesthesia: a union of the senses* (2nd edn.). New York: Springer-Verlag.

Dael, N., Sierro, G., and Mohr, C. (2013). Affect-related synesthesias: a prospective view on their existence, expression and underlying mechanisms. *Frontiers in Psychology*, *4*(754), 1–9 (www.ncbi.nlm.nih.gov/pmc/articles/PMC3798864).

Dailey, A., Martindale, C., and Borkum, J. (1997). Creativity, synesthesia, and physionomic perception. *Creativity Research Journal*, *10*, 1–8.

Dajek, E. R. (2010). *Polska standaryzacja Testu d2, testu badania uwagi R. Brickenkampa* [Polish standardization of Brickenkamp's d2 Test of Attention]. Warszawa: ERDA.

Day, L. B., and MacNeilage, P. F. (1996). Postural asymmetries and language lateralization in humans (*Homo sapiens*). *Journal of Comparative Psychology*, *110*, 88–96.

Day, S. (2005). Some demographic and socio-cultural aspects of synesthesia. In L. C. Robertson and N. Sagiv (Eds.), *Synesthesia: perspectives from cognitive neuroscience* (pp. 11–33). New York: Oxford University Press.

de Pascalis, V., Zawadzki, B., and Strelau, J. (2000). The Formal Characteristics of Behaviour – Temperament Inventory (FCB-TI): preliminary results of the Italian version. *Personality and Individual Differences*, *28*, 287–98.

de Thornley Head, P. (2006). Synaesthesia: pitch-colour isomorphism in RGB-space? Cortex, *42*, 164–74.

Devereux, G. (1966). An unusual audio-motor synesthesia in an adolescent. *Psychiatric Quarterly*, *40*(1–4), 459–71.

de Vignemont, F., and Singer, T. (2006). The empathic brain: how, when and why? *Trends in Cognitive Sciences*, *10*, 435–41.

Díaz, B., Hintz, F., Kiebel, S. J., and von Kriegstein, K. (2012). Dysfunction of the auditory thalamus in developmental dyslexia. *Proceedings of the National Academy of Sciences of the United States of America*, *109*, 13841–6.

Dixon, M. J., and Smilek, D. (2005). The importance of individual differences in grapheme-color synesthesia. *Neuron*, *45*, 821–3.

Dixon, M. J., Smilek, D., Cudahy, C., and Merikle, P. M. (2000). Five plus two equals yellow. *Nature*, *406*, 365.

Dixon, M. J., Smilek, D., Duffy, P. L., Zanna, M. P., and Merikle, P. M. (2006). The role of meaning in grapheme-colour synaesthesia. *Cortex*, *42*, 243–52.

Dixon, M. J., Smilek, D., and Merikle, P. (2004). Not all synaesthetes are created equal: projector versus associator synaesthetes. *Cognitive, Affective and Behavioral Neuroscience*, *4*, 335–43.

Dollinger, S. J., Urban, K. K., and James, T. A. (2004). Creativity and openness: further validation of two creative product measures. *Creativity Research Journal*, *16*, 35–47.

Domino, G. (1989). Synesthesia and creativity in fine arts students: an empirical look. *Creativity Research Journal*, *2*, 17–29.

(1999). Synesthesia. In M. A. Runco and S. R. Pritzker (Eds.), *Encyclopedia of creativity* (vol. II, pp. 597–604). San Diego, CA: Academic Press.

Eagleman, D. M. (2012). Synaesthesia in its protean guises. *British Journal of Psychology*, *103*, 16–19.

Eagleman, D. M., Kagan, A. D., Nelson S. S., Sagaram, D., and Sarma, A. K. (2007). A standardized test battery for the study of synesthesia. *Journal of Neuroscience Methods*, *159*, 139–45.

Easterbrook, J. A. (1959). The effect of emotion on cue utilization and the organization of behavior. *Psychological Review*, *66*, 183–201.

Edgar, C., McRorie, M., and Sneddon, I. (2012). Emotional intelligence, personality and the decoding of non-verbal expressions of emotion. *Personality and Individual Differences*, *52*, 295–300.

Edquist, J., Rich, A. N., Brinkman, C., and Mattingley, J. B. (2006). Do synaesthetic colours act as unique features in visual search? *Cortex*, *42*, 222–31.

Elias, L. J., and Bryden, M. P. (1998). Footedness is a better predictor of language lateralization than handedness. *Laterality, 3*, 41–51.

Elias, L. J., Saucier, D. M., Hardie, C., and Sarty, G. E. (2003). Dissociating semantic and perceptual components of synaesthesia: behavioural and functional neuroanatomical investigations. *Cognitive Brain Research, 16*, 232–7.

Evans, K. K., and Treisman, A. (2010). Natural cross-modal mappings between visual and auditory features. *Journal of Vision, 10*, 1–12.

Eysenck, H. J. (1967). *The biological basis of personality*. Springfield, IL: Thomas.

(1992). A reply to Costa and McCrae. P or A and C - the role of theory. *Personality and Individual Differences, 13*, 867–8.

Eysenck, H. J., and Eysenck, S. B. G. (1964). *Manual of the Eysenck Personality Inventory*. University of London Press.

(1975) *Manual of the Eysenck Personality Questionnaire*. London: Hodder and Stoughton.

(1976). *Psychoticism as a dimension of personality*. London: Hodder and Stoughton.

Eysenck, H. J., Eysenck, S. G. B., and Barrett, P. (1985). A revised version of the Psychoticism Scale. *Personality and Individual Differences, 6*, 21–9.

Eysenck, M. W. (1975). Arousal and speed of recall. *British Journal of Social and Clinical Psychology, 14*, 269–77.

Feist, G. J. (1998). A meta-analysis of personality in scientific and artistic creativity. *Personality and Social Psychology Review, 2*, 290–309.

Finch, J. F., and Graziano, W. G. (2001). Predicting depression from temperament, personality, and patterns of social relations. *Journal of Personality, 69*, 27–55.

Fitzgibbon, B. M., Enticott, P. G., Bradshaw, J. L., Giummarra, M. J., Chou, M., Georgiou-Karistianis, N., and Fitzgerald, P. B. (2012). Enhanced corticospinal response to observed pain in pain synesthetes. *Cognitive, Affective and Behavioral Neuroscience, 12*, 406–18.

Fitzgibbon, B. M., Enticott, P. G., Rich, A. N., Giummarra, M. J., Georgiou-Karistianis, N., and Bradshaw, J. L. (2012). Mirror-sensory synaesthesia: exploring 'shared' sensory experiences as synaesthesia. *Neuroscience and Biobehavioral Reviews, 36*, 645–57.

Fitzgibbon, B. M., Giummarra, M. J., Georgiou-Karistianis, N., Enticott, P. G., and Bradshaw, J. L. (2010). Shared pain: from empathy to synaesthesia. *Neuroscience and Biobehavioral Reviews, 34*, 500–12.

Förster, J. (2012). GLOMO^{sys}: the how and why of global and local processing. *Current Directions in Psychological Science, 21*, 15–19.

Freedberg, D., and Gallese, V. (2007). Motion, emotion and empathy in esthetic experience. *Trends in Cognitive Sciences, 11*, 197–203.

Frith, U. (2003). *Autism: explaining the enigma* (2nd edn.). Oxford: Blackwell Scientific Publications.

Galaburda, A. M., Sherman, G. F., Rosen, G. D., Aboitiz, F., and Geschwind, N. (1985). Developmental dyslexia: four consecutive patients with cortical anomalies. *Annals of Neurology, 18*, 222–33.

Galeyev, B. (1993). The problem of synaesthesia in the arts. *Languages of Design, 1*, 201–3.

Ganiban, J. M., Saudino, K. J., Ulbricht, J., Neiderhiser, J. M., and Reiss, D. (2008). Stability and change in temperament during adolescence. *Journal of Personality and Social Psychology, 95*, 222–36.

Gazor, S., and Zhang, W. (2003). Speech probability distribution. *IEEE Signal Processing Letters, 10*, 204–7.

Gheri, C., Chopping, S., and Morgan, M. J. (2008). Synaesthetic colours do not camouflage form in visual search. *Proceedings of the Royal Society of London. Series B: Biological Sciences, 275*, 841–6.

Giummarra, M. J., and Bradshaw, J. L. (2009). Synaesthesia for pain: feeling pain with another. In J. A. Pineda (Ed.), *Mirror neuron systems* (pp. 287–307). New York: Humana Press.

Glicksohn, J., Alon, A., Perlmutter, A., and Purisman, R. (2001). Symbolic and syncretic cognition among schizophrenics and visual artists. *Creativity Research Journal, 13*, 133–43.

Glicksohn, J., and Barrett, T. R. (2003). Absorption and hallucinatory experience. *Applied Cognitive Psychology, 17*, 833–49.

Glicksohn, J., Salinger, O., and Roychman, A. (1992). An exploratory study of syncretic experience: eidetics, synaesthesia and absorption. *Perception, 21*, 637–42.

Glicksohn, J., Steinbach, I., and Elimalach-Malmilyan, S. (1999). Cognitive dedifferentation in eidetics and synaesthesia: hunting for the ghost once more. *Perception, 28*, 109–20.

Glisky, M. L., Tataryn, D. J., Tobias, B. A., and Kihlstrom, J. F. (1991). Absorption, openness to experience, and hypnotizability. *Journal of Personality and Social Psychology, 60*, 263–72.

Goldsmith, H. H., and Rothbart, J. K. (1991). Contemporary instruments for assessing early temperament by questionnaires and in the laboratory. In J. Strelau and A. Angleitner (Eds.), *Explorations in temperament: international perspectives on theory and measurement* (pp. 249–72). New York: Plenum Press.

Goller, A. I., Richards, K., Novak, S., and Ward, J. (2013). Mirror-touch synaesthesia in the phantom limbs of amputees. *Cortex, 49*(1), 243–51.

Gray, J. A. (1964). Strength of the nervous system and levels of arousal: a reinterpretation. In J. A. Gray (Ed.), *Pavlov's typology: recent theoretical and experimental developments from the laboratory of B. M. Teplov* (pp. 289–366). Oxford: Pergamon Press.

(1981). A critique of Eysenck's theory of personality. In H. J. Eysenck (Ed.), *A model for personality* (pp. 246–76). Berlin: Springer-Verlag.

(2005). Synesthesia: a window on the hard problem of consciousness. In L. C. Robertson and N. Sagiv (Eds.), *Synesthesia: perspectives from cognitive neuroscience* (pp. 127–46). New York: Oxford University Press.

Gray, J. A., Williams, S. C. R., Nunn, J., and Baron-Cohen, S. (1997). Possible implications of synaesthesia for the hard question of consciousness. In S. Baron-Cohen and J. Harrison (Eds.), *Synaesthesia: classic and contemporary readings* (pp. 173–81). Oxford: Blackwell Publishers.

Green, J. A. K., and Goswami, U. (2008). Synesthesia and number cognition in children. *Cognition, 106*, 463–73.

Griffin, M., and McDermott, M. R. (1998). Exploring a tripartite relationship between rebelliousness, openness to experience and creativity. *Social Behavior and Personality*, *26*, 347–56.

Gross, V. C., Neargarderô, S., Caldwell-Harris, C. L., and Cronin-Golomb, A. (2011). Superior encoding enhances recall in color-graphemic synesthesia. *Perception*, *40*, 196–208.

Grossenbacher, P. G. (1997). Perception and sensory information in synesthetic experience. In S. Baron-Cohen and J. Harrison (Eds.), *Synaesthesia: classic and contemporary readings* (pp. 148–72). Oxford: Blackwell.

Grossenbacher, P. G., and Lovelace, C. T. (2001). Mechanisms of synesthesia: cognitive and physiological constraints. *Trends in Cognitive Sciences*, *5*, 36–41.

Guencer, B., and Oral, G. (1993). Relationship between creativity and nonconformity to school discipline as perceived by teachers of Turkish elementary schoolchildren, by controlling for their grade and sex. *Journal of Instructional Psychology*, *20*, 208–14.

Guilford, J. P. (1967). *The nature of human intelligence*. New York: McGraw-Hill.

Habib, M. (2000). The neurological basis of developmental dyslexia: an overview and working hypothesis. *Brain*, *123*, 2373–99.

Halpern, S. F. (1992). *Sex differences in cognitive abilities*. New York: Erlbaum.

Hänggi, J., Wotruba, D., and Jäncke, L. (2011). Globally altered structural brain network topology in grapheme-color synesthesia. *Journal of Neuroscience*, *31*, 5816–28.

Harrison, J. E., and Baron-Cohen, S. (1995). Synaesthesia: reconciling the subjective with the objective. *Endeavour*, *19*, 157–60.

(1997). Synaesthesia: an introduction. In S. Baron-Cohen and J. E. Harrison (Eds.), *Synaesthesia: classic and contemporary readings* (pp. 3–16). Oxford: Blackwell.

Heaton, P., and Wallace, G. L. (2004). Annotation: the savant syndrome. *Journal of Child Psychology and Psychiatry, and Allied Disciplines*, *45*, 899–911.

Heim, S., and Keil, A. (2004). Large-scale neural correlates of developmental dyslexia. *European Child and Adolescent Psychiatry*, *13*, 125–40.

Hernaandez, S., Camacho-Rosales, J., Nieto, A., and Barroso, J. (1997). Cerebral asymmetry and reading performance: effect of language lateralization and hand preference. *Child Neuropsychology*, *3*, 206–25.

Hertz, P. (1999). Synesthetic art – an imaginary number? *Leonardo*, *32*, 399–404.

Hochel, M., and Milán, E. G. (2008). Synaesthesia: the existing state of affairs. *Cognitive Neuropsychology*, *25*, 93–117.

Hochel, M., Milán, E. G., Martín, J. L. M., González, A., García, E. D., Tornay, F., and Vila, J. (2009). Congruence or coherence? Emotional and physiological responses to colours in synaesthesia. *European Journal of Cognitive Psychology*, *21*, 703–23.

Holle, H., Banissy, M., Wright, T., Bowling, N., and Ward, J. (2011). "That's not a real body": identifying stimulus qualities that modulate synaesthetic experiences of touch. *Consciousness and Cognition*, *20*, 720–6.

Holmes, N. P., and Spence, C. (2005). Visual bias of unseen hand position with a mirror: spatial and temporal factors. *Experimental Brain Research*, *166*, 489–97.

Hooper, D., Coughlan, J., and Mullen, M. R. (2008). Structural equation modelling: guidelines for determining model fit. *Electronic Journal of Business Research Methods*, *6*, 53–60.

Houde, O., and Tzourio-Mazoyer, N. (2003). Neural foundations of logical and mathematical cognition. *Nature Reviews: Neuroscience*, *4*, 507–14.

Hubbard, E. M. (2007). Neurophysiology of synesthesia. *Current Psychiatry Reports*, *9*, 193–9.

Hubbard, E. M., and Ramachandran, V. S. (2005). Neurocognitive mechanisms of synesthesia. *Neuron*, *48*, 509–20.

Hubbard, T. I. (1996). Synesthesia-like mappings of lightness, and melodic interval. *American Journal of Psychology*, *109*, 219–28.

Hupka, R. B., Zaleski, Z., Otto, J., Reidl, L., and Tarabrina, N. V. (1997). The colors of anger, envy, fear, and jealousy: a cross-cultural study. *Journal of Cross-Cultural Psychology*, *28*, 156–71.

Jackson, C. J., and Francis, L. J. (1999). Interpreting the correlation between neuroticism and Lie Scale stores. *Personality and Individual Differences*, *26*, 59–63.

Jacome, D. E. (1999). Volitional monocular Lilliputian visual hallucinations and synesthesia. *European Neurology*, *42*, 54–6.

Jäncke, L., Beeli, G., Eulig, C., and Hänggi, J. (2009). The neuroanatomy of grapheme–color synesthesia. *European Journal of Neuroscience*, *29*, 1287–93.

Jansari, A. S., Spiller, M. J., and Redfern, S. (2006). Number synaesthesia: when hearing 'four plus five' looks like gold. *Cortex*, *42*, 253–8.

Jarick, M., Dixon, M. J., and Smilek, D. (2011). 9 is always on top: assessing the automaticity of synaesthetic number-forms. *Brain and Cognition*, *77*, 96–105.

Jarick, M., Dixon, M. J., Stewart, M. T., Maxwell, E. C., and Smilek, D. (2009). A different outlook on time: visual and auditory month names elicit different mental vantage points for a time-space synaesthete. *Cortex*, *45*, 1217–28.

Jawer, M. (2005). Environmental sensitivity: a neurobiological phenomenon? *Seminars in Integrative Medicine*, *3*, 104–9.

Jaworowska, A. (2007). *Test Pamięci Wzrokowej Bentona. Polska normalizacja* [Benton Visual Retention Test. Polish Normalization]. Warszawa: Pracownia Testów Psychologicznych PTP.

Jaworowska, A., and Matczak, A. (2005). *Popularny Kwestionariusz Inteligencji Emocjonalnej PKIE. Podręcznik* [The Popular Emotional Intelligence Questionnaire (PEIQ). Manual]. Warszawa: Pracownia Testów Psychologicznych PTP.

Jaworowska, J., and Szustrowa, T. (2000). *Test Matryc Ravena w wersji Standard. Formy: klasyczna, równoległa, Plus. Polska standaryzacja. Podręcznik* [Polish adaptation of Raven's Progressive Matrices test: Classic, Parallel, and Plus versions. Manual]. Warszawa: Pracownia Testów Psychologicznych PTP.

Jellen, H. G., and Urban, K. K. (1989). Assessing creative potential world-wide: the first cross-cultural application of the Test for Creative Thinking – Drawing Production (TCT-DP). *Gifted Education International*, *6*, 78–86.

Jung, C. G. (1971). *Psychological types*. Princeton University Press.

Jürgens, U. M., and Nikolić, D. (2012). Ideaesthesia: conceptual processes assign similar colours to similar shapes. *Translational Neuroscience*, *3*(1), 22–7.

Just, C. (2011). A review of literature on the general factor of personality. *Personality and Individual Differences*, *50*, 765–71.

Kafka, J. S. (1997). Romantic and classic visions in therapy of psychosis: a personal perspective and evolving theory of schizophrenia. *Psychiatry*, *60*, 262–71.

Kagan, J., and Snidman, N. (1991). Temperamental factors in human development. *American Psychologist*, *46*, 856–62.

Kalbfleisch, M. L. (2009). The neural plasticity of giftedness. In L. V. Shavinina (Ed.), *International handbook on giftedness* (vol. II, pp. 275–93). New York: Springer.

Kansaku, K., and Kitazawa, S. (2001). Imaging studies on sex differences in the lateralization of language. *Neuroscience Research*, *41*, 333–7.

Keith, A. (2009). The connotations of English colour terms: colour-based X-phemisms. *Journal of Pragmatics*, *41*, 626–37.

Kensinger, E. A., and Corkin, S. (2003). Memory enhancement for emotional words: are emotional words more vividly remembered than neutral words? *Memory and Cognition*, *31*, 1169–80.

Kim, C.-Y., Blake, R., and Palmeri, T. J. (2006). Perceptual interaction between real and synesthetic colors. *Cortex*, *42(2)*, 195–203.

King, L. A., McKee Walker, L., and Broyles, S. J. (1996). Creativity and the five factor model. *Journal of Research in Personality*, *30*, 189–203.

Koles, Z. J., Lind, J. C., and Flor-Henry, P. (2010). Gender differences in brain functional organization during verbal and spatial cognitive challenges. *Brain Topography*, *23*, 199–204.

Kosslyn, S. (1994). *Image and brain*. Cambridge, MA: MIT Press.

Kustubayeva, A. (2010). Post-Soviet psychology and individual differences in cognition: a psychophysiological perspective. In A. Gruszka, G. Matthews, and B. Szymura (Eds.), *Handbook of individual differences in cognition: attention, memory and cognition* (pp. 145–68). New York: Springer.

Laeng, B., Hugdahl, K., and Specht, K. (2011). The neural correlate of colour distances revealed with competing synaesthetic and real colours. *Cortex*, *47*, 320–31.

Laeng, B., Svartdal, F., and Oelmann, H. (2004). Does color synaesthesia pose a paradox for early-selection theories of attention? *Psychological Science*, *15*, 277–81.

Lee, K. H., Choi, Y. Y., Gray, J. R., Cho, S. H., Chae, J., Lee, S., and Kim, K. (2006). Neural correlates of superior intelligence: stronger recruitment of posterior parietal cortex. *NeuroImage*, *29*, 578–86.

Lengua, L. J., Long, A. C., Smith, K. I., and Meltzoff, A. N. (2005). Pre-attack symptomatology and temperament as predictors of children's responses to the September 11 terrorist attacks. *Journal of Child Psychology and Psychiatry*, *46*, 631–45.

Linssen, M. I. (2011). Synaesthesia and enhanced memory performance: a review of the literature. *Macquarie Matrix*, *1*, 34–53.

Loring, D. W., Meador, K., Lee, G., Murro, A., Smith, J., Flanigin, B., Gallagher, D., and King, D. (1990). Cerebral language lateralization: evidence from intracarotid amobarbital testing. *Neuropsychologia*, *28*, 831–8.

Luke, D. (2011). Discarnate entities and dimethyltryptamine (DMT): psychopharmacology, phenomenology and ontology. *Journal of the Society for Psychical Research*, *75*, 26–42.

Lupiáñez, J., and Callejas, A. (2006). Automatic perception and synaesthesia: evidence from colour and photism naming in a Stroop-negative priming task. *Cortex*, *42*, 204–12.

Luria, A. R. (1968). *The mind of a mnemonist: a little book about a vast memory*. Cambridge, MA: Harvard University Press.

Makioka, S. A. (2009). Self-organizing learning account of number-form synaesthesia. *Cognition*, *112*, 397–414.

Mann, H., Korzenko, J., Carriere, J. S. A., and Dixon, M. J. (2009). Time–space synaesthesia – a cognitive advantage? *Consciousness and Cognition*, *18*, 619–27.

Marks, L. E. (1975). On colored-hearing synesthesia: cross-modal translations of sensory dimensions. *Psychological Bulletin*, *82*, 303–31.

(1989). On cross-modal similarity: the perceptual structure of pitch, loudness, and brightness. *Journal of Experimental Psychology: Human Perception and Performance*, *15*, 589–602.

Marks, L. E., Hammeal, R. J., and Bornstein, M. H. (1987). Perceiving similarity and comprehending metaphor. *Monographs of the Society for Research in Child Development*, *52*(1), 1–102.

Martino, G., and Marks, L. E. (2001). Synesthesia: strong and weak forms. *Current Directions in Psychological Science*, *10*, 61–5.

Masunaga, H., Kawashima, R., Horn, J. L., Sassa, Y., and Sekiguchi, A. (2008). Neural substrates of the Topology Test to measure fluid reasoning: an fMRI study. *Intelligence*, *36*, 607–15.

Matczak, A., Jaworowska, A., and Stańczak, J. (2000). *Rysunkowy Test Twórczego Myślenia K. K. Urbana i H. G. Jellena TCT-DP. Podręcznik* [Test for Creative Thinking – Drawing Production (TCT-DP) by K. K. Urban and H. G. Jellen. Manual]. Warszawa: Pracownia Testów Psychologicznych PTP.

Mathiesen, K. S., and Tambs, K. (1999). The EAS temperament questionnaire – factor structure, age trends, reliability, and stability in a Norwegian sample. *Journal of Child Psychology and Psychiatry, and Allied Disciplines*, *40*, 431–9.

Mattingley, J. B., Payne, J. M., and Rich, A. N. (2006). Attentional load attenuates synaesthetic priming effects in grapheme-color synaesthesia. *Cortex*, *42*, 213–21.

Mattingley, J. B., Rich, A. N., Yelland, G., and Bradshaw, J. L. (2001). Unconscious priming eliminates automatic binding of colour and alphanumeric form in synaesthesia. *Nature*, *410*, 580–2.

Mayer, J. D., Caruso, D. R., and Salovey, P. (1999). Emotional intelligence meets traditional standards for an intelligence. *Intelligence*, *27*, 267–98.

Mayer, J. D., Salovey, P., Caruso, D. R., and Sitarenios, G. (2001). Emotional intelligence as a standard intelligence. *Emotion*, *1*, 232–42.

McCrae, R. R. (1987). Creativity, divergent thinking, and openness to experience. *Journal of Personality and Social Psychology*, *52*, 1258–65.

McDonald, R. P., and Ho, M.-H. R. (2002). Principles and practice in reporting statistical equation analyses. *Psychological Methods*, *7*, 64–82.

McDougall, S., and Pfeifer, G. (2012). Personality differences in mental imagery and the effects on verbal memory. *British Journal of Psychology*, *103*, 556–73.

Mednick, S. (1962). The associative basis of the creative process. *Psychological Review*, *69*, 220–32.

Mednick, S. A., and Mednick, M. T. (1967). *Examiner's manual: Remote Associates Test*. Boston, MA: Houghton Mifflin.

Meier, B., and Rothen, N. (2007). When conditioned responses 'fire back': bidirectional cross-activation creates learning opportunities in synesthesia. *Neuroscience*, *147*, 569–72.

(2009). Training grapheme-colour associations produces a synaesthetic Stroop effect, but not a conditioned synaesthetic response. *Neuropsychologia*, *47*, 1208–11.

Michielsen, H. J., de Vries, J., and van Heck, G. L. (2003). In search of personality and temperament predictors of chronic fatigue: a prospective study. *Personality and Individual Differences*, *35*, 1073–87.

Mikolaczak, M., Roy, E., Verstrynge, V., and Luminet, O. (2009). An exploration of the moderating effect of trait emotional intelligence on memory and attention in neutral and stressful conditions. *British Journal of Psychology*, *100*, 699–715.

Milán, E. G., Iborra, O., Hochel, M., Artacho, M. A. R., Delgado-Pastor, L. C., Salazar, E., and González-Hernández, A. (2012). Auras in mysticism and synaesthesia: a comparison. *Consciousness and Cognition*, *2*, 258–68.

Mills, C. B., Boteler, E. H., and Oliver, G. K. (1999). Digit synaesthesia: a case study using a Stroop-type test. *Cognitive Neuropsychology*, *16*, 181–91.

Mills, C. B., Innis, J., Westendorf, T., Owsianiecki, L., and McDonald, A. (2006). Effect of a synesthete's photisms on name recall. *Cortex*, *42*, 155–63.

Milne, E., and Szczerbinski, M. (2009). Global and local perceptual style, field-independence, and central coherence: an attempt at concept validation. *Advances in Cognitive Psychology*, *5*, 1–26.

Mon-Williams, M., Wann, J. P., Jenkinson, M., and Rushton, K. (1997). Synaesthesia in the normal limb. *Proceedings of the Royal Society of London. Series B: Biological Sciences*, *264*, 1007–10.

Morton, B. E., and Rafto, S. E. (2010). Behavioral laterality advance: neuroanatomical evidence for the existence of hemisity. *Personality and Individual Differences*, *49*, 34–42.

Moutafi, J., Furnham, A., and Crump, J. (2006). What facets of openness and conscientiousness predict fluid intelligence score? *Learning and Individual Differences*, *16*, 31–42.

Mroczko, A., Metzinger, T., Singer, W., and Nikolić, D. (2009). Immediate transfer of synesthesia to a novel inducer. *Journal of Vision*, *9*, 1–8.

Mulvenna, C. M., and Walsh, V. (2005). Synaesthesia. *Current Biology*, *15*, 399–400.

(2006). Synaesthesia: supernormal integration? *Trends in Cognitive Sciences*, *10*, 350–2.

Murray, A. L. (2010). Can the existence of highly accessible concrete representations explain savant skills? Some insights from synaesthesia. *Medical Hypotheses*, *74*, 1006–12.

Musek, J. (2007). A general factor of personality: evidence for the Big One in the five-factor model. *Journal of Research in Personality, 41*, 1213–33.

Mussell, P. (2010). Epistemic curiosity and related constructs: lacking evidence of discriminant validity. *Personality and Individual Differences, 49*, 506–10.

Myers, I. B., and McCaulley, M. H. (1985). *Manual: a guide to the development and use of the Myers-Briggs Type Indicator*. Palo Alto, CA: Consulting Psychologists Press.

Myles, K. M., Dixon, M. J., Smilek, D., and Merikle, P. M. (2003). Seeing double: the role of meaning in alphanumeric-colour synaesthesia. *Brain and Cognition, 53*, 342–5.

Naerde, A., Røysamb, E., and Tambs, K. (2004). Temperament in adults – reliability, stability, and factor structure of the EAS Temperament Survey. *Journal of Personality Assessment, 82*, 71–9.

Nelson, M. R., and Hitchon, J. C. (1999). Loud tastes, colored fragrances, and scented sounds: how and when to mix the senses in persuasive communications. *Journalism and Mass Communication Quarterly, 76*(2), 354–72.

Newberry, B. H., Clark, W. B., Crawford, R. L., Strelau, J., Angleitner, A., Jones, J. H., and Eliasz, A. (1997). An American English version of the Pavlovian Temperament Survey. *Personality and Individual Differences, 22*, 105–14.

Niccolai, V., van Leeuwen, T. M., Blakemore, C., and Stoerig, P. (2012). Synaesthetic perception of colour and visual space in a blind subject: an fMRI case study. *Consciousness and Cognition, 21*, 889–99.

Nijboer, T. C. W., Satris, G., and van der Stigchel, S. (2011). The influence of synesthesia on eye movements: no synesthetic pop-out in an oculomotor target selection task. *Consciousness and Cognition, 20*, 1193–200.

Nijboer, T. C. W., and van der Stigchel, S. (2009). Is attention essential for inducing synesthetic colors? Evidence from oculomotor distractors. *Journal of Vision, 9*, 1–9.

Nikolić, D. (2009). Is synaesthesia actually ideaesthesia? An inquiry into the nature of the phenomenon. *Proceedings of the Third International Congress on Synaesthesia, Science & Art*, Granada, Spain, 26–29 April (www.danko-nikolic.com/wp-content/uploads/2011/09/Synesthesia2009-Nikolic-Ideaesthesia.pdf).

Nikolić, D., Jürgens, U. M., Rothen, N., Meier, B., and Mroczko, A. (2011). Swimming-style synesthesia. *Cortex, 47*, 874–9.

Nold, M. G. (1997). Synesthesia and blindness: a personal account and informal survey. *Journal of Visual Impairment and Blindness, 91*, 14–15.

Nosal, C. S. (1992). *Diagnoza typów umysłu* [Diagnosis of types of mind]. Warszawa: Wydawnictwo Naukowe PWN.

(2001). *Psychologia myślenia i działania menadżera* [Psychology of the thinking and acting of a manager]. Kraków: Wydawnictwo AKADE.

Novich, S., Cheng, S., and Eagleman, D. M. (2011). Is synaesthesia one condition or many? A large-scale analysis reveals subgroups. *Journal of Neuropsychology, 5*, 353–71.

O'Donovan, D. (1969). An historical review of the Lie Scale: with particular reference to the Maudsley Personality Inventory. *Papers in Psychology, 3*, 13–19.

O'Grady, K. (1980). The absorption scale: a factor analytic study. *International Journal of Clinical and Experimental Hypnosis*, *28*, 281–8.

Oniszczenko, W. (1997). *Kwestionariusz temperamentu EAS Arnolda Bussa i Roberta Plomina. Wersje dla dorosłych i dla dzieci. Adaptacja polska. Podręcznik* [Arnold Buss and Robert Plomin's EAS Temperament Survey for adults and children: Polish adaptation. Manual]. Warsaw: Pracownia Testów Psychologicznych PTP.

Ott, U., Reuter, M., Hennig, J., and Vaitl, D. (2005). Evidence for a common biological basis of the absorption trait, hallucinogen effects, and positive symptoms: epistasis between 5-HT2a and COMT polymorphisms. *American Journal of Medical Genetics, Neuropsychiatric Genetics*, *137B*, 29–32.

Paivio, A. (1986). *Mental representations: a dual coding approach*. Oxford University Press.

Palmeri, T. J., Blake, R., Marois, R., Flanery, M. A., and Whetsell, W., Jr. (2002). The perceptual reality of synesthetic colors. *Proceedings of the National Academy of Sciences of the United States of America*, *99*, 4127–31.

Patrick, C. J., Curtin, J. J., and Tellegen, A. (2002). Development and validation of a brief form of the Multidimensional Personality Questionnaire. *Psychological Assessment*, *14*, 150–63.

Pavlov, I. P. (1941). The conditioned reflex. In W. H. Gantt (Ed.), *Lectures on conditioned reflexes: conditioned reflexes and psychiatry* (vol. II, pp. 168–70). New York: International Publishers.

Pekala, R. J., Wenger, C. F., and Levine, R. L. (1985). Individual differences in phenomenological experience: states of consciousness as a function of absorption. *Journal of Personality and Social Psychology*, *48*, 125–32.

Pernet, C. R., Poline, J. B., Demonet, J. F., and Rousselet, G. A. (2009). Brain classification reveals the right cerebellum as the best biomarker of dyslexia. *BMC Neuroscience*, *10*, 1–19.

Perona-Garcelán, S., Carrascoso-López, F., García-Montes, J. M., Vallina-Fernández, O., Pérez-Álvarez, M., Ductor-Recuerda, M. J., Salas-Azcona, R., Cuevas-Yust, C., and Gómez-Gómez, M. T. (2011). Depersonalization as a mediator in the relationship between self-focused attention and auditory hallucinations. *Journal of Trauma and Dissociation*, *12*, 535–48.

Peters, M. (1995). Handedness and its relation to other indices of cerebral lateralization. In R. Davidson and A. Hugdahl (Eds.), *Brain asymmetry* (pp. 183–215). Cambridge, MA: MIT Press.

Piaget, J. (1936). *Origins of intelligence in the child*. London: Routledge and Kegan Paul.

(1952). *The origins of intelligence in children*. New York: International Universities Press.

Podoll, K., and Robinson, D. (2002). Auditory-visual synaesthesia in a patient with basilar migraine. *Journal of Neurology*, *249*, 476–7.

Popek, S. (2000). *Kwestionariusz Twórczego Zachowania KANH* [The Creative Behaviour Questionnaire (KANH)]. Lublin: UMCS.

Powell, J. L., Kemp, G. J., and García-Finaña, M. (2012). Association between language and spatial laterality and cognitive ability: an fMRI study. *NeuroImage*, *59*, 1818–29.

Pozella, D. J., and Hassen, J. L. (1997). Aesthetic preferences for combinations of color and music. *Perceptual and Motor Skills*, *85*, 960–2.

Prabhakaran, V., Smith, J. A. L., Desmond, J. E., Glover, G. H., and Gabrieli, J. D. E. (1997). Neural substrates of fluid reasoning: an fMRI study of neocortical activation during performance of Raven's Progressive Matrices Test. *Cognitive Psychology*, *33*, 43–63.

Price, M. (2009). Spatial forms and mental imagery. *Cortex*, *45*, 1229–45.

Putnam, S. P., Ellis, L. K., and Rothbart, M. K. (2001). The structure of temperament from infancy through adolescence. In A. Eliasz and A. Angeleitner (Eds.), *Advances in research on temperament* (pp. 165–82). Lengerich: Pabst Science Publishers.

Rader, C. M., and Tellegen, A. (1981). A comparison of synesthetes and non-synesthetes. In E. Klinger (Ed.), *Imagery: concepts, results, and applications* (vol. II, pp. 153–63). New York: Plenum Press.

(1987). An investigation of synesthesia. *Journal of Personality and Social Psychology*, *52*, 981–7.

Radvansky, G. A., Gibson, B. S., and McNerney, M. W. (2011). Synesthesia and memory: color congruency, von Restorff, and false memory effects. *Journal of Experimental Psychology. Learning, Memory, and Cognition*, *37*, 219–29.

Ramachandran, V. S., and Brang, D. (2008). Tactile-emotion synesthesia. *Neurocase*, *14*, 390–9.

Ramachandran, V. S., and Hubbard, E. M. (2001a). Psychophysical investigations into the neural basis of synaesthesia. *Proceedings of the Royal Society of London. Series B: Biological Sciences*, *268*, 979–83.

(2001b). Synaesthesia – a window into perception, thought and language. *Journal of Consciousness Studies*, *8*, 3–34.

Ramachandran, V. S., and Rogers-Ramachandran, D. (1996). Synaesthesia in phantom limbs induced with mirrors. *Proceedings of the Royal Society of London. Series B: Biological Sciences*, *263*, 377–86.

(2000). Phantom limbs and neural plasticity. *Archives of Neurology*, *57*, 317–20.

Ramachandran, V. S., Rogers-Ramachandran, D., and Cobb, S. (1995). Touching the phantom limb. *Nature*, *377*, 489–90.

Ramus, F., Rosen, S., Dakin, S. C., Day, B. L., Castellote, J. M., White, S., and Frith, U. (2003). Theories of developmental dyslexia: insights from a multiple case study of dyslexic adults. *Brain*, *126*, 841–65.

Rao, A., Nobre, A. C., Alexander, I., and Ceowy, A. (2007). Auditory evoked visual awareness following sudden ocular blindness: an EEG and TMS investigation. *Experimental Brain Research*, *176*, 288–98.

Raven, J., Raven, J. C., and Court, J. H. (1998). *Raven manual: Section 3. Standard Progressive Matrices* (this edition introduces the Parallel and Plus versions). Oxford Psychologists Press.

Reeves, A., Fuller, H., and Fine, E. M. (2005). The role of attention in binding shape to color. *Vision Research*, *45*, 3343–55.

Rich, A. N., Bradshaw, J. L., and Mattingley, J. B. (2005). A systematic, large-scale study of synaesthesia: implications for the role of early experience in lexical-colour associations. *Cognition*, *98*, 53–84.

Rich, A. N., and Mattingley, J. B. (2002). Anomalous perception in synaesthesia: a cognitive neuroscience perspective. *Nature Reviews Neuroscience*, *3*, 43–52.

(2005). Can attention modulate colour–graphemic synaesthesia? In L. C. Robertson and N. Sagiv (Eds.), *Synaesthesia: perspectives from cognitive neuroscience* (pp. 108–23). New York: Oxford University Press.

(2010). Out of sight, out of mind: the attentional blink can eliminate synaesthetic colours. *Cognition*, *114*, 320–8.

Rich, A. N., Williams, M. A., Puce, A., Syngeniotis, A., Howard, M. A., McGlone, F., and Mattingley, J. B. (2006). Neural correlates of imagined and synaesthetic colours. *Neuropsychologia*, *44*, 2918–25.

Rizzo, M., and Eslinger, P. I. (1989). Colored hearing synesthesia: an investigation of neural factors. *Neurology*, *39*, 781–4.

Ro, T., Farne, A., Johnson, R. M., Wedeen, V., Chu, Z., Wang, Z. J., and Beauchamp, M. S. (2007). Feeling sounds after a thalamic lesion. *Annals of Neurology*, *62*, 433–41.

Robertson, L. C. (2003). Binding, spatial attention and perceptual awareness. *Nature Reviews Neuroscience*, *4*, 93–102.

Roche, S. M., and McConkey, K. M. (1990). Absorption: nature, assessment, and correlates. *Journal of Personality and Social Psychology*, *59*, 91–101.

Rogowska, A. (2007). *Synestezja* [Synaesthesia]. Opole: Oficyna Wydawnicza PO.

(2011). Categorization of synaesthesia. *Review of General Psychology*, *15*, 213–27.

Rollins, M. (2001). The strategic eye: Kosslyn's theory of imagery and perception. *Minds and Machines*, *11*, 267–86.

Rothbart, M. K., and Bates, J. E. (1998). Temperament. In W. Damon (Series Ed.) and N. Eisenberg (Vol. Ed.), *Handbook of child psychology: social, emotional and personality development* (5th edn., vol. III, pp. 105–76). New York: Wiley.

Rothen, N., and Meier, B. (2009). Do synesthetes have a general advantage in visual search and episodic memory? A case for group studies. *PLoS ONE*, *4*, e5037.

(2010a). Grapheme-colour synesthesia yields an ordinary rather than extraordinary memory advantage: evidence from a group study. *Memory*, *18*, 258–64.

(2010b). Higher prevalence of synaesthesia in art students. *Perception*, *39*, 718–20.

Rothen, N., Meier, B., and Ward, J. (2012). Enhanced memory ability: insights from synaesthesia. *Neuroscience and Biobehavioral Reviews*, *36*, 1952–63.

Rothen, N., Nyffeler, T., von Wartburg, R., Müri, R., and Meier, B. (2010). Parieto-occipital suppression eliminates implicit bidirectionality in grapheme-colour synaesthesia. *Neuropsychologia*, *48*, 3482–7.

Rouw, R., and Scholte, H. S. (2007). Increased structural connectivity in grapheme-color synesthesia. *Nature Neuroscience*, *10*, 792–7.

(2010). Neural basis of individual differences in synesthetic experiences. *Journal of Neuroscience*, *30*, 6205–13.

Rouw, R., Scholte, H. S., and Colizoli, O. (2011). Brain areas involved in synaesthesia: a review. *Journal of Neuropsychology*, *5*, 214–42.

Royce, J. R., and Diamond, S. R. (1980). *A multifactor-system dynamics theory of emotion: cognitive-affective interaction*. Edmonton: Center for Advanced Study in Theoretical Psychology, University of Alberta.

Runco, M. A. (2007). *Creativity: theories and themes: research, development, and practice*. Burlington, MA: Elsevier Academic Press.

Rushton, J. P. (1985). Differential K theory: the sociobiology of individual and group differences. *Personality and Individual Differences*, *6*, 441–52.

(1990). Sir Francis Galton, epigenetic rules, genetic similarity theory, and human life history analysis. *Journal of Personality*, *58*, 117–40.

Rushton, J. P., and Irwing, P. (2011). The general factor of personality: normal and abnormal. In T. Chamorro-Premuzic, S. von Stumm, and A. Furnham (Eds.), *The Wiley-Blackwell handbook of individual differences* (pp. 134–63). Malden, MA: Blackwell Publishing.

Sacks, O., Wasserman, R. L., Zeki, S., and Siegel, R. M. (1988). Sudden colour blindness of cerebral origin. *Society for Neuroscience Abstracts*, *14*, 1251.

Sagiv, N., Heer, J., and Robertson, L. (2006). Does binding of synaesthetic color to the evoking grapheme require attention? *Cortex*, *42*, 232–42.

Sagiv, N., and Robertson, L. C. (2005). Synaesthesia and the binding problem. In L. C. Robertson and N. Sagiv (Eds.), *Synaesthesia: perspectives from cognitive neuroscience* (pp. 90–107). New York: Oxford University Press.

Schaefer, M., Noennig, N., Heinze, H. J., and Rotte, M. (2006). Fooling your feelings: artificially induced referred sensations are linked to a modulation of the primary somatosensory cortex. *NeuroImage*, *29*, 67–73.

Schlegel, K., Grandjean, D., and Scherer, K. R. (2012). Emotion recognition: unidimensional ability or a set of modality- and emotion-specific skills? *Personality and Individual Differences*, *53*, 16–21.

Schmid, J., and Leiman, J. M. (1957). The development of hierarchical factor solutions. *Psychometrika*, *22*, 83–90.

Schwenzer, M., and Mathiak, K. (2012). The correlation of inductive reasoning with multi-dimensional perception. *Personality and Individual Differences*, *52*, 903–7.

Seitz, J. A. (2005). The neural, evolutionary, developmental, and bodily basis of metaphor. *New Ideas in Psychology*, *23*, 74–95.

Shaywitz, B. A., Shaywitz, S. E., Pugh, K. R., Mencl, W. E., Fulbright, R. K., Skudlarksi, P., Constable, T., Marchione, K. E., Fletcher, J. M., Lyon, G. R., and Gore, J. C. (2002). Disruption of posterior brain systems for reading in children with developmental dyslexia. *Biological Psychiatry*, *52*, 101–10.

Shaywitz, S. E., Shaywitz, B. A., Pugh, K. R., Fulbright, R. K., Constable, R. T., Mencl, W. E., Shankweiler, D. P., Liberman, A. M., Skudlarski, P., Fletcher, J. M., Katz, L., Marchione, K. E., Lacadie, C., Gatenby, C., and Gore, J. C. (1998). Functional disruption in the organization of the brain for reading in dyslexia. *Proceedings of the National Academy of Sciences of the United States of America*, *95*, 2636–41.

Simner, J. (2007). Beyond perception: synaesthesia as a psycholinguistic phenomenon. *Trends in Cognitive Sciences*, *11*, 23–9.

(2012a). Defining synaesthesia. *British Journal of Psychology*, *103*, 1–15.

(2012b). Defining synaesthesia: a response to two excellent commentaries. *British Journal of Psychology*, *103*, 24–7.

Simner, J., Gärtner, O., and Taylor, M. D. (2011). Cross-modal personality attributions in synaesthetes and non-synaesthetes. *Journal of Neuropsychology*, *5*, 283–301.

Simner, J., Glover, L., and Mowat, A. (2006). Linguistic determinants of word colouring in grapheme-colour synaesthesia. *Cortex*, *42*, 281–9.

Simner, J., Harrold, J., Creed, H., Monro, L., and Foulkes, L. (2009). Early detection of markers for synaesthesia in childhood populations. *Brain: A Journal of Neurology*, *132*, 57–64.

Simner, J., and Holenstein, E. (2007). Ordinal linguistic personification as a variant of synesthesia. *Journal of Cognitive Neuroscience*, *19*, 694–703.

Simner, J., and Hubbard, E. M. (2006). Variants of synesthesia interact in cognitive tasks: evidence for implicit associations and late connectivity in cross-talk theories. *Neuroscience*, *143*, 805–14.

Simner, J., Mayo, N., and Spiller, M. J. (2009). A foundation for savantism? Visuo-spatial synaesthetes present with cognitive benefits. *Cortex*, *45*, 1246–60.

Simner, J., Mulvenna, C., Sagiv, N., Tsakanikos, E., Witherby, S. A., Fraser, C., Scott, K., and Ward, J. (2006). Synaesthesia: the prevalence of atypical cross-modal experiences. *Perception*, *35*, 1024–33.

Simner, J., Ward, J., Lanz, M., Jansari, A., Noonan, K., Glover, L., and Oakley, D. A. (2005). Non-random associations of graphemes to colours in synaesthetic and non-synaesthetic populations. *Cognitive Neuropsychology*, *22*, 1069–85.

Simos, P. G., Breier, J. I., Fletcher, J. M., Bergman, E., and Papanicolaou, A. C. (2000). Cerebral mechanisms involved in word reading in dyslexic children: a magnetic source imaging approach. *Cerebral Cortex*, *10*, 809–16.

Sinke, C., Halpern, J. H., Zedler, M., Neufeld, J., Emrich, H. M., and Passie, T. (2012). Genuine and drug-induced synesthesia: a comparison. *Consciousness and Cognition*, *12*, 1419–34.

Siuta, J. (1987). Zastosowanie Inwentarza Wyobraźni T. X. Barbera i S. C. Wilson w badaniach nad hipnozą [Application of the Imagination Inventory in T. X. Barber and S. C. Wilson's research on hypnosis]. *Przegląd Psychologiczny*, *1*, 245–57.

(1996). The Imagination Inventory and its correlates with imagery and hypnotizability. *American Journal of Clinical Hypnosis*, *39*, 115–25.

Skelton, R., Ludwig, C., and Mohr, C. (2009). A novel, illustrated questionnaire to distinguish projector and associator synaesthetes. *Cortex*, *45*, 721–9.

Smilek, D., Callejas, A., Dixon, M. J., and Merikle, P. M. (2007). Ovals of time: time-space associations in synaesthesia. *Consciousness and Cognition*, *16*, 507–19.

Smilek, D., and Dixon, M. J. (2002). Towards a synergistic understanding of synaesthesia: combining current experimental findings with synaesthetes' subjective descriptions. *Psyche*, *8*, Article 01 (www.theassc.org/files/assc/2529.pdf).

Smilek, D., Dixon, M. J., Cudahy, C., and Merikle, P. M. (2001). Synaesthetic photisms influence visual perception. *Journal of Cognitive Neuroscience*, *13*, 930–6.

(2002). Synesthetic color experiences influence memory. *Psychological Science, 13*, 548–52.

Smilek, D., Dixon, M. J., and Merikle, P. M. (2003). Synaesthetic photisms guide attention. *Brain and Cognition, 53*, 364–7.

(2005). Synaesthesia: discordant male monozygotic twins. *Neurocase, 11*, 363–70.

(2006). Revisiting the category effect: the influence of meaning and search strategy on the efficiency of visual search. *Brain Research, 1080*, 73–90.

Smilek, D., Moffatt, B. A., Pasternak, J., White, B. N., Dixon, M. J., and Merikle, P. M. (2002). Synaesthesia: a case study of discordant monozygotic twins. *Neurocase, 8*, 338–42.

Smith, G. J. W. (1999). Trait and process in personality theory: defined within two contemporary research traditions. *Scandinavian Journal of Psychology, 40*, 269–76.

Sneath, P. H. A., and Sokal, R. R. (1973). *Numerical taxonomy: the principles and practice of numerical classification*. San Francisco, CA: W. H. Freeman.

Spalding, J. M. K., and Zangwill, O. L. (1950). Disturbance of number-form in a case of brain injury. *Journal of Neurology, Neurosurgery & Psychiatry, 13*, 24–9.

Spence, C. (2011). Crossmodal correspondences: a tutorial review. *Attention, Perception, & Psychophysics, 73*, 971–95.

Sperling, J. M., Prvulovic, D., Linden, D. E. J., Singer, W., and Stirn, A. (2006). Neuronal correlatates of colour-graphemic synaesthesia: an fMRI study. *Cortex, 42*, 295–303.

Spiller, M. J., and Jansari, A. S. (2008). Mental imagery and synaesthesia: is synaesthesia from internally-generated stimuli possible? *Cognition, 109*, 143–51.

Springer, S. P., and Deutsch, G. (1997). *Left brain, right brain: perspectives from cognitive neuroscience* (5th edn.). New York: Worth Publishers.

Steen, C. (2001). Visions shared: a firsthand look into synesthesia and art. *Leonardo, 34*, 203–8.

Stefanics, G., Fosker, T., Huss, M., Mead, N., Szucs, D., and Goswami, U. (2011). Auditory sensory deficits in developmental dyslexia: a longitudinal ERP study. *NeuroImage, 57*, 723–32.

Strelau, J. (1983). *Temperament-personality-activity*. London: Academic Press.

(1987). The concept of temperament in personality research. *European Journal of Personality, 1*, 107–17.

(1996). The regulative theory of temperament: current status. *Personality and Individual Differences, 20*, 131–42.

(1998). *Temperament: a psychological perspective*. New York: Plenum.

Strelau, J., and Angleitner, A. (1994). Cross-cultural studies on temperament: theoretical considerations and empirical studies based on the Pavlovian Temperament Survey (PTS). *Personality and Individual Differences, 16*, 331–42.

Strelau, J., Angleitner, A., and Newberry, B. H. (1999). *The Pavlovian Temperament Survey (PTS): an international handbook*. Goettingen: Hogrefe and Huber.

Strelau, J., and Zawadzki, B. (1993). The Formal Characteristics of Behavior-Temperament Inventory (FCB-TI): theoretical assumptions and scale construction. *European Journal of Personality*, *7*, 313–36.

(1995). The Formal Characteristics of Behaviour – Temperament Inventory (FCB-TI): validity studies. *European Journal of Personality*, *9*, 207–29.

(1998). *Kwestionariusz temperamentu PTS. Podręcznik* [Temperament Questionnaire PTS. Manual]. Warszawa: Pracowania Testów Psychologicznych PTP.

Strelau, J., Zawadzki, B., and Angleitner, A. (1995). Kwestionariusz Temperamentu PTS: próba psychologicznej interpretacji podstawowych cech układu nerwowego według Pawłowa [The Pavlovian Temperament Survey (PTS): an attempt at a psychological interpretation of the Pavlovian dimensions of basic nervous system properties]. *Studia Psychologiczne*, *33*, 9–48.

Studerus, E., Gamma, A., Kometer, M., and Vollenweider, F. X. (2012). Prediction of psilocybin response in healthy volunteers. *PLoS ONE* *7*(2), e30800.

Studerus, E., Gamma, A., and Vollenweider, F. X. (2010). Psychometric evaluation of the Altered States of Consciousness Rating Scale (OAV). *PLoS ONE*, *5*(8), 1–19, e12412.

Swenson, R. S. (2006). Review of clinical and functional neuroscience. In G. L. Holmes, M. Levin, and J. A. Cohen (Eds.), *Educational review manual in neurology*. New York: Castle Connolly Graduate Medical Publishing (www.dartmouth.edu/~rswenson/NeuroSci/).

Tammet, D. (2006). *Born on a blue day: the gift of an extraordinary mind*. London: Hodder and Stoughton.

Tellegen, A. (1982). *Manual for the Multidimensional Personality Questionnaire*. Unpublished manuscript. Minneapolis, University of Minnesota.

Tellegen, A., and Atkinson, G. (1974). Openness to absorbing and self-altering experiences ('absorption'), a trait related to hypnotic susceptibility. *Journal of Abnormal Psychology*, *83*, 268–77.

Terhune, D. B. (2009). The incidence and determinants of visual phenomenology during out-of-body experiences. *Cortex*, *45*, 236–42.

Terhune, D. B., Cardeña, E., and Lindgren, M. (2010). Disruption of synaesthesia by posthypnotic suggestion: an ERP study. *Neuropsychologia*, *48*, 3360–4.

Terhune, D. B., Tai, S., Cowey, A., Popescu, T, and Cohen Kadosh, R. (2011). Enhanced cortical excitability in grapheme-color synesthesia and its modulation. *Current Biology*, *21*, 2006–9.

Thalbourne, M. A., Houran, J., Alias, A. G., and Grugger, P. (2001). Transliminality, brain function, and synesthesia. *Journal of Nervous and Mental Disease*, *189*, 190–2.

Thingujam, N. S., Laukka, P., and Elfenbein, H. A. (2012). Distinct emotional abilities converge: evidence from emotional understanding and emotion recognition through the voice. *Journal of Research in Personality*, *46*, 350–4.

Thomas, A., and Chess, S. (1985). The behavioral study of temperament. In J. Strelau, F. H. Farley, and A. Gale (Eds.), *The biological bases of personality and behavior: theories, measurement techniques, and development* (pp. 213–25). Washington, DC: Hemisphere.

Tomson, S. N., Avidan, N., Lee, K., Sarma, A. K., Tushe, R., Milewicz, D. M., Bray, M., Leal, S. M., and Eagleman, D. M. (2011). The genetics of colored

sequence synesthesia: suggestive evidence of linkage to 16q and genetic heterogeneity for the condition. *Behavioural Brain Research*, *223*, 48–52.
Torrance, E. P. (1966). *The Torrance Tests of Creative Thinking – Norms-Technical Manual Research Edition – Verbal Tests, Forms A and B – Figural Tests, Forms A and B*. Princeton, NJ: Personnel Press.
Toyota, H. (2011). Individual differences in emotional intelligence and incidental memory of words. *Japanese Psychological Research*, *53*, 213–20.
Treisman, A., and Gelade, G. (1980). A feature-integration theory of attention. *Cognitive Psychology*, *12*, 97–136.
Urban, K. K. (1996). *Test for Creative Thinking – Drawing Production (TCT-DP) by K. K. Urban and H. G. Jellen. Manual*. Frankfurt: Swets and Zeitlinger.
(2005). Assessing creativity: the Test for Creative Thinking – Drawing Production (TCT-DP). *International Education Journal*, *6*, 272–80.
van Campen, C. (2008). *The hidden sense: synesthesia in art and science*. Cambridge MA: MIT Press.
van Campen, C., and Froger, C. (1999). Artistic and psychological experiments with synesthesia. *Leonardo*, *32*, 9–14.
van der Ven, A. H. G. S., and Ellis, J. L. (2000). A Rasch analysis of Raven's Standard Progressive Matrices. *Personality and Individual Differences*, *29*, 45–64.
van de Ven, V., and Merckelbach, H. (2003). The role of schizotypy, mental imagery, and fantasy proneness in hallucinatory reports of undergraduate students. *Personality and Individual Differences*, *35*, 889–96.
van Leeuwen, T. M., den Ouden, H. E. M., and Hagoort, P. (2011). Effective connectivity determines the nature of subjective experience in grapheme-color synesthesia. *Journal of Neuroscience*, *31*, 9879–84.
van Leeuwen, T. M., Petersson, K. M., and Hagoort, P. (2010). Synaesthetic colour in the brain: beyond colour areas. A functional magnetic resonance imaging study of synaesthetes and matched controls. *PLoS ONE*, *5*(8), e12074.
van Leeuwen, T. M., van den Peper, J. S., Berg, S. M., Brouwer, R. M., Hulshoff Pol, H. E., Kahn, R. S., and Boomsma, D. I. (2009). A genetic analysis of brain volumes and IQ in children. *Intelligence*, *37*, 181–91.
van Prooijen, J.-W., and van der Kloot, W. A. (2001). Confirmatory analysis of exploratively obtained factor structures. *Educational and Psychological Measurement*, *61*, 777–92.
Villemure, C., Wassimi, S., Bennett, G. J., Shir, Y., and Bushnell, M. C. (2006). Unpleasant odors increase pain processing in a patient with neuropathic pain: psychophysical and fMRI investigation. *Pain*, *120*, 213–20.
Voyer, D. (1996). On the magnitude of laterality effects and sex differences in functional lateralities. *Laterality*, *1*, 51–83.
Waldo, T. G., and Merritt, R. D. (2000). Fantasy proneness, dissociation, and DSM–IV Axis II symptomatology. *Journal of Abnormal Psychology*, *109*, 355–8.
Ward, J. (2004). Emotionally mediated synaesthesia. *Cognitive Neuropsychology*, *21*, 761–72.
(2007). Acquired auditory-tactile synesthesia. *Annals of Neurology*, *62*, 429–30.

Ward, J., Huckstep, B., and Tsakanikos, E. (2006). Sound-colour synaesthesia: to what extent does it use cross-modal mechanisms common to us all? *Cortex*, *42*, 264–80.

Ward, J., Jonas, C., Dienes, Z., and Seth, A. (2010). Grapheme-colour synaesthesia improves detection of embedded shapes but without pre-attentive 'pop--out' of synaesthetic colour. *Proceedings of the Royal Society of London. Section B: Biological Sciences*, *277*, 1021–6.

Ward, J., Li, R., Salih, S., and Sagiv, N. (2007). Varieties of grapheme-colour synaesthesia: a new theory of phenomenological and behavioural differences. *Consciousness and Cognition*, *16*, 913–31.

Ward, J., and Simner, J. (2003). Lexical-gustatory synaesthesia: linguistic and conceptual factors. *Cognition*, *89*, 237–61.

Ward, J., Simner, J., and Auyeung, V. (2005). A comparison of lexical-gustatory and grapheme-colour synaesthesia. *Cognitive Neuropsychology*, *22*, 28–41.

Ward, J., Thompson-Lake, D., Ely, R., and Kaminski, F. (2008). Synaesthesia, creativity and art: what is the link? *British Journal of Psychology*, *99*, 127–41.

Ward, J., Tsakanikos, E., and Bray, A. (2006). Synaesthesia for reading and playing musical notes. *Neurocase*, *12*, 27–34.

Watson, M. R., Akins, K. A., and Enns, J. T. (2012). Second-order mappings in grapheme–color synesthesia. *Psychonomic Bulletin and Review*, *19*, 211–17.

Weiss, P. H., and Fink, G. R. (2009). Grapheme-colour synaesthetes show increased grey matter volumes of parietal and fusiform cortex. *Brain*, *132*, 65–70.

Weiss, P. H., Shah, N. J., Toni, I., Zilles, K., and Fink, G. R. (2001). Associating colours with people: a case of chromatic-lexical synaesthesia. *Cortex*, *37*, 750–3.

Wherry, R. J. (1959). Hierarchical factor solutions without rotation. *Psychometrika*, *24*, 45–51.

Wicker, F. W., and Holahan, C. K. (1978). Analogy training and synesthetic phenomena. *Journal of General Psychology*, *98*, 113–22.

Wild, T. C., Kuiken, D., and Schopflocher, D. (1995). The role of absorption in experiential involvement. *Journal of Personality and Social Psychology*, *69*, 569–679.

Wilson, S. C., and Barber, T. X. (1978). The creative imagination scale as a measure of hypnotic responsiveness: applications to experimental and clinical hypnosis. *American Journal of Clinical Hypnosis*, *20*, 235–49.

(1981). Vivid fantasy and hallucinatory abilities in the life histories of excellent hypnotic subjects ('somnambules'): preliminary report with female subjects. In E. Klinger (Ed.), *Imagery: concepts, results, and applications* (vol. II, pp. 133–49). New York: Plenum.

(1983a). *Inventory of Childhood Memories and Imaginings*. Framingham, MA: Cushing Hospital.

(1983b). The fantasy-prone personality: implications for understanding imagery, hypnosis, and parapsychological phenomena. In A. A. Sheikh (Ed.), *Imagery: current theory, research and application* (pp. 340–90). New York: Wiley.

Witkin, H. A., Dyk, R. B., Faterson, H. F., Goodenough, D. R., and Karp, S. (1962). *Psychological differentiation: studies of development*. New York: Wiley.

Witten, I. H., Frank, E., and Hall, M. A. (2011). *Data mining: practical machine learning tools and techniques* (3rd edn.). Burlington, MA: Morgan Kaufmann Publishers.

Witthoft, N., and Winawer, J. (2006). Synesthetic colors determined by having colored refrigerator magnets in childhood. *Cortex*, *42*, 175–83.

(2013). Learning, memory, and synesthesia. *Psychological Science*, *24*(3), 258–65.

Wold, H. (1966). Estimation of principal components and related models by iterative least squares. In P. R. Krishnaiah (Ed.), *Multivariate analysis* (pp. 391–420). New York: Academic Press.

Yaro, C., and Ward, J. (2007). Searching for Shereshevskii: what is superior about the memory of synaesthetes? *Quarterly Journal of Experimental Psychology*, *60*, 681–95.

Zawadzki, B., and Strelau, J. (1997) *Formalna charakterystyka zachowania–kwestionariusz temperamentu (FCZ–KT). Podręcznik* [Formal Characteristics of Behavior–Temperament Inventory (FCB–TI). Manual]. Warszawa: Pracownia Testów Psychologicznych PTP.

(2010). Structure of personality: search for a general factor viewed from a temperament perspective. *Personality and Individual Differences*, *49*, 77–82.

Zawadzki, B., Strelau, J., Szczepaniak, P., and Śliwińska, M. (1998). *Inwentarz osobowości NEO-FFI Costy i McCrae: adaptacja polska. Podręcznik* [Personality inventory NEO-FFI by Costa and McCrae: Polish adaptation. Manual]. Warszawa: Pracownia Testów Psychologicznych PTP.

Zingrone, N. L., Alvarado, C. S., and Agee, N. (2009). Psychological correlates of aura vision: psychic experiences, dissociation, absorption, and synaesthesia-like experiences. *Australian Journal of Clinical and Experimental Hypnosis*, *37*, 131–68.

Zuckerman, M. (1979). *Sensation seeking: beyond the optimal level of arousal.* London: Wiley.

Index

23

C2

106